# *Reader's Guide*
# *to*
# GEORGE BERNARD SHAW

# *Reader's Guide*

# *to*

# GEORGE BERNARD SHAW

**Rudolf Eisler**

CENTRUM PRESS
NEW DELHI-110002 (INDIA)

**CENTRUM PRESS**

**H.O.:** 4360/4, Ansari Road, Daryaganj,
New Delhi-110 002 (India)
Ph.: 23278000, 23261597

**B.O.:** No. 1015, Ist Main Road, BSK IIIrd Stage
IIIrd Phase, IIIrd Block,
Bangalore - 560 085 (India)
Tel.: 080-41723429
*Visit us at*: www.centrumpress.com

*Reader's Guide to George Bernard Shaw*



First Edition, 2009

ISBN 978-93-80106-68-7

PRINTED IN INDIA

*Printed at* Salasar Imaging Systems, Delhi-110035 (India)

# Contents

# Preface

George Bernard Shaw was born in Dublin, where he grew up in something close to genteel poverty. Irish dramatist, literary critic, a socialist spokesman, and a leading figure in the 20th century Theater. Bernard Shaw was a freethinker, defender of women's rights, and advocate of equality of income. In 1925 he was awarded the Nobel Prize for Literature. Shaw accepted the honour but refused the money.

In 1866 the family moved to a better neighbourhood. Shaw went to the Wesleyan Connexional School, then moved to a private school near Dalkey, and from there to Dublin's Central Model School. Shaw finished his formal education at the Dublin English Scientific and Commercial Day School. At the age of 15, he started to work as a junior clerk. In 1876 he went to London, joining his sister and mother. Shaw did not return to Ireland for nearly thirty years.

In his plays Shaw combined contemporary moral problems with ironic tone and paradoxes, "Shavian" wit, which has produced such phrases as "He who can, does. He who cannot, teaches", "England and America are two countries divided by a common language", "Christianity might be a good thing if anyone ever tried it", and "I never resist temptation because I have found that things are bad for me do not tempt me."

Author

## Chapter 1

# Introduction

George Bernard Shaw, (26 July 1856 – 2 November 1950) was an Irish playwright. Although Shaw's first profitable writing was music and literary criticism, his talent was for drama, and he authored more than 60 plays. Nearly all of his writings deal sternly with prevailing social problems, but have a vein of comedy to make their stark themes more palatable. Shaw examined education, marriage, religion, government, health care, and class privilege and found them all defective. He was most angered by the exploitation of the working class, and most of his writings censure that abuse.

An ardent socialist, Shaw wrote many brochures and speeches for the Fabian Society. He became an accomplished orator in the furtherance of its causes, which included gaining equal political rights for men and women, alleviating abuses of the working class, rescinding private ownership of productive land, and promoting healthful lifestyles. He supported the Stalinist regime, dismissing the reports on famine as falsehoods.

Shaw married Charlotte Payne-Townshend, a fellow Fabian, whom he survived. They settled in Ayot St. Lawrence in a house now called Shaw's Corner. Shaw died there, aged 94, from chronic problems exacerbated by injuries he incurred by falling.

He is the only person to have been awarded both the Nobel Prize for Literature (1925) and an Oscar (1938). These were for his contributions to literature and for his work on the film *Pygmalion,* respectively. Shaw wanted to refuse his Nobel Prize outright because he had no desire for public honors, but accepted it at his wife's behest: she considered it a tribute to Ireland. He did reject the monetary award, requesting it be used to finance translation of Swedish books to English.

George Bernard Shaw was born in Synge Street, Dublin in 1856 to George Carr Shaw (1814–1885), whose father was Bernard Shaw, an unsuccessful grain merchant and sometime civil servant, and Lucinda Elizabeth Shaw, born Gurly (1830–1913), a professional singer. He had two sisters, Lucinda Frances (1853–1920), a singer of musical comedy and light opera, and Elinor Agnes (1854–1876).

George briefly attended the Wesleyan Connexional School, a grammar school operated by the Methodist New Connexion, before moving to a private school near Dalkey and then transferring to Dublin's Central Model School. He ended his formal education at the Dublin English Scientific and Commercial Day School.

He harbored a lifelong animosity toward schools and teachers, saying, "Schools and schoolmasters, as we have them today, are not popular as places of education and teachers, but rather prisons and turnkeys in which children are kept to prevent them disturbing and chaperoning their parents."

Shaw expressed this attitude in the astringent prologue to Cashel Byron's Profession where young Byron's educational experience is a fictionalized description of Shaw's own schooldays. Later he painstakingly detailed the reasons for his aversion to formal education in his *Treatise on Parents and Children.* In brief, he considered the standardized curricula useless, deadening to the spirit and stifling to the intellect. He particularly deplored the use of corporal punishment, which was prevalent in his time.

When his mother left home and followed her voice teacher, George Vandeleur Lee, to London, Shaw was almost sixteen years old. His sisters accompanied their mother but Shaw remained in Dublin with his father, first as a reluctant pupil, then as a clerk in an estate office. He worked efficiently, albeit discontentedly, for several years. In 1876, Shaw joined his mother's London household. She, Vandeleur Lee, and his sister

Lucy, provided him with a pound a week while he frequented public libraries and the British Museum reading room where he studied earnestly and began writing novels. He earned his allowance by ghostwriting Vandeleur Lee's music column, which appeared in the London *Hornet*. His novels were rejected, however, so his literary earnings remained negligible until 1885, when he became self-supporting as a critic of the arts.

Influenced by his reading, he became a dedicated Socialist and a charter member of the Fabian Society, a middle class organization established in 1884 to promote the gradual spread of socialism by peaceful means. In the course of his political activities he met Charlotte Payne-Townshend, an Irish heiress and fellow Fabian; they married in 1898.

In 1906 the Shaws moved into a house, now called Shaw's Corner, in Ayot St Lawrence, a small village in Hertfordshire; it was to be their home for the remainder of their lives, although they also maintained a residence at 29 Fitzroy Square in London.

Shaw's plays were first performed in the 1890s. By the end of the decade he was an established playwright. He wrote sixty-three plays and his output as novelist, critic, pamphleteer, essayist and private correspondent was prodigious. He is known to have written more than 250,000 letters.

Along with Fabian Society members Sidney Webb and Beatrice Webb and Graham Wallas, Shaw founded the London School of Economics and Political Science in 1895 with funding provided by private philanthropy, including a bequest of £20,000 from Henry Hunt Hutchinson to the Fabian Society. One of the libraries at the LSE is named in Shaw's honour; it contains collections of his papers and photographs.

During his final years Shaw enjoyed attending to the grounds at Shaw's Corner. His death, at 94, from renal failure, was precipitated by injuries incurred by falling while pruning a tree. His ashes, mixed with those of his wife, were scattered along footpaths and around the statue of Saint Joan in their garden.

## LITERARY WORKS

The International Shaw Society provides a detailed chronological listing of Shaw's writings. View Shaw's Works for listings of his novels and plays, with links to their electronic texts, if those exist.

## CRITICISM

Shaw became a critic of the arts when, sponsored by William Archer, he joined the reviewing staff of the *Pall Mall Gazette* in 1885. There he wrote under the pseudonym "*Corno di Bassetto*" ("basset horn")—chosen because it sounded European and nobody knew what a *corno di basseto* was. In a miscellany of other periodicals, including *Dramatic Review* (1885–86), *Our Corner* (1885–86), and the *Pall Mall Gazette* (1885–88) his byline was "GBS".

From 1895 to 1898, Shaw was the drama critic for Frank Harris' *Saturday Review*, in which position he campaigned brilliantly to displace the artificialities and hypocrisies of the Victorian stage with a theater of actuality and thought. His earnings as a critic made him self-supporting as an author and his articles for the *Saturday Review* made his name well-known.

Much of Shaw's music criticism, ranging from short comments to the book-length essay—*The Perfect Wagnerite*—extols the work of the German composer Richard Wagner. Wagner worked 25 years composing *Nibelung's Ring*, a massive four-part musical dramatization drawn from the Teutonic mythology of gods, giants, dwarves and Rhine maidens; Shaw considered it a work of genius and reviewed it in detail.

Beyond the music, he saw it as an allegory of social evolution where workers, driven by "the invisible whip of hunger", seek freedom from their wealthy masters. Wagner did have socialistic sympathies, as Shaw carefully points out, but made no such claim about his opus.

Conversely, Shaw disparaged Brahms, deriding *A German Requiem* by saying "it could only have come from the establishment of a first-class undertaker".

Although he found Brahms lacking in intellect, he praised

his musicality, saying "...nobody can listen to Brahms' natural utterance of the richest absolute music, especially in his chamber compositions, without rejoicing in his natural gift." Shaw's writings about music gained great popularity because they were understandable and fair, as well as pleasantly light-hearted and free of affectation, thus contrasting starkly with the dourly pretentious pedantry of most critiques in that era.

All of his music critiques have been collected in *Shaw's Music*. As the drama critic for the *Saturday Review*, a post he held from 1895 to 1898, Shaw championed Henrik Ibsen whose realistic plays scandalized the Victorian public. His influential *Quintessence of Ibsenism* was written in 1891.

**NOVELS**

Shaw wrote five unsuccessful novels at the start of his career between 1879 and 1883. Eventually all were published. The first to be printed was *Cashel Byron's Profession* (1886), which was written in 1882. Its eponymous character, Cashel, a rebellious schoolboy with an unsympathetic mother, runs away to Australia where he becomes a famed prizefighter. He returns to England for a boxing match, and falls in love with erudite and wealthy Lydia Carew.

Lydia, drawn by sheer animal magnetism, eventually consents to marry despite the disparity of their social positions. This breach of propriety is nullified by the unpresaged discovery that Cashel is of noble lineage and heir to a fortune comparable to Lydia's.

With those barriers to happiness removed, the couple settles down to prosaic family life with Lydia dominant; Cashel attains a seat in Parliament. In this novel Shaw first expresses his conviction that productive land and all other natural resources should belong to everyone in common, rather than being owned and exploited privately. The book was written in the year when Shaw first heard the lectures of Henry George who advocated such reforms.

Written in 1883, *An Unsocial Socialist* was published in 1887. The tale begins with a hilarious description of student antics at a girl's school then changes focus to a seemingly uncouth laborer who, it soon develops, is really a wealthy gentleman in hiding from his overly affectionate wife. He needs the freedom gained by matrimonial truancy to promote the socialistic cause, to which he is an active convert.

Once the subject of socialism emerges, it dominates the story, allowing only space enough in the final chapters to excoriate the idle upper class and allow the erstwhile schoolgirls, in their earliest maturity, to marry suitably. *Love Among the Artists* was published in the United States in 1900 and in England in 1914, but it was written in 1881.

In the ambiance of chit-chat and frivolity among members of Victorian polite society a youthful Shaw describes his views on the arts, romantic love and the practicalities of matrimony. Dilettantes, he thinks, can love and settle down to marriage, but artists with real genius are too consumed by their work to fit that pattern.

The dominant figure in the novel is Owen Jack, a musical genius, somewhat mad and quite bereft of social graces. From an abysmal beginning he rises to great fame and is lionized by socialites despite his unremitting crudity. *The Irrational Knot* was written in 1880 and published in 1905. Within a framework of leisure class preoccupations and frivolities Shaw disdains hereditary status and proclaims the nobility of workers.

Marriage, as the knot in question, is exemplified by the union of Marian Lind, a lady of the upper class, to Edward Conolly, always a workman but now a magnate, thanks to his invention of an electric motor that makes steam engines obsolete. The marriage soon deteriorates, primarily because Marian fails to rise above the preconceptions and limitations of her social class and is, therefore, unable to share her husband's interests.

Eventually she runs away with a man who is her social peer, but he proves himself a scoundrel and abandons her in desperate circumstances. Her husband rescues her and offers to take her back, but she pridefully refuses, convinced she is unworthy and certain that she faces life as a pariah to her family and friends. The preface, written when Shaw was 49, expresses gratitude to his parents for their support during the lean years while he learned to write and includes details of his early life in London.

Shaw's first novel, *Immaturity,* was written in 1879 but was the last one to be printed in 1931. It relates tepid romances, minor misfortunes and subdued successes in the developing career of Robert Smith, an energetic young Londoner and outspoken agnostic.

Condemnation of alcoholic behaviour is the prime message in the book, and derives from Shaw's familial memories. This is made clear in the books's preface, which was written by the mature Shaw at the time of its belated publication. The preface is a valuable resource because it provides autobiographical details not otherwise available.

## SHORT STORIES

A collection of Shaw's short stories, *The Black Girl in Search of God and Some Lesser Tales,* was published in 1934. The Black Girl, an enthusiastic but misguided convert to Christianity, goes searching for God, whom she believes to be an actual person. Written as an allegory, somewhat reminiscent of Bunyan's *The Pilgrim's Progress,* Shaw uses her adventures to expose flaws and fallacies in the religions of the world.

At the story's happy ending, the Black Girl quits her searchings in favour of rearing a family with the aid of a red-haired Irishman who has no metaphysical inclination. One of the Lesser Tales is *The Miraculous Revenge* (1885), which relates the misadventures of an alcoholic investigator while he probes the mystery of a graveyard—full of saintly corpses—that migrates across a stream to escape association with the body of a newly buried sinner. The story is so different from Shaw's ordinary style that it is hard to believe he wrote it.

## PLAYS

The texts of plays by Shaw mentioned in this section, with the dates when they were written and first performed can be found in *Complete Plays and Prefaces.* Shaw began working on his first play destined for production, *Widowers' Houses,* in 1885 in collaboration with critic William Archer, who supplied the structure. Archer decided that Shaw could not write a play, so the project was abandoned. Years later, Shaw tried again and, in 1892, completed the play without collaboration.

*Widower's Houses*, a scathing attack on slumlords, was first performed at London's Royalty Theatre on 9 December 1892. Shaw would later call it one of his worst works, but he had found his medium. His first significant financial success as a playwright came from Richard Mansfield's American production of *The Devil's Disciple* (1897). He went on to write 63 plays, most of them full-length.

Often his plays succeeded in the United States and Germany before they did in London. Although major London productions of many of his earlier pieces were delayed for years, they are still being performed there. Examples include *Mrs. Warren's Profession* (1893), *Arms and the Man* (1894), *Candida* (1894) and *You Never Can Tell* (1897).

Shaw's plays, like those of Oscar Wilde, were fraught with incisive humour, which was exceptional among playwrights of the Victorian era; both authors are remembered for their comedy.

However, Shaw's wittiness should not obscure his important role in revolutionizing British drama. In the Victorian Era, the London stage had been regarded as a place for frothy, sentimental entertainment. Shaw made it a forum for considering moral, political and economic issues, possibly his most lasting and important contribution to dramatic art.

In this, he considered himself indebted to Henrik Ibsen, who pioneered modern realistic drama, meaning drama designed to heighten awareness of some important social issue. Significantly, *Widowers Houses*—an example of the realistic genre—was completed after William Archer, Shaw's friend, had translated some of Ibsen's plays to English and Shaw had written *The Quintessence of Ibsensism*.

As Shaw's experience and popularity increased, his plays and prefaces became more voluble about reforms he advocated, without diminishing their success as entertainments. Such works, including *Caesar and Cleopatra* (1898), *Man and Superman*

(1903), *Major Barbara* (1905) and *The Doctor's Dilemma* (1906), display Shaw's matured views, for he was approaching 50 when he wrote them.

From 1904 to 1907, several of his plays had their London premieres in notable productions at the Court Theatre, managed by Harley Granville-Barker and J. E. Vedrenne. The first of his new plays to be performed at the Court Theatre, *John Bull's Other Island* (1904), while not especially popular today, made his reputation in London when King Edward VII laughed so hard during a command performance that he broke his chair.

By the 1910s, Shaw was a well-established playwright. New works such as *Fanny's First Play* (1911) and *Pygmalion* (1912)—on which the award-winning *My Fair Lady* (1956) is based—had long runs in front of large London audiences.

A musical adaptation of *Arms and the Man* (1894)—*The Chocolate Soldier* by Oscar Strauss (1908)—was also very popular, but Shaw detested it and, for the rest of his life, forbade musicalization of his work, including a proposed Franz Lehár operetta based on *Pygmalion*; the Broadway musical *My Fair Lady* could be produced only after Shaw's death.

Shaw's outlook was changed by World War I, which he uncompromisingly opposed despite incurring outrage from the public as well as from many friends. His first full-length piece, presented after the War, written mostly during it, was *Heartbreak House* (1919). A new Shaw had emerged—the wit remained, but his faith in humanity had dwindled. In the preface to *Heartbreak House* he said:

"It is said that every people has the Government it deserves. It is more to the point that every Government has the electorate it deserves; for the orators of the front bench can edify or debauch an ignorant electorate at will. Thus our democracy moves in a vicious circle of reciprocal worthiness and unworthiness."

Shaw had previously supported gradual democratic change toward socialism, but now he saw more hope in government by benign strong men. This sometimes made him oblivious to the dangers of dictatorships. Near his life's end that hope failed him too. In the first act of *Buoyant Billions* (1946–48), his last full-length play, his protagonist asks:

"Why appeal to the mob when ninetyfive per cent of them do not understand politics, and can do nothing but mischief without leaders? And what sort of leaders do they vote for? For Titus Oates and Lord George Gordon with their Popish plots, for Hitlers who call on them to exterminate Jews, for Mussolinis who rally them to nationalist dreams of glory and empire in which all foreigners are enemies to be subjugated."

In 1921, Shaw completed *Back to Methuselah*, his "Metabiological Pentateuch".

The massive, five-play work starts in the Garden of Eden and ends thousands of years in the future; it showcases Shaw's postulate that a "Life Force" directs evolution toward ultimate perfection by trial and error. Shaw proclaimed the play a masterpiece, but many critics disagreed. The theme of a benign force directing evolution reappears in *Geneva* (1938), wherein Shaw maintains humans must develop longer lifespans in order to acquire the wisdom needed for self-government.

*Methuselah* was followed by *Saint Joan* (1923), which is generally considered to be one of his better works. Shaw had long considered writing about Joan of Arc, and her canonization supplied a strong incentive. The play was an international success, and is believed to have led to his Nobel Prize in Literature. He wrote plays for the rest of his life, but very few of them are as notable—or as often revived—as his earlier work. *The Apple Cart* (1929) was probably his most popular work of this era. Later full-length plays like *Too True to Be Good* (1931), *On the Rocks* (1933), *The Millionairess* (1935), and *Geneva* (1938) have been seen as marking a decline. His last significant play, *In Good King Charles Golden Days* has, according to St. John Ervine, passages that are equal to Shaw's major works.

Shaw's published plays come with lengthy prefaces. These tend to be more about Shaw's opinions on the issues addressed by the plays than about the plays themselves. Often his prefaces are longer than the plays they introduce. For example, the Penguin Books edition of his one-act *The Shewing-up Of Blanco Posnet* (1909) has a 67-page preface for the 29-page playscript.

## POLEMICAL WRITING

In a letter to Henry James dated 17 January 1909,[36] Shaw said:

"I, as a Socialist, have had to preach, as much as anyone, the enormous power of the environment. We can change it; we must change it; there is absolutely no other sense in life than the task of changing it. What is the use of writing plays, what is the use of writing anything, if there is not a will which finally moulds chaos itself into a race of gods."

Thus he viewed writing as a way to further his humanitarian and political agendas. His works were very popular because of their comedic content, but the public tended to disregard his messages and enjoy his work as pure entertainment. He was acutely aware of that. His preface to *Heartbreak House* (1919) attributes the rejection to the need of post-World War I audiences for frivolities, after four long years of grim privation, more than to their inborn distaste of instruction. His crusading nature led him to adopt and tenaciously hold a variety of causes, which he furthered with fierce intensity, heedless of opposition and ridicule. For example, *Common Sense about the War* (1914) lays out Shaw's strong objections at the onset of World War I. His stance ran counter to public sentiment and cost him dearly at the box-office, but he never compromised.

Shaw joined in the public opposition to vaccination against smallpox, calling it "a particularly filthy piece of witchcraft", despite having nearly died from the disease when he contracted it in 1881. In the preface to *Doctor's Dilemma* he made it plain he regarded traditional medical treatment as dangerous quackery that should be replaced with sound public sanitation, good personal hygiene and diets devoid of meat. Shaw became a vegetarian while he was twenty-five, after hearing a lecture by H. F. Lester. In 1901, remembering the experience, he said "I was a cannibal for twenty-five years.

For the rest I have been a vegetarian." As a staunch vegetarian, he was a firm anti-vivisectionist and antagonistic to cruel sports for the remainder of his life. The belief in the immorality of eating animals was one of the Fabian causes near his heart and is frequently a topic in his plays and prefaces. His position, succinctly stated, was "A man of my spiritual intensity does not eat corpses."

As well as plays and prefaces, Shaw wrote long political treatises, such as *Fabian Essays in Socialism* (1889), and *The Intelligent Woman's Guide to Socialism and Capitalism* (1912), a 495-page book detailing all aspects of socialistic theory as Shaw interpreted it. Excerpts of the latter were republished in 1928 as *Socialism and Liberty,* Late in his life he wrote another guide to political issues, *Everybody's Political What's What* (1944).

## FRIENDS AND CORRESPONDENTS

Shaw corresponded with an array of people, many of them well-known. His letters to and from Mrs. Patrick Campbell were adapted for the stage by Jerome Kilty as *Dear Liar: A Comedy of Letters,* as was his correspondence with the poet Lord Alfred 'Bosie' Douglas (the intimate friend of Oscar Wilde), into the drama *Bernard and Bosie: A Most Unlikely Friendship* by Anthony Wynn.

His letters to the prominent actress, Ellen Terry, to the boxer Gene Tunney, and to H.G. Wells, have also been published. Eventually the volume of his correspondence became insupportable, as can be inferred from apologetic letters written by assistants. Shaw campaigned against the executions of the rebel leaders of the Easter Rising, and he became a personal friend of the Cork-born IRA leader Michael Collins, whom he invited to his home for dinner while Collins was negotiating the Anglo-Irish Treaty with Lloyd George in London. After Collins's assassination in 1922, Shaw sent a personal message of condolence to one of Collins's sisters. He had an enduring friendship with G. K. Chesterton, the Roman Catholic-convert British writer.

Another friend was the composer Edward Elgar. The latter dedicated one of his late works, *Severn Suite,* to Shaw;

and Shaw exerted himself (eventually with success) to persuade the BBC to commission from Elgar a third symphony, though this piece remained incomplete at Elgar's death. Shaw's correspondence with the motion picture producer Gabriel Pascal, who was the first to successfully bring Shaw's plays to the screen and who later tried to put into motion a musical adaptation of *Pygmalion*, but died before he could realise it, is published in a book titled *Bernard Shaw and Gabriel Pascal*. A stage play based on a book by Hugh Whitmore, *The Best of Friends*, provides a window on the friendships of Dame Laurentia McLachlan, OSB (late Abbess of Stanbrook) with Sir Sydney Cockerell and Shaw through adaptations from their letters and writings.

## SOCIALISM AND POLITICAL BELIEFS

Shaw asserted that each social class strove to serve its own ends, and that the upper and middle classes won in the struggle while the working class lost. He condemned the democratic system of his time, saying that workers, ruthlessly exploited by greedy employers, lived in abject poverty and were too ignorant and apathetic to vote intelligently. He believed this deficiency would ultimately be corrected by the emergence of long-lived supermen with experience and intelligence enough to govern properly. He called the developmental process *elective breeding* but it is sometimes referred to as *shavian eugenics*, largely because he thought it was driven by a "Life Force" that led women—subconsciously—to select the mates most likely to give them superior children. The outcome Shaw envisioned is dramatised in *Back to Methuselah*, a monumental play depicting human development from its beginning in the Garden of Eden until the distant future.

In 1882, influenced by Henry George's views on land nationalization, Shaw concluded that private ownership of land and its exploitation for personal profit was a form of theft, and advocated equitable distribution of land and natural resources and their control by governments intent on promoting the commonwealth. Shaw believed that income for individuals should come solely from the sale of their own labour and that poverty could be eliminated by giving equal pay to everyone. These concepts led Shaw to apply for membership in the Social Democratic Federation (SDF), led by H. M. Hyndman who introduced him to the works of Karl Marx. Shaw never joined the SDF, which favored forcible reforms. Instead, in 1884, he joined the newly formed Fabian Society, which accorded with his belief that reform should be gradual and induced by peaceful means rather than by outright revolution. Shaw was an active Fabian. He wrote many of their pamphlets, lectured tirelessly on behalf of their causes and provided money to set up the *The New Age*, an independent socialist journal.

As a Fabian, he participated in the formation of the Labour Party. *The Intelligent Woman's Guide to Socialism and Capitalism* provides a clear statement of his socialistic views. As evinced in plays like *Major Barbara* and *Pygmalion*, class struggle is a motif in much of Shaw's writing. Shaw opposed the execution of Sir Roger Casement in 1916. He wrote a letter "as an Irishman" to The Times newspaper, which was rejected by The Times, but was subsequently printed by the Manchester Guardian on 22 July 1916, and New York American on 13 August 1916.

After visiting the USSR in the 1930s where he met Stalin, Shaw became an ardent supporter of the Stalinist USSR. The preface to his play *On the Rocks* (1933) is primarily an effort to justify the pogroms conducted by the State Political Directorate (OGPU). In an open letter to the Manchester Guardian, he dismisses stories of a Soviet famine as slanderous and calls reports of its exploited workers falsehoods. Asked why he did not stay permanently in the Soviet 'earthly paradise', Shaw jokingly explained that England was a hell and he was a small devil. He wrote a defence of Stalin's espousal of Lysenkoism in a letter to *Labour Monthly*.

## LEGACY

In his old age, Shaw was a household name both in Britain and Ireland, and was famed throughout the world.

His ironic wit endowed English with the adjective "Shavian", used to characterize observations such as: "My way of joking is to tell the truth. It's the funniest joke in the world." Concerned about the vagaries of English spelling, Shaw willed a portion of his wealth (probated at £367,233 13s) to fund the creation of a new phonemic alphabet for the English language. However, the money available was insufficient to support the project, so it was neglected for a time.

This changed when his estate began earning significant royalties from the rights to *Pygmalion*, once *My Fair Lady*—a musical adapted from the play by Alan Jay Lerner and Frederick Loewe—became a hit. However, the Public Trustee found the intended trust to be invalid because its intent was to serve a private interest instead of a charitable purpose. In the end an out-of-court settlement granted only £8600 for promoting the new alphabet, which is now called the Shavian alphabet. The National Gallery of Ireland, RADA and the British Museum all received substantial bequests.

Shaw's home, now called Shaw's Corner, in the small village of Ayot St Lawrence, Hertfordshire is a National Trust property, open to the public. The Shaw Theatre, Euston Road, London, opened in 1971, was named in his honour. Near its entrance, opposite the new British Library, a contemporary statue of *Saint Joan* commemorates Shaw as author of that play.

The Shaw Festival, an annual theater festival in Niagara-on-the-Lake, Ontario, began as an eight week run of *Don Juan in Hell* (as the long third act dream sequence of *Man And Superman* is called when staged alone) and *Candida* in 1962, and has grown into an annual festival with over 800 performances a year, dedicated to producing the works of Shaw and his contemporaries. He is also remembered as one of the pivotal founders of the London School of Economics, whose library is now called the British Library of Political and Economic Science. The Fabian Window designed by Shaw, hangs in the Shaw Library in the main building of the LSE.

## Chapter 2

# First Aid to Critics Bernard Shaw

The Euripidean verses in the second act of Major Barbara are not by me, or even directly by Euripides. They are by Professor Gilbert Murray, whose English version of The Baccha; came into our dramatic literature with all the impulsive power of an original work shortly before Major Barbara was begun. The play, indeed, stands indebted to him in more ways than one. G. B. S. Before dealing with the deeper aspects of Major Barbara, let me, for the credit of English literature, make a protest against an unpatriotic habit into which many of my critics have fallen.

Whenever my view strikes them as being at all outside the range of, say, an ordinary suburban churchwarden, they conclude that I am echoing Schopenhauer, Nietzsche, Ibsen, Strindberg, Tolstoy, or some other heresiarch in northern or eastern Europe. I confess there is something flattering in this simple faith in my accomplishment as a linguist and my erudition as a philosopher. But I cannot tolerate the assumption that life and literature is so poor in these islands that we must go abroad for all dramatic material that is not common and all ideas that are not superficial. I therefore venture to put my critics in possession of certain facts concerning my contact with modern ideas.

About half a century ago, an Irish novelist, Charles Lever, wrote a story entitled A Day's Ride: A Life's Romance. It was published by Charles Dickens in Household Words, and proved so strange to the public taste that Dickens pressed Lever to make short work of it. I read scraps of this novel when I was a child; and it made an enduring impression on me. The hero was a very romantic hero, trying to live bravely, chivalrously, and powerfully by dint of mere romance-fed imagination, without courage, without means, without knowledge, without skill, without anything real except his bodily appetites.

Even in my childhood I found in this poor devil's unsuccessful encounters with the facts of life, a poignant quality that romantic fiction lacked. The book, in spite of its first failure, is not dead: I saw its title the other day in the catalogue of Tauchnitz. Now why is it that when I also deal in the tragi-comic irony of the conflict between real life and the romantic imagination, no critic ever affiliates me to my countryman and immediate forerunner, Charles Lever, whilst they confidently derive me from a Norwegian author of whose language I do not know three words, and of whom I knew nothing until years after the Shavian Anschauung was already unequivocally declared in books full of what came, ten years later, to be perfunctorily labelled Ibsenism. I was not Ibsenist even at second hand; for Lever, though he may have read Henri Beyle, alias Stendhal, certainly never read Ibsen.

Of the books that made Lever popular, such as Charles O'Malley and Harry Lorrequer, I know nothing but the names and some of the illustrations. But the story of the day's ride and life's romance of Potts (claiming alliance with Pozzo di Borgo) caught me and fascinated me as something strange and significant, though I already knew all about Alnaschar and Don Quixote and Simon Tappertit and many another romantic hero mocked by reality. From the plays of Aristophanes to the tales of Stevenson that mockery has been made familiar to all who are properly saturated with letters.

Where, then, was the novelty in Lever's tale? Partly, I think, in a new seriousness in dealing with Potts's disease. Formerly, the contrast between madness and sanity was deemed comic: Hogarth shows us how fashionable people went in parties to Bedlam to laugh at the lunatics. I myself have had a village idiot exhibited to me as some thing irresistibly funny. On the stage the madman was once a regular comic figure; that was how Hamlet got his opportunity before Shakespeare touched him.

The originality of Shakespeare's version lay in his taking the lunatic sympathetically and seriously, and thereby making an advance towards the eastern consciousness of the fact that lunacy may be inspiration in disguise, since a man who has more brains than his fellows necessarily appears as mad to them as one who has less.

But Shakespeare did not do for Pistol and Parolles what he did for Hamlet. The particular sort of madman they represented, the romantic make believer, lay outside the pale of sympathy in literature: he was pitilessly despised and ridiculed here as he was in the east under the name of Alnaschar, and was doomed to be, centuries later, under the name of Simon Tappertit. When Cervantes relented over Don Quixote, and Dickens relented over Pickwick, they did not become impartial: they simply changed sides, and became friends and apologists where they had formerly been mockers.

In Lever's story there is a real change of attitude. There is no relenting towards Potts: he never gains our affections like Don Quixote and Pickwick: he has not even the infatuate courage of Tappertit. But we dare not laugh at him, because, somehow, we recognize ourselves in Potts. We may, some of us, have enough nerve, enough muscle, enough luck, enough tact or skill or address or knowledge to carry things off better than he did; to impose on the people who saw through him; to fascinate Katinka (who cut Potts so ruthlessly at the end of the story); but for all that, we know that Potts plays an enormous part in ourselves and in the world, and that the social problem is not a problem of story-book heroes of the older pattern, but a problem of Pottses, and of how to make men of them.

To fall back on my old phrase, we have the feeling—one that Alnaschar, Pistol, Parolles, and Tappertit never gave us—that Potts is a piece of really scientific natural history as distinguished from comic story telling. His author is not throwing a stone at a creature of another and inferior order, but making a confession, with the effect that the stone hits everybody full in the conscience and causes their self-esteem to smart very sorely.

Hence the failure of Lever's book to please the readers of Household Words. That pain in the self-esteem nowadays causes critics to raise a cry of Ibsenism. I therefore assure them that the sensation first came to me from Lever and may have come to him from Beyle, or at least out of the Stendhalian atmosphere. I exclude the hypothesis of complete originality on Lever's part, because a man can no more be completely original in that sense than a tree can grow out of air. Another mistake as to my literary ancestry is made whenever I violate the romantic convention that all women are angels when they are not devils; that they are better looking than men; that their part in courtship is entirely passive; and that the human female form is the most beautiful object in nature.

Schopenhauer wrote a splenetic essay which, as it is neither polite nor profound, was probably intended to knock this nonsense violently on the head. A sentence denouncing the idolized form as ugly has been largely quoted. The English critics have read that sentence; and I must here affirm, with as much gentleness as the implication will bear, that it has yet to be proved that they have dipped any deeper.

At all events, whenever an English playwright represents a young and marriageable woman as being anything but a romantic heroine, he is disposed of without further thought as an echo of Schopenhauer. My own case is a specially hard one, because, when I implore the critics who are obsessed with the Schopenhaurian formula to remember that playwrights, like sculptors, study their figures from life, and not from philosophic essays, they reply passionately that I am not a playwright and that my stage figures do not live.

But even so, I may and do ask them why, if they must give the credit of my plays to a philosopher, they do not give it to an English philosopher? Long before I ever read a word by Schopenhauer, or even knew whether he was a philosopher or a chemist, the Socialist revival of the eighteen-eighties brought me into contact, both literary and personal, with Mr Ernest Belfort Bax, an English Socialist and philosophic essayist, whose handling of modern feminism would provoke romantic protests from Schopenhauer himself, or even Strindberg.

As a matter of fact I hardly noticed Schopenhauer's disparagements of women when they came under my notice later on, so thoroughly had Mr Bax familiarized me with the homoist attitude, and forced me to recognize the extent to which public opinion, and consequently legislation and jurisprudence, is corrupted by feminist sentiment. But Mr Bax's essays were not confined to the Feminist question. He was a ruthless critic of current morality. Other writers have gained sympathy for dramatic criminals by eliciting the alleged "soul of goodness in things evil"; but Mr Bax would propound some quite undramatic and apparently shabby violation of our commercial law and morality, and not merely defend it with the most disconcerting ingenuity, but actually prove it to be a positive duty that nothing but the certainty of police persecution should prevent every right-minded man from at once doing on principle.

The Socialists were naturally shocked, being for the most part morbidly moral people; but at all events they were saved later on from the delusion that nobody but Nietzsche had ever challenged our mercanto-Christian morality. I first heard the name of Nietzsche from a German mathematician, Miss Borchardt, who had read my Quintessence of Ibsenism, and told me that she saw what I had been reading: namely, Nietzsche's Jenseits von Gut and Bose.

Which I protest I had never seen, and could not have read with any comfort, for want of the necessary German, if I had seen it. Nietzsche, like Schopenhauer, is the victim in England of a single much quoted sentence containing the phrase "big blonde beast." On the strength of this alliteration it is assumed that Nietzsche gained his European reputation by a senseless glorification of selfish bullying as the rule of life, just as it is assumed, on the strength of the single word Superman (Ubermensch) borrowed by me from Nietzsche, that I look for the salvation of society to the despotism of a single Napoleonic Superman, in spite of my careful demonstration of the folly of that outworn infatuation. But even the less recklessly superficial critics seem to believe that the modern objection to Christianity as a pernicious slave-morality was first put forward by Nietzsche.

It was familiar to me before I ever heard of Nietzsche. The late Captain Wilson, author of several queer pamphlets, propagandist of a metaphysical system called Comprehensionism, and inventor of the term "Crosstianity" to distinguish the retrograde element in Christendom, was wont thirty years ago, in the discussions of the Dialectical Society, to protest earnestly against the beatitudes of the Sermon on the Mount as excuses for cowardice and servility, as destructive of our will, and consequently of our honour and manhood.

Now it is true that Captain Wilson's moral criticism of Christianity was not a historical theory of it, like Nietzsche's; but this objection cannot be made to Mr Stuart-Glennie, the successor of Buckle as a philosophic historian, who has devoted his life to the elaboration and propagation of his theory that Christianity is part of an epoch (or rather an aberration, since it began as recently as 6000BC and is already collapsing) produced by the necessity in which the numerically inferior white races found themselves to impose their domination on the colored races by priestcraft, making a virtue and a popular religion of drudgery and submissiveness in this world not only as a means of achieving saintliness of character but of securing a reward in heaven.

Here you have the slave-morality view formulated by a Scotch philosopher long before English writers began chattering about Nietzsche.

As Mr Stuart-Glennie traced the evolution of society to the conflict of races, his theory made some sensation among Socialists—that is, among the only people who were seriously thinking about historical evolution at all—by its collision with the class-conflict theory of Karl Marx. Nietzsche, as I gather, regarded the slave-morality as having been invented and imposed on the world by slaves making a virtue of necessity and a religion of their servitude. Mr Stuart-Glennie regards the slave-morality as an invention of the superior white race to subjugate the minds of the inferior races whom they wished to exploit, and who would have destroyed them by force of numbers if their minds had not been subjugated. As this process is in operation still, and can be studied at first hand not only in our Church schools and in the struggle between our modern proprietary classes and the proletariat, but in the part played by Christian missionaries in reconciling the black races of Africa to their subjugation by European Capitalism, we can judge for ourselves whether the initiative came from above or below.

My object here is not to argue the historical point, but simply to make our theatre critics ashamed of their habit of treating Britain as an intellectual void, and assuming that every philosophical idea, every historic theory, every criticism of our moral, religious and juridical institutions, must necessarily be either imported from abroad, or else a fantastic sally (in rather questionable taste) totally unrelated to the existing body of thought.

I urge them to remember that this body of thought is the slowest of growths and the rarest of blossomings, and that if there is such a thing on the philosophic plane as a matter of course, it is that no individual can make more than a minute contribution to it. In fact, their conception of clever persons parthenogenetically bringing forth complete original cosmogonies by dint of sheer "brilliancy" is part of that ignorant credulity which is the despair of the honest philosopher, and the opportunity of the religious impostor.

## THE GOSPEL OF ST. ANDREW UNDERSHAFT

It is this credulity that drives me to help my critics out with Major Barbara by telling them what to say about it. In the millionaire Undershaft I have represented a man who has become intellectually and spiritually as well as practically conscious of the irresistible natural truth which we all abhor and repudiate: to wit, that the greatest of evils and the worst of crimes is poverty, and that our first duty—a duty to which every other consideration should be sacrificed—is not to be poor. "Poor but honest," "the respectable poor," and such phrases are as intolerable and as immoral as "drunken but amiable," "fraudulent but a good after-dinner speaker," "splendidly criminal," or the like.

Security, the chief pretence of civilization, cannot exist where the worst of dangers, the danger of poverty, hangs over everyone's head, and where the alleged protection of our persons from violence is only an accidental result of the existence of a police force whose real business is to force the poor man to see his children starve whilst idle people overfeed pet dogs with the money that might feed and clothe them.

It is exceedingly difficult to make people realise that an evil is an evil. For instance, we seize a man and deliberately do him a malicious injury: say, imprison him for years. One would not suppose that it needed any exceptional clearness of wit to recognize in this an act of diabolical cruelty. But in England such a recognition provokes a stare of surprise, followed by an explanation that the outrage is punishment or justice or something else that is all right, or perhaps by a heated attempt to argue that we should all be robbed and murdered in our beds if such senseless villainies as sentences of imprisonment were not committed daily. It is useless to argue that even if this were true, which it is not, the alternative to adding crimes of our own to the crimes from which we suffer is not helpless submission.

Chickenpox is an evil; but if I were to declare that we must either submit to it or else repress it sternly by seizing everyone who suffers from it and punishing them by inoculation with smallpox, I should be laughed at; for though nobody could deny that the result would be to prevent chickenpox to some extent by making people avoid it much more carefully, and to effect a further apparent prevention by making them conceal it very anxiously, yet people would have sense enough to see that the deliberate propagation of smallpox was a creation of evil, and must therefore be ruled out in favour of purely humane and hygienic measures.

Yet in the precisely parallel case of a man breaking into my house and stealing my wife's diamonds I am expected as a matter of course to steal ten years of his life, torturing him all the time. If he tries to defeat that monstrous retaliation by shooting me, my survivors hang him. The net result suggested by the police statistics is that we inflict atrocious injuries on the burglars we catch in order to make the rest take effectual precautions against detection; so that instead of saving our wives' diamonds from burglary we only greatly decrease our chances of ever getting them back, and increase our chances of being shot by the robber if we are unlucky enough to disturb him at his work.

But the thoughtless wickedness with which we scatter sentences of imprisonment, torture in the solitary cell and on the plank bed, and flogging, on moral invalids and energetic rebels, is as nothing compared to the stupid levity with which we tolerate poverty as if it were either a wholesome tonic for lazy people or else a virtue to be embraced as St Francis embraced it. If a man is indolent, let him be poor. If he is drunken, let him be poor. If he is not a gentleman, let him be poor. If he is addicted to the fine arts or to pure science instead of to trade and finance, let him be poor.

If he chooses to spend his urban eighteen shillings a week or his agricultural thirteen shillings a week on his beer and his family instead of saving it up for his old age, let him be poor. Let nothing be done for "the undeserving": let him be poor. Serve him right! Also—somewhat inconsistently—blessed are the poor! Now what does this Let Him Be Poor mean? It means let him be weak. Let him be ignorant. Let him become a nucleus of disease.

Let him be a standing exhibition and example of ugliness and dirt. Let him have rickety children. Let him be cheap and let him drag his fellows down to his price by selling himself to do their work. Let his habitations turn our cities into poisonous congeries of slums. Let his daughters infect our young men with the diseases of the streets and his sons revenge him by turning the nation's manhood into scrofula, cowardice, cruelty, hypocrisy, political imbecility, and all the other fruits of oppression and malnutrition. Let the undeserving become still less deserving; and let the deserving lay up for himself, not treasures in heaven, but horrors in hell upon earth.

This being so, is it really wise to let him be poor? Would he not do ten times less harm as a prosperous burglar, incendiary, ravisher or murderer, to the utmost limits of humanity's comparatively negligible impulses in these directions? Suppose we were to abolish all penalties for such activities, and decide that poverty is the one thing we will not tolerate—that every adult with less than, say, 365 pounds a year, shall be painlessly but inexorably killed, and every hungry half naked child forcibly fattened and clothed, would not that be an enormous improvement on our existing system, which has already destroyed so many civilizations, and is visibly destroying ours in the same way?

Is there any radicle of such legislation in our parliamentary system? Well, there are two measures just sprouting in the political soil, which may conceivably grow to something valuable. One is the institution of a Legal Minimum Wage. The other, Old Age Pensions. But there is a better plan than either of these. Some time ago I mentioned the subject of Universal Old Age Pensions to my fellow Socialist Mr Cobden-Sanderson, famous as an artist-craftsman in bookbinding and printing. "Why not Universal Pensions for Life?" said Cobden-Sanderson.

In saying this, he solved the industrial problem at a stroke. At present we say callously to each citizen: "If you want money, earn it," as if his having or not having it were a matter that concerned himself alone. We do not even secure for him the opportunity of earning it: on the contrary, we allow our industry to be organized in open dependence on the maintenance of "a reserve army of unemployed" for the sake of "elasticity." The sensible course would be Cobden-Sanderson's: that is, to give every man enough to live well on, so as to guarantee the community against the possibility of a case of the malignant disease of poverty, and then (necessarily) to see that he earned it.

Undershaft, the hero of Major Barbara, is simply a man who, having grasped the fact that poverty is a crime, knows that when society offered him the alternative of poverty or a lucrative trade in death and destruction, it offered him, not a choice between opulent villainy and humble virtue, but between energetic enterprise and cowardly infamy. His conduct stands the Kantian test, which Peter Shirley's does not.

Peter Shirley is what we call the honest poor man. Undershaft is what we call the wicked rich one: Shirley is Lazarus, Undershaft Dives. Well, the misery of the world is due to the fact that the great mass of men act and believe as Peter Shirley acts and believes. If they acted and believed as Undershaft acts and believes, the immediate result would be a revolution of incalculable beneficence. To be wealthy, says Undershaft, is with me a point of honour for which I am prepared to kill at the risk of my own life. This preparedness is, as he says, the final test of sincerity.

Like Froissart's medieval hero, who saw that "to rob and pill was a good life," he is not the dupe of that public sentiment against killing which is propagated and endowed by people who would otherwise be killed themselves, or of the mouth-honour paid to poverty and obedience by rich and insubordinate do-nothings who want to rob the poor without courage and command them without superiority. Froissart's knight, in placing the achievement of a good life before all the other duties—which indeed are not duties at all when they conflict with it, but plain wickednesses—behaved bravely, admirably, and, in the final analysis, public-spiritedly. Medieval society, on the other hand, behaved very badly indeed in organizing itself so stupidly that a good life could be achieved by robbing and pilling.

If the knight's contemporaries had been all as resolute as he, robbing and pilling would have been the shortest way to the gallows, just as, if we were all as resolute and clearsighted as Undershaft, an attempt to live by means of what is called "an independent income" would be the shortest way to the lethal chamber. But as, thanks to our political imbecility and personal cowardice (fruits of poverty both), the best imitation of a good life now procurable is life on an independent income, all sensible people aim at securing such an income, and are, of course, careful to legalize and moralize both it and all the actions and sentiments which lead to it and support it as an institution. What else can they do? They know, of course, that they are rich because others are poor. But they cannot help that: it is for the poor to repudiate poverty when they have had enough of it. The thing can be done easily enough: the demonstrations to the contrary made by the economists, jurists, moralists and sentimentalists hired by the rich to defend them, or even doing the work gratuitously out of sheer folly and abjectness, impose only on the hirers.

The reason why the independent income-tax payers are not solid in defence of their position is that since we are not medieval rovers through a sparsely populated country, the poverty of those we rob prevents our having the good life for which we sacrifice them. Rich men or aristocrats with a developed sense of life—men like Ruskin and William Morris and Kropotkin—have enormous social appetites and very fastidious personal ones.

They are not content with handsome houses: they want handsome cities. They are not content with bediamonded wives and blooming daughters: they complain because the charwoman is badly dressed, because the laundress smells of gin, because the sempstress is anemic, because every man they meet is not a friend and every woman not a romance. They turn up their noses at their neighbors' drains, and are made ill by the architecture of their neighbors' houses. Trade patterns made to suit vulgar people do not please them (and they can get nothing else): they cannot sleep nor sit at ease upon "slaughtered" cabinet makers' furniture. The very air is not good enough for them: there is too much factory smoke in it. They even demand abstract conditions: justice, honour, a noble moral atmosphere, a mystic nexus to replace the cash nexus.

Finally they declare that though to rob and pill with your own hand on horseback and in steel coat may have been a good life, to rob and pill by the hands of the policeman, the bailiff, and the soldier, and to underpay them meanly for doing it, is not a good life, but rather fatal to all possibility of even a tolerable one. They call on the poor to revolt, and, finding the poor shocked at their ungentlemanliness, despairingly revile the proletariat for its "damned wantlessness" (verdammte Bedurfnislosigkeit).

So far, however, their attack on society has lacked simplicity. The poor do not share their tastes nor understand their art-criticisms. They do not want the simple life, nor the esthetic life; on the contrary, they want very much to wallow in all the costly vulgarities from which the elect souls among the rich turn away with loathing. It is by surfeit and not by abstinence that they will be cured of their hankering after unwholesome sweets. What they do dislike and despise and are ashamed of is poverty. To ask them to fight for the difference between the Christmas number of the Illustrated London News and the Kelmscott Chaucer is silly: they prefer the News.

The difference between a stockbroker's cheap and dirty starched white shirt and collar and the comparatively costly and carefully dyed blue shirt of William Morris is a difference so disgraceful to Morris in their eyes that if they fought on the subject at all, they would fight in defence of the starch. "Cease to be slaves, in order that you may become cranks" is not a very inspiring call to arms; nor is it really improved by substituting saints for cranks.

Both terms denote men of genius; and the common man does not want to live the life of a man of genius: he would much rather live the life of a pet collie if that were the only alternative. But he does want more money. Whatever else he may be vague about, he is clear about that. He may or may not prefer Major Barbara to the Drury Lane pantomime; but he always prefers five hundred pounds to five hundred shillings. Now to deplore this preference as sordid, and teach children that it is sinful to desire money, is to strain towards the extreme possible limit of impudence in lying, and corruption in hypocrisy. The universal regard for money is the one hopeful fact in our civilization, the one sound spot in our social conscience.

Money is the most important thing in the world. It represents health, strength, honour, generosity and beauty as conspicuously and undeniably as the want of it represents illness, weakness, disgrace, meanness and ugliness. Not the least of its virtues is that it destroys base people as certainly as it fortifies and dignifies noble people. It is only when it is cheapened to worthlessness for some, and made impossibly dear to others, that it becomes a curse.

In short, it is a curse only in such foolish social conditions that life itself is a curse. For the two things are inseparable: money is the counter that enables life to be distributed socially: it is life as truly as sovereigns and bank notes are money. The first duty of every citizen is to insist on having money on reasonable terms; and this demand is not complied with by giving four men three shillings each for ten or twelve hours' drudgery and one man a thousand pounds for nothing. The crying need of the nation is not for better morals, cheaper bread, temperance, liberty, culture, redemption of fallen sisters and erring brothers, nor the grace, love and fellowship of the Trinity, but simply for enough money.

And the evil to be attacked is not sin, suffering, greed, priestcraft, kingcraft, demagogy, monopoly, ignorance, drink, war, pestilence, nor any other of the scapegoats which reformers sacrifice, but simply poverty. Once take your eyes from the ends of the earth and fix them on this truth just under your nose; and Andrew Undershaft's views will not perplex you in the least.

Unless indeed his constant sense that he is only the instrument of a Will or Life Force which uses him for purposes wider than his own, may puzzle you. If so, that is because you are walking either in artificial Darwinian darkness, or to mere stupidity.

All genuinely religious people have that consciousness. To them Undershaft the Mystic will be quite intelligible, and his perfect comprehension of his daughter the Salvationist and her lover the Euripidean republican natural and inevitable. That, however, is not new, even on the stage. What is new, as far as I know, is that article in Undershaft's religion which recognizes in Money the first need and in poverty the vilest sin of man and society. This dramatic conception has not, of course, been attained per saltum.

Nor has it been borrowed from Nietzsche or from any man born beyond the Channel. The late Samuel Butler, in his own department the greatest English writer of the latter half of the XIX century, steadily inculcated the necessity and morality of a conscientious Laodiceanism in religion and of an earnest and constant sense of the importance of money.

It drives one almost to despair of English literature when one sees so extraordinary a study of English life as Butler's posthumous Way of All Flesh making so little impression that when, some years later, I produce plays in which Butler's extraordinarily fresh, free and future-piercing suggestions have an obvious share, I am met with nothing but vague cacklings about Ibsen and Nietzsche, and am only too thankful that they are not about Alfred de Musset and Georges Sand. Really, the English do not deserve to have great men.

They allowed Butler to die practically unknown, whilst I, a comparatively insignificant Irish journalist, was leading them by the nose into an advertisement of me which has made my own life a burden. In Sicily there is a Via Samuele Butler. When an English tourist sees it, he either asks "Who the devil was Samuele Butler?" or wonders why the Sicilians should perpetuate the memory of the author of Hudibras. Well, it cannot be denied that the English are only too anxious to recognize a man of genius if somebody will kindly point him out to them.

Having pointed myself out in this manner with some success, I now point out Samuel Butler, and trust that in consequence I shall hear a little less in future of the novelty and foreign origin of the ideas which are now making their way into the English theatre through plays written by Socialists.

There are living men whose originality and power are as obvious as Butler's; and when they die that fact will be discovered. Meanwhile I recommend them to insist on their own merits as an important part of their own business.

## THE SALVATION ARMY

When Major Barbara was produced in London, the second act was reported in an important northern newspaper as a withering attack on the Salvation Army, and the despairing ejaculation of Barbara deplored by a London daily as a tasteless blasphemy. And they were set right, not by the professed critics of the theatre, but by religious and philosophical publicists like Sir Oliver Lodge and Dr Stanton Coit, and strenuous Nonconformist journalists like Mr William Stead, who not only understood the act as well as the Salvationists themselves, but also saw it in its relation to the religious life of the nation, a life which seems to lie not only outside the sympathy of many of our theatre critics, but actually outside their knowledge of society. Indeed nothing could be more ironically curious than the confrontation Major Barbara effected of the theatre enthusiasts with the religious enthusiasts.

On the one hand was the playgoer, always seeking pleasure, paying exorbitantly for it, suffering unbearable discomforts for it, and hardly ever getting it. On the other hand was the Salvationist, repudiating gaiety and courting effort and sacrifice, yet always in the wildest spirits, laughing, joking, singing, rejoicing, drumming, and tambourining: his life flying by in a flash of excitement, and his death arriving as a climax of triumph. And, if you please, the playgoer despising the Salvationist as a joyless person, shut out from the heaven of the theatre, self-condemned to a life of hideous gloom; and the Salvationist mourning over the playgoer as over a prodigal with vine leaves in his hair, careering outrageously to hell amid the popping of champagne corks and the ribald laughter of sirens!

Could misunderstanding be more complete, or sympathy worse misplaced? Fortunately, the Salvationists are more accessible to the religious character of the drama than the playgoers to the gay energy and artistic fertility of religion. They can see, when it is pointed out to them, that a theatre, as a place where two or three are gathered together, takes from that divine presence an inalienable sanctity of which the grossest and profanest farce can no more deprive it than a hypocritical sermon by a snobbish bishop can desecrate Westminster Abbey.

But in our professional playgoers this indispensable preliminary conception of sanctity seems wanting. They talk of actors as mimes and mummers, and, I fear, think of dramatic authors as liars and pandars, whose main business is the voluptuous soothing of the tired city speculator when what he calls the serious business of the day is over. Passion, the life of drama, means nothing to them but primitive sexual excitement: such phrases as "impassioned poetry" or "passionate love of truth" have fallen quite out of their vocabulary and been replaced by "passional crime" and the like.

They assume, as far as I can gather, that people in whom passion has a larger scope are passionless and therefore uninteresting. Consequently they come to think of religious people as people who are not interesting and not amusing. And so, when Barbara cuts the regular Salvation Army jokes, and snatches a kiss from her lover across his drum, the devotees of the theatre think they ought to appear shocked, and conclude that the whole play is an elaborate mockery of the Army.

And then either hypocritically rebuke me for mocking, or foolishly take part in the supposed mockery! Even the handful of mentally competent critics got into difficulties over my demonstration of the economic deadlock in which the Salvation Army finds itself. Some of them thought that the Army would not have taken money from a distiller and a cannon founder: others thought it should not have taken it: all assumed more or less definitely that it reduced itself to absurdity or hypocrisy by taking it. On the first point the reply of the Army itself was prompt and conclusive.

As one of its officers said, they would take money from the devil himself and be only too glad to get it out of his hands and into God's. They gratefully acknowledged that publicans not only give them money but allow them to collect it in the bar—sometimes even when there is a Salvation meeting outside preaching teetotalism. In fact, they questioned the verisimilitude of the play, not because Mrs Baines took the money, but because Barbara refused it. On the point that the Army ought not to take such money, its justification is obvious. It must take the money because it cannot exist without money, and there is no other money to be had.

Practically all the spare money in the country consists of a mass of rent, interest, and profit, every penny of which is bound up with crime, drink, prostitution, disease, and all the evil fruits of poverty, as inextricably as with enterprise, wealth, commercial probity, and national prosperity. The notion that you can earmark certain coins as tainted is an unpractical individualist superstition. None the less the fact that all our money is tainted gives a very severe shock to earnest young souls when some dramatic instance of the taint first makes them conscious of it.

When an enthusiastic young clergyman of the Established Church first realizes that the Ecclesiastical Commissioners receive the rents of sporting public houses, brothels, and sweating dens; or that the most generous contributor at his last charity sermon was an employer trading in female labour cheapened by prostitution as unscrupulously as a hotel keeper trades in waiters' labour cheapened by tips, or commissionaire's labour cheapened by pensions; or that the only patron who can afford to rebuild his church or his schools or give his boys' brigade a gymnasium or a library is the son-in-law of a Chicago meat King, that young clergyman has, like Barbara, a very bad quarter hour.

But he cannot help himself by refusing to accept money from anybody except sweet old ladies with independent incomes and gentle and lovely ways of life. He has only to follow up the income of the sweet ladies to its industrial source, and there he will find Mrs Warren's profession and the poisonous canned meat and all the rest of it. His own stipend has the same root.

He must either share the world's guilt or go to another planet. He must save the world's honour if he is to save his own. This is what all the Churches find just as the Salvation Army and Barbara find it in the play. Her discovery that she is her father's accomplice; that the Salvation Army is the accomplice of the distiller and the dynamite maker; that they can no more escape one another than they can escape the air they breathe; that there is no salvation for them through personal righteousness, but only through the redemption of the whole nation from its vicious, lazy, competitive anarchy: this discovery has been made by everyone except the Pharisees and (apparently) the professional playgoers, who still wear their Tom Hood shirts and underpay their washerwomen without the slightest misgiving as to the elevation of their private characters, the purity of their private atmospheres, and their right to repudiate as foreign to themselves the coarse depravity of the garret and the slum.

Not that they mean any harm: they only desire to be, in their little private way, what they call gentlemen. They do not understand Barbara's lesson because they have not, like her, learnt it by taking their part in the larger life of the nation.

## BARBARA'S RETURN TO THE COLORS

Barbara's return to the colors may yet provide a subject for the dramatic historian of the future. To go back to the Salvation Army with the knowledge that even the Salvationists themselves are not saved yet; that poverty is not blessed, but a most damnable sin; and that when General Booth chose Blood and Fire for the emblem of Salvation instead of the Cross, he was perhaps better inspired than he knew: such knowledge, for the daughter of Andrew Undershaft, will clearly lead to something hopefuller than distributing bread and treacle at the expense of Bodger.

It is a very significant thing, this instinctive choice of the military form of organization, this substitution of the drum for the organ, by the Salvation Army. Does it not suggest that the Salvationists divine that they must actually fight the devil instead of merely praying at him? At present, it is true, they have not quite ascertained his correct address. When they do, they may give a very rude shock to that sense of security which he has gained from his experience of the fact that hard words, even when uttered by eloquent essayists and lecturers, or carried unanimously at enthusiastic public meetings on the motion of eminent reformers, break no bones.

It has been said that the French Revolution was the work of Voltaire, Rousseau and the Encyclopedists. It seems to me to have been the work of men who had observed that virtuous indignation, caustic criticism, conclusive argument and instructive pamphleteering, even when done by the most earnest and witty literary geniuses, were as useless as praying, things going steadily from bad to worse whilst the Social Contract and the pamphlets of Voltaire were at the height of their vogue.

Eventually, as we know, perfectly respectable citizens and earnest philanthropists connived at the September massacres because hard experience had convinced them that if they contented themselves with appeals to humanity and patriotism, the aristocracy, though it would read their appeals with the greatest enjoyment and appreciation, flattering and admiring the writers, would none the less continue to conspire with foreign monarchists to undo the revolution and restore the old system with every circumstance of savage vengeance and ruthless repression of popular liberties.

The nineteenth century saw the same lesson repeated in England. It had its Utilitarians, its Christian Socialists, its Fabians (still extant): it had Bentham, Mill, Dickens, Ruskin, Carlyle, Butler, Henry George, and Morris. And the end of all their efforts is the Chicago described by Mr Upton Sinclair, and the London in which the people who pay to be amused by my dramatic representation of Peter Shirley turned out to starve at forty because there are younger slaves to be had for his wages, do not take, and have not the slightest intention of taking, any effective step to organize society in such a way as to make that everyday infamy impossible.

I, who have preached and pamphleteered like any Encyclopedist, have to confess that my methods are no use, and would be no use if I were Voltaire, Rousseau, Bentham, Mill, Dickens, Carlyle, Ruskin, George, Butler, and Morris all rolled into one, with Euripides, More, Moliere, Shakespeare, Beaumarchais, Swift, Goethe, Ibsen, Tolstoy, Moses and the prophets all thrown in (as indeed in some sort I actually am, standing as I do on all their shoulders).

The problem being to make heroes out of cowards, we paper apostles and artist-magicians have succeeded only in giving cowards all the sensations of heroes whilst they tolerate every abomination, accept every plunder, and submit to every oppression.

Christianity, in making a merit of such submission, has marked only that depth in the abyss at which the very sense of shame is lost. The Christian has been like Dickens' doctor in the debtor's prison, who tells the newcomer of its ineffable peace and security: no duns; no tyrannical collectors of rates, taxes, and rent; no importunate hopes nor exacting duties; nothing but the rest and safety of having no further to fall. Yet in the poorest corner of this soul-destroying Christendom vitality suddenly begins to germinate again.

Joyousness, a sacred gift long dethroned by the hellish laughter of derision and obscenity, rises like a flood miraculously out of the fetid dust and mud of the slums; rousing marches and impetuous dithyrambs rise to the heavens from people among whom the depressing noise called "sacred music" is a standing joke; a flag with Blood and Fire on it is unfurled, not in murderous rancor, but because fire is beautiful and blood a vital and splendid red; Fear, which we flatter by calling Self, vanishes; and transfigured men and women carry their gospel through a transfigured world, calling their leader General, themselves captains and brigadiers, and their whole body an Army: praying, but praying only for refreshment, for strength to fight, and for needful MONEY (a notable sign, that); preaching, but not preaching submission; daring ill-usage and abuse, but not putting up with more of it than is inevitable; and practising what the world will let them practise, including soap and water, colour and music. There is danger in such Activity; and where there is danger there is hope. Our present security is nothing, and can be nothing, but evil made irresistible.

## WEAKNESSES OF THE SALVATION ARMY

For the present, however, it is not my business to flatter the Salvation Army. Rather must I point out to it that it has almost as many weaknesses as the Church of England itself. It is building up a business organization which will compel it eventually to see that its present staff of enthusiast-commanders shall be succeeded by a bureaucracy of men of business who will be no better than bishops, and perhaps a good deal more unscrupulous.

That has always happened sooner or later to great orders founded by saints; and the order founded by St William Booth is not exempt from the same danger. It is even more dependent than the Church on rich people who would cut off supplies at once if it began to preach that indispensable revolt against poverty which must also be a revolt against riches. It is hampered by a heavy contingent of pious elders who are not really Salvationists at all, but Evangelicals of the old school. It still, as Commissioner Howard affirms, "sticks to Moses," which is flat nonsense at this time of day if the Commissioner means, as I am afraid he does, that the Book of Genesis contains a trustworthy scientific account of the origin of species, and that the god to whom Jephthah sacrificed his daughter is any less obviously a tribal idol than Dagon or Chemosh.

Further, there is still too much other-worldliness about the Army. Like Frederick's grenadier, the Salvationist wants to live for ever (the most monstrous way of crying for the moon); and though it is evident to anyone who has ever heard General Booth and his best officers that they would work as hard for human salvation as they do at present if they believed that death would be the end of them individually, they and their followers have a bad habit of talking as if the Salvationists were heroically enduring a very bad time on earth as an investment which will bring them in dividends later on in the form, not of a better life to come for the whole world, but of an eternity spent by themselves personally in a sort of bliss which would bore any active person to a second death. Surely the truth is that the Salvationists are unusually happy people. And is it not the very diagnostic of true salvation that it shall overcome the fear of death?

Now the man who has come to believe that there is no such thing as death, the change so called being merely the transition to an exquisitely happy and utterly careless life, has not overcome the fear of death at all: on the contrary, it has overcome him so completely that he refuses to die on any terms whatever.

I do not call a Salvationist really saved until he is ready to lie down cheerfully on the scrap heap, having paid scot and lot and something over, and let his eternal life pass on to renew its youth in the battalions of the future. Then there is the nasty lying habit called confession, which the Army encourages because it lends itself to dramatic oratory, with plenty of thrilling incident. For my part, when I hear a convert relating the violences and oaths and blasphemies he was guilty of before he was saved, making out that he was a very terrible fellow then and is the most contrite and chastened of Christians now, I believe him no more than I believe the millionaire who says he came up to London or Chicago as a boy with only three halfpence in his pocket.

Salvationists have said to me that Barbara in my play would never have been taken in by so transparent a humbug as Snobby Price; and certainly I do not think Snobby could have taken in any experienced Salvationist on a point on which the Salvationist did not wish to be taken in. But on the point of conversion all Salvationists wish to be taken in; for the more obvious the sinner the more obvious the miracle of his conversion. When you advertize a converted burglar or reclaimed drunkard as one of the attractions at an experience meeting, your burglar can hardly have been too burglarious or your drunkard too drunken. As long as such attractions are relied on, you will have your Snobbies claiming to have beaten their mothers when they were as a matter of prosaic fact habitually beaten by them, and your Rummies of the tamest respectability pretending to a past of reckless and dazzling vice.

Even when confessions are sincerely autobiographic there is no reason to assume at once that the impulse to make them is pious or the interest of the hearers wholesome. It might as well be assumed that the poor people who insist on showing appalling ulcers to district visitors are convinced hygienists, or that the curiosity which sometimes welcomes such exhibitions is a pleasant and creditable one. One is often tempted to suggest that those who pester our police superintendents with confessions of murder might very wisely be taken at their word and executed, except in the few cases in which a real murderer is seeking to be relieved of his guilt by confession and expiation.

For though I am not, I hope, an unmerciful person, I do not think that the inexorability of the deed once done should be disguised by any ritual, whether in the confessional or on the scaffold. And here my disagreement with the Salvation Army, and with all propagandists of the Cross (to which I object as I object to all gibbets) becomes deep indeed. Forgiveness, absolution, atonement, are figments: punishment is only a pretence of cancelling one crime by another; and you can no more have forgiveness without vindictiveness than you can have a cure without a disease.

You will never get a high morality from people who conceive that their misdeeds are revocable and pardonable, or in a society where absolution and expiation are officially provided for us all. The demand may be very real; but the supply is spurious. Thus Bill Walker, in my play, having assaulted the Salvation Lass, presently finds himself overwhelmed with an intolerable conviction of sin under the skilled treatment of Barbara.

Straightway he begins to try to unassault the lass and deruffianize his deed, first by getting punished for it in kind, and, when that relief is denied him, by fining himself a pound to compensate the girl. He is foiled both ways. He finds the Salvation Army as inexorable as fact itself. It will not punish him: it will not take his money. It will not tolerate a redeemed ruffian: it leaves him no means of salvation except ceasing to be a ruffian. In doing this, the Salvation Army instinctively grasps the central truth of Christianity and discards its central superstition: that central truth being the vanity of revenge and punishment, and that central superstition the salvation of the world by the gibbet.

For, be it noted, Bill has assaulted an old and starving woman also; and for this worse offence he feels no remorse whatever, because she makes it clear that her malice is as great as his own. "Let her have the law of me, as she said she would," says Bill: "what I done to her is no more on what you might call my conscience than sticking a pig." This shows a perfectly natural and wholesome state of mind on his part. The old woman, like the law she threatens him with, is perfectly ready to play the game of retaliation with him: to rob him if he steals, to flog him if he strikes, to murder him if he kills.

By example and precept the law and public opinion teach him to impose his will on others by anger, violence, and cruelty, and to wipe off the moral score by punishment. That is sound Crosstianity. But this Crosstianity has got entangled with something which Barbara calls Christianity, and which unexpectedly causes her to refuse to play the hangman's game of Satan casting out Satan.

She refuses to prosecute a drunken ruffian; she converses on equal terms with a blackguard whom no lady could be seen speaking to in the public street: in short, she behaves as illegally and unbecomingly as possible under the circumstances. Bill's conscience reacts to this just as naturally as it does to the old woman's threats. He is placed in a position of unbearable moral inferiority, and strives by every means in his power to escape from it, whilst he is still quite ready to meet the abuse of the old woman by attempting to smash a mug on her face.

And that is the triumphant justification of Barbara's Christianity as against our system of judicial punishment and the vindictive villain-thrashings and "poetic justice" of the romantic stage. For the credit of literature it must be pointed out that the situation is only partly novel. Victor Hugo long ago gave us the epic of the convict and the bishop's candlesticks, of the Crosstian policeman annihilated by his encounter with the Christian Valjean. But Bill Walker is not, like Valjean, romantically changed from a demon into an angel.

There are millions of Bill Walkers in all classes of society to-day; and the point which I, as a professor of natural psychology, desire to demonstrate, is that Bill, without any change in his character whatsoever, will react one way to one sort of treatment and another way to another. In proof I might point to the sensational object lesson provided by our commercial millionaires to-day.

They begin as brigands: merciless, unscrupulous, dealing out ruin and death and slavery to their competitors and employees, and facing desperately the worst that their competitors can do to them. The history of the English factories, the American trusts, the exploitation of African gold, diamonds, ivory and rubber, outdoes in villainy the worst that has ever been imagined of the buccaneers of the Spanish Main. Captain Kidd would have marooned a modern Trust magnate for conduct unworthy of a gentleman of fortune.

The law every day seizes on unsuccessful scoundrels of this type and punishes them with a cruelty worse than their own, with the result that they come out of the torture house more dangerous than they went in, and renew their evil doing (nobody will employ them at anything else) until they are again seized, again tormented, and again let loose, with the same result. But the successful scoundrel is dealt with very differently, and very Christianly. He is not only forgiven: he is idolized, respected, made much of, all but worshipped. Society returns him good for evil in the most extravagant overmeasure.

And with what result? He begins to idolize himself, to respect himself, to live up to the treatment he receives. He preaches sermons; he writes books of the most edifying advice to young men, and actually persuades himself that he got on by taking his own advice; he endows educational institutions; he supports charities; he dies finally in the odor of sanctity, leaving a will which is a monument of public spirit and bounty. And all this without any change in his character.

The spots of the leopard and the stripes of the tiger are as brilliant as ever; but the conduct of the world towards him has changed; and his conduct has changed accordingly. You have only to reverse your attitude towards him— to lay hands on his property, revile him, assault him, and he will be a brigand again in a moment, as ready to crush you as you are to crush him, and quite as full of pretentious moral reasons for doing it.

In short, when Major Barbara says that there are no scoundrels, she is right: there are no absolute scoundrels, though there are impracticable people of whom I shall treat presently. Every practicable man (and woman) is a potential scoundrel and a potential good citizen. What a man is depends on his character; but what he does, and what we think of what he does, depends on his circumstances. The characteristics that ruin a man in one class make him eminent in another. The characters that behave differently in different circumstances behave alike in similar circumstances. Take a common English character like that of Bill Walker. We meet Bill everywhere: on the judicial bench, on the episcopal bench, in the Privy Council, at the War Office and Admiralty, as well as in the Old Bailey dock or in the ranks of casual unskilled labour.

And the morality of Bill's characteristics varies with these various circumstances. The faults of the burglar are the qualities of the financier: the manners and habits of a duke would cost a city clerk his situation. In short, though character is independent of circumstances, conduct is not; and our moral judgments of character are not: both are circumstantial. Take any condition of life in which the circumstances are for a mass of men practically alike: felony, the House of Lords, the factory, the stables, the gipsy encampment or where you please!

In spite of diversity of character and temperament, the conduct and morals of the individuals in each group are as predicable and as alike in the main as if they were a flock of sheep, morals being mostly only social habits and circumstantial necessities. Strong people know this and count upon it. In nothing have the master-minds of the world been distinguished from the ordinary suburban season-ticket holder more than in their straightforward perception of the fact that mankind is practically a single species, and not a menagerie of gentlemen and bounders, villains and heroes, cowards and daredevils, peers and peasants, grocers and aristocrats, artisans and laborers, washerwomen and duchesses, in which all the grades of income and caste represent distinct animals who must not be introduced to one another or intermarry.

Napoleon constructing a galaxy of generals and courtiers, and even of monarchs, out of his collection of social nobodies; Julius Caesar appointing as governor of Egypt the son of a freedman—one who but a short time before would have been legally disqualified for the post even of a private soldier in the Roman army; Louis XI making his barber his privy councillor: all these had in their different ways a firm hold of the scientific fact of human equality, expressed by Barbara in the Christian formula that all men are children of one father. A man who believes that men are naturally divided into upper and lower and middle classes morally is making exactly the same mistake as the man who believes that they are naturally divided in the same way socially.

And just as our persistent attempts to found political institutions on a basis of social inequality have always produced long periods of destructive friction relieved from time to time by violent explosions of revolution; so the attempt—will Americans please note—to found moral institutions on a basis of moral inequality can lead to nothing but unnatural Reigns of the Saints relieved by licentious Restorations; to Americans who have made divorce a public institution turning the face of Europe into one huge sardonic smile by refusing to stay in the same hotel with a Russian man of genius who has changed wives without the sanction of South Dakota; to grotesque hypocrisy, cruel persecution, and final utter confusion of conventions and compliances with benevolence and respectability.

It is quite useless to declare that all men are born free if you deny that they are born good. Guarantee a man's goodness and his liberty will take care of itself. To guarantee his freedom on condition that you approve of his moral character is formally to abolish all freedom whatsoever, as every man's liberty is at the mercy of a moral indictment, which any fool can trump up against everyone who violates custom, whether as a prophet or as a rascal.

This is the lesson Democracy has to learn before it can become anything but the most oppressive of all the priesthoods. Let us now return to Bill Walker and his case of conscience against the Salvation Army. Major Barbara, not being a modern Tetzel, or the treasurer of a hospital, refuses to sell Bill absolution for a sovereign. Unfortunately, what the Army can afford to refuse in the case of Bill Walker, it cannot refuse in the case of Bodger. Bodger is master of the situation because he holds the purse strings. "Strive as you will," says Bodger, in effect: "me you cannot do without. You cannot save Bill Walker without my money."

And the Army answers, quite rightly under the circumstances, "We will take money from the devil himself sooner than abandon the work of Salvation." So Bodger pays his conscience-money and gets the absolution that is refused to Bill. In real life Bill would perhaps never know this. But I, the dramatist, whose business it is to show the connexion between things that seem apart and unrelated in the haphazard order of events in real life, have contrived to make it known to Bill, with the result that the Salvation Army loses its hold of him at once.

But Bill may not be lost, for all that. He is still in the grip of the facts and of his own conscience, and may find his taste for blackguardism permanently spoiled. Still, I cannot guarantee that happy ending. Let anyone walk through the poorer quarters of our cities when the men are not working, but resting and chewing the cud of their reflections; and he will find that there is one expression on every mature face: the expression of cynicism.

The discovery made by Bill Walker about the Salvation Army has been made by every one of them. They have found that every man has his price; and they have been foolishly or corruptly taught to mistrust and despise him for that necessary and salutary condition of social existence. When they learn that General Booth, too, has his price, they do not admire him because it is a high one, and admit the need of organizing society so that he shall get it in an honorable way: they conclude that his character is unsound and that all religious men are hypocrites and allies of their sweaters and oppressors. They know that the large subscriptions which help to support the Army are endowments, not of religion, but of the wicked doctrine of docility in poverty and humility under oppression; and they are rent by the most agonizing of all the doubts of the soul, the doubt whether their true salvation must not come from their most abhorrent passions, from murder, envy, greed, stubbornness, rage, and terrorism, rather than from public spirit, reasonableness, humanity, generosity, tenderness, delicacy, pity and kindness.

The confirmation of that doubt, at which our newspapers have been working so hard for years past, is the morality of militarism; and the justification of militarism is that circumstances may at any time make it the true morality of the moment. It is by producing such moments that we produce violent and sanguinary revolutions, such as the one now in progress in Russia and the one which Capitalism in England and America is daily and diligently provoking.

At such moments it becomes the duty of the Churches to evoke all the powers of destruction against the existing order. But if they do this, the existing order must forcibly suppress them. Churches are suffered to exist only on condition that they preach submission to the State as at present capitalistically organized. The Church of England itself is compelled to add to the thirty-six articles in which it formulates its religious tenets, three more in which it apologetically protests that the moment any of these articles comes in conflict with the State it is to be entirely renounced, abjured, violated, abrogated and abhorred, the policeman being a much more important person than any of the Persons of the Trinity.

And this is why no tolerated Church nor Salvation Army can ever win the entire confidence of the poor. It must be on the side of the police and the military, no matter what it believes or disbelieves; and as the police and the military are the instruments by which the rich rob and oppress the poor (on legal and moral principles made for the purpose), it is not possible to be on the side of the poor and of the police at the same time.

Indeed the religious bodies, as the almoners of the rich, become a sort of auxiliary police, taking off the insurrectionary edge of poverty with coals and blankets, bread and treacle, and soothing and cheering the victims with hopes of immense and inexpensive happiness in another world when the process of working them to premature death in the service of the rich is complete in this.

## CHRISTIANITY AND ANARCHISM

Such is the false position from which neither the Salvation Army nor the Church of England nor any other religious organization whatever can escape except through a reconstitution of society. Nor can they merely endure the State passively, washing their hands of its sins. The State is constantly forcing the consciences of men by violence and cruelty. Not content with exacting money from us for the maintenance of its soldiers and policemen, its gaolers and executioners, it forces us to take an active personal part in its proceedings on pain of becoming ourselves the victims of its violence.

As I write these lines, a sensational example is given to the world. A royal marriage has been celebrated, first by sacrament in a cathedral, and then by a bullfight having for its main amusement the spectacle of horses gored and disembowelled by the bull, after which, when the bull is so exhausted as to be no longer dangerous, he is killed by a cautious matador. But the ironic contrast between the bullfight and the sacrament of marriage does not move anyone.

Another contrast—that between the splendor, the happiness, the atmosphere of kindly admiration surrounding the young couple, and the price paid for it under our abominable social arrangements in the misery, squalor and degradation of millions of other young couples—is drawn at the same moment by a novelist, Mr Upton Sinclair, who chips a corner of the veneering from the huge meat packing industries of Chicago, and shows it to us as a sample of what is going on all over the world underneath the top layer of prosperous plutocracy.

One man is sufficiently moved by that contrast to pay his own life as the price of one terrible blow at the responsible parties. Unhappily his poverty leaves him also ignorant enough to be duped by the pretence that the innocent young bride and bridegroom, put forth and crowned by plutocracy as the heads of a State in which they have less personal power than any policeman, and less influence than any chairman of a trust, are responsible.

At them accordingly he launches his sixpennorth of fulminate, missing his mark, but scattering the bowels of as many horses as any bull in the arena, and slaying twenty-three persons, besides wounding ninety-nine. And of all these, the horses alone are innocent of the guilt he is avenging: had he blown all Madrid to atoms with every adult person in it, not one could have escaped the charge of being an accessory, before, at, and after the fact, to poverty and prostitution, to such wholesale massacre of infants as Herod never dreamt of, to plague, pestilence and famine, battle, murder and lingering death—perhaps not one who had not helped, through example, precept, connivance, and even clamor, to teach the dynamiter his well-learnt gospel of hatred and vengeance, by approving every day of sentences of years of imprisonment so infernal in its unnatural stupidity and panic-stricken cruelty, that their advocates can disavow neither the dagger nor the bomb without stripping the mask of justice and humanity from themselves also.

Be it noted that at this very moment there appears the biography of one of our dukes, who, being Scotch, could argue about politics, and therefore stood out as a great brain among our aristocrats. And what, if you please, was his grace's faviurite historical episode, which he declared he never read without intense satisfaction?

Why, the young General Bonapart's pounding of the Paris mob to pieces in 1795, called in playful approval by our respectable classes "the whiff of grapeshot," though Napoleon, to do him justice, took a deeper view of it, and would fain have had it forgotten.

And since the Duke of Argyll was not a demon, but a man of like passions with ourselves, by no means rancorous or cruel as men go, who can doubt that all over the world proletarians of the ducal kidney are now revelling in "the whiff of dynamite" (the flavour of the joke seems to evaporate a little, does it not?) because it was aimed at the class they hate even as our argute duke hated what he called the mob. In such an atmosphere there can be only one sequel to the Madrid explosion. All Europe burns to emulate it. Vengeance! More blood!

Tear "the Anarchist beast" to shreds. Drag him to the scaffold. Imprison him for life. Let all civilized States band together to drive his like off the face of the earth; and if any State refuses to join, make war on it. This time the leading London newspaper, anti-Liberal and therefore anti-Russian in politics, does not say "Serve you right" to the victims, as it did, in effect, when Bobrikofl; and De Plehve, and Grand Duke Sergius, were in the same manner unofficially fulminated into fragments.

No: fulminate our rivals in Asia by all means, ye brave Russian revolutionaries; but to aim at an English princess-monstrous! hideous! hound down the wretch to his doom; and observe, please, that we are a civilized and merciful people, and, however much we may regret it, must not treat him as Ravaillac and Damiens were treated. And meanwhile, since we have not yet caught him, let us soothe our quivering nerves with the bullfight, and comment in a courtly way on the unfailing tact and good taste of the ladies of our royal houses, who, though presumably of full normal natural tenderness, have been so effectually broken in to fashionable routine that they can be taken to see the horses slaughtered as helplessly as they could no doubt be taken to a gladiator show, if that happened to be the mode just now.

Strangely enough, in the midst of this raging fire of malice, the one man who still has faith in the kindness and intelligence of human nature is the fulminator, now a hunted wretch, with nothing, apparently, to secure his triumph over all the prisons and scaffolds of infuriate Europe except the revolver in his pocket and his readiness to discharge it at a moment's notice into his own or any other head. Think of him setting out to find a gentleman and a Christian in the multitude of human wolves howling for his blood.

Think also of this: that at the very first essay he finds what he seeks, a veritable grandee of Spain, a noble, high-thinking, unterrified, malice-void soul, in the guise—of all masquerades in the world!—of a modern editor. The Anarchist wolf, flying from the wolves of plutocracy, throws himself on the honour of the man. The man, not being a wolf (nor a London editor), and therefore not having enough sympathy with his exploit to be made bloodthirsty by it, does not throw him back to the pursuing wolves—gives him, instead, what help he can to escape, and sends him off acquainted at last with a force that goes deeper than dynamite, though you cannot make so much of it for sixpence. That righteous and honorable high human deed is not wasted on Europe, let us hope, though it benefits the fugitive wolf only for a moment.

The plutocratic wolves presently smell him out. The fugitive shoots the unlucky wolf whose nose is nearest; shoots himself; and then convinces the world, by his photograph, that he was no monstrous freak of reversion to the tiger, but a good looking young man with nothing abnormal about him except his appalling courage and resolution (that is why the terrified shriek Coward at him): one to whom murdering a happy young couple on their wedding morning would have been an unthinkably unnatural abomination under rational and kindly human circumstances.

Then comes the climax of irony and blind stupidity. The wolves, balked of their meal of fellow-wolf, turn on the man, and proceed to torture him, after their manner, by imprisonment, for refusing to fasten his teeth in the throat of the dynamiter and hold him down until they came to finish him. Thus, you see, a man may not be a gentleman nowadays even if he wishes to.

As to being a Christian, he is allowed some latitude in that matter, because, I repeat, Christianity has two faces. Popular Christianity has for its emblem a gibbet, for its chief sensation a sanguinary execution after torture, for its central mystery an insane vengeance bought off by a trumpery expiation. But there is a nobler and profounder Christianity which affirms the sacred mystery of Equality, and forbids the glaring futility and folly of vengeance, often politely called punishment or justice. The gibbet part of Christianity is tolerated. The other is criminal felony. Connoisseurs in irony are well aware of the fact that the only editor in England who denounces punishment as radically wrong, also repudiates Christianity; calls his paper The Freethinker; and has been imprisoned for two years for blasphemy.

And now I must ask the excited reader not to lose his head on one side or the other, but to draw a sane moral from these grim absurdities. It is not good sense to propose that laws against crime should apply to principals only and not to accessories whose consent, counsel, or silence may secure impunity to the principal. If you institute punishment as part of the law, you must punish people for refusing to punish. If you have a police, part of its duty must be to compel everybody to assist the police. No doubt if your laws are unjust, and your policemen agents of oppression, the result will be an unbearable violation of the private consciences of citizens.

But that cannot be helped: the remedy is, not to license everybody to thwart the law if they please, but to make laws that will command the public assent, and not to deal cruelly and stupidly with lawbreakers. Everybody disapproves of burglars; but the modern burglar, when caught and overpowered by a householder usually appeals, and often, let us hopes, with success, to his captor not to deliver him over to the useless horrors of penal servitude. In other cases the lawbreaker escapes because those who could give him up do not consider his breech of the law a guilty action.

Sometimes, even, private tribunals are formed in

opposition to the official tribunals; and these private tribunals employ assassins as executioners, as was done, for example, by Mahomet before he had established his power officially, and by the Ribbon lodges of Ireland in their long struggle with the landlords. Under such circumstances, the assassin goes free although everybody in the district knows who he is and what he has done. They do not betray him, partly because they justify him exactly as the regular Government justifies its official executioner, and partly because they would themselves be assassinated if they betrayed him: another method learnt from the official government.

Given a tribunal, employing a slayer who has no personal quarrel with the slain; and there is clearly no moral difference between official and unofficial killing. In short, all men are anarchists with regard to laws which are against their consciences, either in the preamble or in the penalty. In London our worst anarchists are the magistrates, because many of them are so old and ignorant that when they are called upon to administer any law that is based on ideas or knowledge less than half a century old, they disagree with it, and being mere ordinary homebred private Englishmen without any respect for law in the abstract, naively set the example of violating it.

In this instance the man lags behind the law; but when the law lags behind the man, he becomes equally an anarchist. When some huge change in social conditions, such as the industrial revolution of the eighteenth and nineteenth centuries, throws our legal and industrial institutions out of date, Anarchism becomes almost a religion.

The whole force of the most energetic geniuses of the time in philosophy, economics, and art, concentrates itself on demonstrations and reminders that morality and law are only conventions, fallible and continually obsolescing. Tragedies in which the heroes are bandits, and comedies in which law-abiding and conventionally moral folk are compelled to satirize themselves by outraging the conscience of the spectators every time they do their duty, appear simultaneously with economic treatises entitled "What is Property? Theft!" and with histories of "The Conflict between Religion and Science." Now this is not a healthy state of things. The advantages of living in society are proportionate, not to the freedom of the individual from a code, but to the complexity and subtlety of the code he is prepared not only to accept but to uphold as a matter of such vital importance that a lawbreaker at large is hardly to be tolerated on any plea.

Such an attitude becomes impossible when the only men who can make themselves heard and remembered throughout the world spend all their energy in raising our gorge against current law, current morality, current respect ability, and legal property. The ordinary man, uneducated in social theory even when he is schooled in Latin verse, cannot be set against all the laws of his country and yet persuaded to regard law in the abstract as vitally necessary to society.

Once he is brought to repudiate the laws and institutions he knows, he will repudiate the very conception of law and the very groundwork of institutions, ridiculing human rights, extolling brainless methods as "historical," and tolerating nothing except pure empiricism in conduct, with dynamite as the basis of politics and vivisection as the basis of science. That is hideous; but what is to be done? Here am I, for instance, by class a respectable man, by common sense a hater of waste and disorder, by intellectual constitution legally minded to the verge of pedantry, and by temperament apprehensive and economically disposed to the limit of old-maidishness; yet I am, and have always been, and shall now always be, a revolutionary writer, because our laws make law impossible; our liberties destroy all freedom; our property is organized robbery; our morality is an impudent hypocrisy; our wisdom is administered by inexperienced or malexperienced dupes, our power wielded by cowards and weaklings, and our honour false in all its points. I am an enemy of the existing order for good reasons; but that does not make my attacks any less encouraging or helpful to people who are its enemies for bad reasons.

The existing order may shriek that if I tell the truth about it, some foolish person may drive it to become still worse by trying to assassinate it. I cannot help that, even if I could see what worse it could do than it is already doing. And the disadvantage of that worst even from its own point of view is that society, with all its prisons and bayonets and whips and ostracisms and starvations, is powerless in the face of the Anarchist who is prepared to sacrifice his own life in the battle with it. Our natural safety from the cheap and devastating explosives which every Russian student can make, and every Russian grenadier has learnt to handle in Manchuria, lies in the fact that brave and resolute men, when they are rascals, will not risk their skins for the good of humanity, and, when they are sympathetic enough to care for humanity, abhor murder, and never commit it until their consciences are outraged beyond endurance. The remedy is, simply not to outrage their consciences. Do not be afraid that they will not make allowances.

All men make very large allowances indeed before they stake their own lives in a war to the death with society. Nobody demands or expects the millennium. But there are two things that must be set right, or we shall perish, like Rome, of soul atrophy disguised as empire. The first is, that the daily ceremony of dividing the wealth of the country among its inhabitants shall be so conducted that no crumb shall go to any able-bodied adults who are not producing by their personal exertions not only a full equivalent for what they take, but a surplus sufficient to provide for their superannuation and pay back the debt due for their nurture.

The second is that the deliberate infliction of malicious injuries which now goes on under the name of punishment be abandoned; so that the thief, the ruffian, the gambler, and the beggar, may without inhumanity be handed over to the law, and made to understand that a State which is too humane to punish will also be too thrifty to waste the life of honest men in watching or restraining dishonest ones. That is why we do not imprison dogs. We even take our chance of their first bite. But if a dog delights to bark and bite, it goes to the lethal chamber.

That seems to me sensible. To allow the dog to expiate

his bite by a period of torment, and then let him loose in a much more savage condition (for the chain makes a dog savage) to bite again and expiate again, having meanwhile spent a great deal of human life and happiness in the task of chaining and feeding and tormenting him, seems to me idiotic and superstitious. Yet that is what we do to men who bark and bite and steal. It would be far more sensible to put up with their vices, as we put up with their illnesses, until they give more trouble than they are worth, at which point we should, with many apologies and expressions of sympathy, and some generosity in complying with their last wishes, then, place them in the lethal chamber and get rid of them. Under no circumstances should they be allowed to expiate their misdeeds by a manufactured penalty, to subscribe to a charity, or to compensate the victims. If there is to be no punishment there can be no forgiveness.

We shall never have real moral responsibility until everyone knows that his deeds are irrevocable, and that his life depends on his usefulness. Hitherto, alas! humanity has never dared face these hard facts. We frantically scatter conscience money and invent systems of conscience banking, with expiatory penalties, atonements, redemptions, salvations, hospital subscription lists and what not, to enable us to contract-out of the moral code. Not content with the old scapegoat and sacrificial lamb, we deify human saviors, and pray to miraculous virgin intercessors. We attribute mercy to the inexorable; soothe our consciences after committing murder by throwing ourselves on the bosom of divine love; and shrink even from our own gallows because we are forced to admit that it, at least, is irrevocable—as if one hour of imprisonment were not as irrevocable as any execution!

If a man cannot look evil in the face without illusion, he will never know what it really is, or combat it effectually. The few men who have been able (relatively) to do this have been called cynics, and have sometimes had an abnormal share of evil in themselves, corresponding to the abnormal strength of their minds; but they have never done mischief unless they intended to do it. That is why great scoundrels have been beneficent rulers whilst amiable and privately harmless monarchs have ruined their countries by trusting to the hocus-pocus of innocence and guilt, reward and punishment, virtuous indignation and pardon, instead of standing up to the facts without either malice or mercy. Major Barbara stands up to Bill Walker in that way, with the result that the ruffian who cannot get hated, has to hate himself.

To relieve this agony be tries to get punished; but the Salvationist whom he tries to provoke is as merciless as Barbara, and only prays for him. Then he tries to pay, but can get nobody to take his money. His doom is the doom of Cain, who, failing to find either a savior, a policeman, or an almoner to help him to pretend that his brother's blood no longer cried from the ground, had to live and die a murderer. Cain took care not to commit another murder, unlike our railway shareholders (I am one) who kill and maim shunters by hundreds to save the cost of automatic couplings, and make atonement by annual subscriptions to deserving charities. Had Cain been allowed to pay off his score, he might possibly have killed Adam and Eve for the mere sake of a second luxurious reconciliation with God afterwards. Bodger, you may depend on it, will go on to the end of his life poisoning people with bad whisky, because he can always depend on the Salvation Army or the Church of England to negotiate a redemption for him in consideration of a trifling percentage of his profits.

There is a third condition too, which must be fulfilled before the great teachers of the world will cease to scoff at its religions. Creeds must become intellectually honest. At present there is not a single credible established religion in the world. That is perhaps the most stupendous fact in the whole world-situation. This play of mine, Major Barbara, is, I hope, both true and inspired; but whoever says that it all happened, and that faith in it and understanding of it consist in believing that it is a record of an actual occurrence, is, to speak according to Scripture, a fool and a liar, and is hereby solemnly denounced and cursed as such by me, the author, to all posterity.

# Chapter 3

# Lilith

The conclusion of Back to Methuselah by George Bernard Shaw presents a fertile area for investigation inasmuch as the last major speech, that of Lilith, brings a new character on stage, one who has been previously referred to only in the most perfunctory way and who has not appeared before. Lilith has a mythological function in Judaic legend as Adam's first wife but her function in Back to Methuselah seems to be different, to be more symbolic of certain things that are expressed in the play. This symbolism is accomplished by the use of anaphora in her concluding speech which serves to summarize the events of the play and bring a cyclical structure to the play as a whole.

The segment of the play in which Lilith is introduced and which includes her concluding speech is as follows:

A Voice. There is one that came before the serpent. The Serpent. That is the voice of Lilith, in whom the father and mother were one. Hail, Lilith! Lilith becomes visible between Cain and Adam. Lilith. I suffered unspeakably; I tore myself asunder; I lost my life, to make of my one flesh these twain, man woman. And this is what has become of it. What do you make of it, Adam, my son?

Adam. I made the earth bring forth by my labour, and the woman bring forth by my love. And this is what has come of it. What do you make of it, Eve, my wife? Eve. I nourished the egg in my body and fed it with my blood. And now they let it fall as the birds did, and suffer not at all. What do you make of it, Cain, my first-born? Cain. I invented killing and conquest and mastery and the winnowing out of the weak by the strong. And now the strong have slain one another; and the weak live for ever; and their deeds do nothing for the doer more than for another. What do you make of it, snake? The Serpent. I am justified. For I chose wisdom and the knowledge of good and evil; and now there is no evil; and wisdom and good are one. It is enough. [She vanishes].

Cain. There is no place for me on earth any longer. You cannot deny that mine was a splendid game while it lasted. But now! Out, out, brief candle! [He vanishes]. Eve. The clever ones were always my favorites. The diggers and the fighters have dug themselves in with the worms. My clever ones have inherited the earth.

All's well [She fades away]. Adam. I can make nothing of it, neither head nor tail. What is it all for? Why? Whither? Whence? We were well enough in the garden. And now the fools have killed all the animals; and they are dissatisfied because they cannot be bothered with their bodies! Foolishness, I call it. [He disappears].

Lilith. They have accepted the burden of eternal life. They have taken the agony from birth; and their life does not fail them even in the hour of their destruction. Their breasts are without milk: Their bowels are gone: the very shapes of them are only ornaments for their children to admire and caress without understanding. Is this enough; or shall I labour again? Shall I bring forth something that will sweep them away and make an end of them as they have swept away the beasts of the garden, and made an end of the crawling things and the flying things and of all them that refuse to live for ever? I had patience with them for many ages: they tried me very sorely.

They did terrible things: I stood amazed at the malice and destructiveness of the things I had made: Mars blushed as he looked down on the shame of his sister planet: cruelty and hypocrisy became so hideous that the face of the earth was pitted with the graves of little children among which living skeletons crawled in search of horrible food. The pangs of another birth were already upon me when one man repented and lived three hundred years; and I waited to see what would come of that. And so much came of it that the horrors of that time seem now but an evil dream. They have redeemed themselves from their vileness, and turned away from their sins.

Best of all, they are still not satisfied: the impulse I gave them in that day when I sundered myself in twain and launched Man and Woman on the earth still urges them: after passing a million goals they press on to the goal of redemption from the flesh, to the vortex freed from matter, to the whirlpool in pure intelligence that, when the world began, was a whirlpool in pure force. And though all that they have done seems but the first hour of the infinite work of creation, yet I will not supersede them until they have forded this last stream that lies between flesh and spirit, and disentangled their life from the matter that has always mocked it. I can wait: waiting and patience mean nothing to the eternal. I gave the woman the greatest of gifts: curiosity.

By that her seed has been saved from my wrath; for I also am curious; and I have waited always to see what they will do tomorrow. Let them feed that appetite well for me. I say, let them dread, of all things, stagnation; for from the moment I, Lilith, lose hope and faith in them, they are doomed. In that hope and faith I have let them live for a moment; and in that moment I have spared them many times. But mightier creatures than they have killed hope and faith, and perished from the earth; and I may not spare them for ever. I am Lilith: I brought life into the whirlpool of force, and compelled my enemy, Matter, to obey a living soul.

But in enslaving Life's enemy I made him Life's master; for that is the end of all slavery; and now I shall see the slave set free and the enemy reconciled, the whirlpool become all life and no matter. And because these infants that call themselves ancients are reaching out towards that, I will have patience with them still; though I know well that when they attain it they shall become one with me and supersede me, and Lilith will be only a legend and a lay that has lost its meaning. Of Life only is there no end; and though of its million starry mansions many are empty and many still unbuilt, and though its vast domain is as yet unbearably desert, my seed shall one day fill it and master its matter to its uttermost confines. And for what may be beyond, the eyesight of Lilith is too short. It is enough that there is a beyond. [She vanishes].

Before proceeding with an analysis of the text the overall background for the scene needs to be established.

Back to Methuselah bears the subtitle A Metabiological Pentateuch. Shaw is referring in the title and the subtitle to several things. First, the Biblical character Methuselah, the oldest person mentioned in the Bible; secondly the title is a itself a cataphoric reference to the rallying cry of the brothers Barnabas in the second play, The Gospel of the Brothers' Barnabas.

The subtitle combines two ideas, metabiology, a word that is unique to Shaw and one that is constructed along the same lines and conveys the same import as metaphysics, in other words metabiology is analogous to metaphysics in that it is philosophically oriented. Then the word pentateuch appears in the subtitle. Pentateuch means simply five books but is most often found in discussions of the first five books of the Bible, so the play is linked to other texts from the outset by the use of the name Methuselah, which is a direct Biblical reference, to philosophy through the neologistic formation of metabiological and then refers back to the Bible in a formal sense by adding the word pentateuch.

Shaw could have called the play a quintet and seems to have chosen the word pentateuch precisely because of the Biblical associations; the word quintet would have musical connotations which Shaw apparently wanted to avoid. It is important to realise that Shaw, in other texts, expressed the view that what he advocated was a religion and that his plays were in some sense religious texts.

This Biblical patterning is exhibited in the first two plays In the Beginning and The Gospel of the Brothers' Barnabas. The first title echoes the opening of the first book of the Bible, Genesis, whose opening words are "In the beginning...." This play deals with Adam and Eve and the temptation in the garden in its first act and with Cain in its second. The second play, which uses the word gospel in its title is intended to echo the gospels of the Bible, as such the connotative meanings of the word include those of message or news that is promulgated and doctrinal belief.

The third, fourth, and fifth plays within the cycle are entitled The Thing Happens, The Tragedy of an Elderly Gentleman, and As Far as Thought Can Reach respectively.

The plays trace the evolution of the human race and predict its future evolution and vary from mythological and symbolic significance in the first play to standard drawing room comedy and satire in the second and third plays to melodrama in the fourth and depiction of a utopian society in the fifth.

The main concern, however, of this paper is an analysis, which makes use of the terms and concepts of discourse analysis, of Lilith's concluding speech. In order to do this it is necessary to provide a brief summary of the plots and thematic content of both plays.

## BACKGROUND SUMMARY

Back to Methuselah opens with In the Beginning, which is designed to parallel the opening chapters of Genesis. The cast of characters in the first act is limited to Adam, Eve, and the Serpent. The first act hinges on the discovery, by the human characters, of a dead deer. They realise that it is possible for them to die by accident, as the deer has and so Adam decides that he shall set a limit on the span of his life and live for a thousand years. Eve acquiesces in this decision after she has been told about sex by the Serpent. It is the serpent who mentions Lilith and says,

I remember Lilith, who came before Adam and Eve. I was her darling, as I am yours. She was alone: there was no man with her. She saw death as you saw it when the fawn fell; and she knew then that she must find out how to renew herself and cast the skin like me. She had a mighty will; she strove to renew herself and strove and willed and willed for more moons than there are leaves on all the trees of the garden.

Her pangs were terrible: her groans drove sleep from Eden. She said it must never be again: that the burden of renewing life was past bearing: that it was too much for one. And when she cast her skin, lo! there was not one new Lilith but two: one like herself, the other like Adam. You were the one: Adam was the other.

It is noteworthy that rather then being Adam's first wife and a demonic character, as she is in Judaic legend, Lilith is here described as a proto-being, one who is almost divine.

The second act of the play takes place several hundred years later and the characters are Adam, Eve, and Cain. This episode takes place after Cain has killed Abel and is the scene in which the symbolic nature of the characters is brought to the fore. Cain is representative of the hunters and warriors; Adam and the dead Abel are representative of the farmers; the unseen Tubal and Enoch are representative of the clever artificers and religious mystics and Eve is, of course, the mother of all of them.

The fifth play, As Far as Thought Can Reach, takes place in 31,920 AD and presents a typical day in the life of a utopian community of a race of people who represent the next step in evolution, as such it has no plot to speak of, there is merely a succession of incidents which include the birth of a new member of the community (the people are oviparous and are born at what we would take for the biological age of seventeen); a visit by some older people, referred to as Ancients, who live an eremitical existence on the periphery of the community; an exhibition of a scientific exhibit (laboratory created human beings) by Pygmalion, who is killed by his creations; the departure of a young person who has started to turn old, to become one of the ancients and, finally, when the day is over, the ghostly appearances of Adam, Eve, Cain, the Serpent, and Lilith.

In the course of the fifth play there is discussion of evolution and the teleological impulse behind evolution, which is, for the Ancients, to achieve power, specifically intellectual power, and to eliminate the body and become immortal spirits without bodies, to become vortices.

It is at the end of the fifth play that our fragment of discourse appears, after the characters from the 30th millennium have left the stage the characters appear one by one and converse until finally Lilith appears.

Before giving a detailed analysis of Lilith's speech it seems advisable to discuss the overall patterns of reference in the fragment given here.

## THE SCENE

The first thing that is noticeable about this fragment is the identification A Voice. The character is not named until another character has used the character's name, this pattern of character identification only after the character has been identified by another is typical of printed Shavian dramatic texts and is found throughout the corpus of his work.

The voice states that it came before the serpent, thereby indicating its antiquity. The serpent responds by recognizing it as "the voice of Lilith, in whom the father and mother were one." This is the first reference in our scene fragment in which the reference is to the first play. Lilith was described in the first play as coming before Adam and Eve and has not been mentioned again until now.

Lilith then becomes visible between Cain and Adam, not between Adam and Eve or between Eve and the Serpent but between the two representatives of distinctly different types of men, between Adam, the gardener and farmer, and Cain, the hunter and warrior. Lilith then speaks and continues the reference begun by the Serpent and describes the pain she endured in bringing about the creation of Adam and Eve from herself. She then asks Adam what he makes of it and refers to him by his relationship to her, i.e., "my son." This pattern of statement and reference will be repeated by each character in turn, except for the Serpent, first they will state what they have done, then say what has become of it, and then ask another character what they make of it. The Serpent, however, varies the formula by saying "I am justified," and then making his statement.

All the statements refer to events depicted or described in

the first play. Further, no character in his or her statement refers directly to what the character preceding him has stated. The reference in each case is to what the character did or represented in the first play of the cycle. Lilith's statement is about cleaving herself in two and making man and woman but Adam's is about his life as a farmer and Eve's is about nourishing the egg in her body; Cain's statement is about conquest and mastery and the snake's is about choosing wisdom.

This apparent irrelevance, however, is dependent upon the reference, in each case, of the word it in "What do you make of it...." In order for the reference not to be irrelevant it is necessary for the anaphora to be not to the statement that the character has just made but to the scene which has just been played out and to which Lilith, Adam, Eve, Cain and the Serpent have just been unseen spectators. This reference to the scene is something that will be emphasized in Lilith's concluding speech.

The formulaic nature of these utterance serves at least two purpose, topical statement and symbolic representation. The speaker is at once presenting a topic, one which has been discussed or dealt with throughout the cycle and also presenting themselves as the symbolic inventor of the thing (sexual duality, war, and so on). The question then becomes not one of what someone thinks about what has happened but "Was I justified in doing what I did; does the course of events bear witness to my success or failure?" The Serpent therefore is the last to speak in this sequence and the first to vanish and his speech states that he was justified and pleased with the results of his decision.

Since each of these utterances by the character refers to something which is not immediate to the reader or audience and which lies outside the fragment of the play which is presented here it is unclear whether this should be construed as exophoric or endophoric. Insofar as the episodes, in a staged production, would be seen with one or more breaks of uncertain duration between them or even with a break of one or more days, it would be exophoric and each play within the cycle would be a separate event. From the standpoint of the author, or of a person who reads the cycle at one sitting, the lines are endophoric inasmuch as the plays form, from his perspective, a unified whole.

From the viewpoint of an audience, which may experience the plays as a series of events over a number of days, the references are exophoric. Insofar as the plays form a unified whole and represent a single work the pattern of pronominal reference could be construed as endophoric and it is as an endophoric reference based on the act of reading rather than as an audience viewing the cycle that we shall take as the pattern of pronominal reference.

Cain is the last human to speak in this sequence and he addresses the Serpent who makes his statement and then vanishes. At this point the characters begin to disappear from the stage in the opposite of the order in which they have just spoken. Cain makes a statement, which contains a quotation from Shakespeare, and then vanishes; Eve and Adam then speak and disappear so that only Lilith is left alone on the stage. It then falls to her to draw together the themes of the five plays and bring about an overall unity to what would otherwise be five isolated plays of varying quality strung together in a haphazard fashion.

This is accomplished indirectly and in part by the nature of the anaphoric reference in her speech. The use of they in the first sentence "They have accepted the burden of eternal life" makes no sense if it is to be understood as referring to the spirits who have just vanished, particularly since Adam and Eve are explicitly represented in the first play as having rejected "the burden of eternal life." Subsequent pronomial references then must be understood as having for their antecedents not the most immediate preceding direct statement but some other event or person or scene that precedes it.

The reference of the pronouns continues to be to the actors of the scene we have just witnessed up until Lilith says "I had patience with them for many ages...." At this point the reference seems to shift away from the immediately preceding scene to something else and this shift in reference is accompanied by a shift in tense from the perfect tense of "They have accepted...They have taken...their life does not fail them..." to the past tense of "I had patience...they did terrible things." The reference cannot be to the ancients and the children of the fifth play because it has already been established that they live in a utopia so the reference must be to something or someone else.

The reference remains ambiguous until Lilith says "one man repented" here the reference is to a character in the second and third plays, the Reverend Haslam, who is the first man, since Biblical times, to live for three hundred years. At this point the immediately preceding references become clear, the reference is to the people that lived up until the time when Haslam "repented" and chose to live for three hundred years.

The reference immediately shifts again, however, and the they in "They have redeemed themselves..." cannot be understood as referring to Haslam and to those preceding him so it must be to something subsequent to Haslam's time and this is the ancients and children of the utopian community depicted in As Far as Thought Can Reach. This point is the last time the reference shifts in a major way or for an extended period of time to the generation of man that has just stepped off the stage although there are references to "the woman," who is most likely Eve, as Lilith's daughter or female side.

Lilith's speech takes a different turn when she says, "I will not supersede them." Prior to this point she had been a symbol of a sexual unity that diverged and became a duality, at this point, however, she begins a process that can only be called an apotheosis. The implicature of "I will not supersede them" is that she, Lilith, has the power or capability of supplanting the human race. Her next sentence, "I can wait: waiting and patience mean nothing to the eternal." is ambiguous in its use of the word eternal.

The word eternal is used in an anaphoric way referring back to the I of the opening. What is ambiguous, however, is whether "the eternal" is used as referring to one of a number of eternal things of which Lilith is but one or whether it is used as referring to the concept of the eternal itself. The meaning seems to be clarified when Lilith says, "I am Lilith: I brought life into the whirlpool of force, and compelled my enemy, Matter, to obey a living soul."

Here the identification of Lilith seems to be with some eternal force, an immaterial force that is opposed to matter. The statement "I am Lilith" is in this context more than a simple statement of identity, the qualifications that are added after this clause indicate that it is said as the result of an apotheosis so that the meaning of "I am Lilith" becomes identical with the the statement "I am God." This continues in the next utterance of the speech in which Lilith says "I will have patience..." and then ends. At this point Lilith switches and speaks of being superseded by the ancients and then proceeds to an encomium on Life. Finally she concludes that whatever may lay beyond that point is too far away for her to see but that it is sufficient that there is a beyond. She vanishes and the final play is concluded.

The speech of Lilith then brings to a conclusion the cycle of plays that Shaw has presented and it does this by the use of a pattern of reference to the previous scenes but it does not conclude by simply summarizing the events of the play, for example the fourth play, The Tragedy of an Elderly Gentleman is not referred to at all by Lilith and the second play, The Gospel of the Brothers Barnabas is referred to only indirectly insofar as the Reverend Haslam, the one who repents and lives for three hundred years, is a part of that play.

The central points of reference then are the first play, In The Beginning; the third play, The Thing Happens; and the fifth play, As Far as Thought Can Reach. These are the plays that contain events that Lilith refers to by indirection rather than coming out and saying something like "You remember Haslam, he chose to live for three hundred years." The pronomial reference then is indirect and serves to bring the play to a complete close by repetition of the important philosophical ideas of the play.

Lilith, however, conveys new ideas that are themselves of philosophical importance. Specifically the opposition of Matter and Life as entities has never been broached before;

also the identity of Lilith with the creative principle itself is not made until her line beginning "I am Lilith," which is a new idea that has never been suggested before.

The speech summarizes and brings to a close the cycle and it also points to what may be beyond the far future when Lilith says "And for what may be beyond, the eyesight of Lilith is too short. It is enough that there is a beyond."

A detailed analysis of Lilith's speech is given in an appendix below, immediately following the summary.

Lilith's speech brings a very long dramatic cycle to a close. The entire cycle occupies over two hundred and sixty pages of type and would probably take six or seven hours to present in its entirety on the stage. Since the play represents not only a dramatic fiction but also a philosophical and religious statement, as evidenced by the subtitle A Metabiological Pentateuch it is necessary to bring the play not only to a dramatic conclusion but also to a philosophical one. This is done in Lilith's speech which acts as a topical coda to the plays and summarizes and introduces new material as part of the statement of the play's topic.

The topic of the cycle is not necessarily the dramatic events that are portrayed in the play but what motivates the play, in this case a presentation of biological and philosophical doctrine. Lilith presents these doctrines in a summary form in her final discourse, a discourse that breaks down into three major sections, and a possible fourth section, or coda, that are marked by changes in tense and apparent changes in the reference of the third person pronouns which are used throughout the analyzed text. This may be referred to as the macro-structure of the text and can be determined by looking at the changes in tense and in pronominal reference that accompany the change in tense.

The macro- structure can be seen by breaking the speech into sections on the basis of the shift in tense from the perfect to the past and by the shift in pronominal usage from "they" to "I". Based on this it can be seen that the first part includes some material marked by the use of "I" but which is put into the first part because it is conjoined with the use of the perfect tense. The second section begins with Lilith asserting she had patience with them for many ages and is marked by a shift to the past tense. The third section is marked by a shift to the perfect tense again and the fourth by a shift in tense and mood, which goes from the indicative to the imperative and then alternates back and forth between the two moods before finally settling down into the indicative again.

In the first part of the speech, which is presented in the perfect tense she is referring to the ancients and to the fact that they have evolved into a race of long- lived human beings. The second part is presented through a shift to the past tense and is a description of the pain and suffering that ensued as a result of the First World War.

The third section seems to shift back to the ancients and to the evolved race of humans that have inherited the earth. Lilith then moves into what can only be described as an apotheosis or coda, which marks a fourth section, distinguished from the other three by the use of the first person singular, in which she reveals herself or identifies herself with life and with God and finally concludes with a vision of life's many mansions and the statement that for what may lie beyond the next step in evolution her, that is Lilith's, eyesight is too short.

The play is brought to a conclusion by the summation that refers back to the events and descriptions of the last play, by the shift in reference to the character of Haslam, the man who repented and chose to live for three hundred years, and then by shifting back to the ancients again. This serves to establish the relationship between the ancients and their short-lived ancestors and to provide the topical links between the second and third plays and the fifth play.

When Lilith refers to herself, or to "the woman," as she does in fragment 55, she is referring to the personages of the first play and to the event which the Serpent describes as giving birth to sexual duality and this sets the stage for her apotheosis.

The difficulty with the text arises from the shift in reference and in tense. A cursory reading would suggest that the third person pronouns that are used throughout the speech always refer to mankind in general but a closer examination, such as this, shows that in some cases it is clearly necessary for the reference to be to the ancients and in others to their short-lived predecessors.

This ambiguity, however, can be resolved by noting that it is accompanied by a shift from the perfect tense to the past and back again so that two different groups are clearly referred to, one of which is acting in the present and one which did something in the past. Topical links between the plays are then established by the constant back and forth reference to events and scenes that are presumably still fresh in the viewer's/reader's mind. The play is therefore summarized and new directions are indicated by the concluding speech and the play is thus brought to a satisfying dramatic and philosophical conclusion.

## DETAILED ANALYSIS

In the analysis that follows Lilith's speech has been broken up into a series of fragments based on two principles, that of punctuation, where a pause has been indicated by a period, comma, semicolon, or colon that portion has been treated as a separate fragment, and by breaking on what seem to be minor pauses, which are not indicated by punctuation marks, but which also seem to be relatively complete information units.

Each fragment in the original version of this paper was preceded by a number in a bold typeface and then given immediately below it in a contrasting bold typeface.This feature has been omitted in this HTML version.

Each fragment, except for those fragments that are composed of single words, contains information that is, in terms of discourse analysis, of both the given and new types, however, rather than attempting a mechanical breakdown of the information into these categories it has been mentioned only in those places where it seemed to affect the interpretation of the text or its oral interpretation by someone portraying Lilith on the stage.

Lilith is identified as the speaker of the text.

They have accepted the burden of eternal life.

The first problem is the anaphoric reference of they. The characters who have vanished could be the they but this seems not to be warranted because they are described earlier as having rejected eternal life. It is precisely because Adam set a limit on the human life span that life has been shortened. The reference therefore must be to some other group of characters. The only characters that the description would fit are those that are characterized as ancients.

They have taken the agony from birth;

Once again the pronoun refers to the ancients. The new information that is conveyed here is that these people have taken the agony from birth. They have done this by becoming oviparous as we witnessed at the opening of the fifth play and their life does not fail them

"Their life" in this instance refers to either their individual lives or to the principle of life. This seems to be ambiguous even in the hour of their destruction.

The ambiguity is resolved here. It, "their life," does not fail them even in the hour of death. There is a kind of immortality predicated about the ancients.

Their breasts are without milk:

The children are presented as being born at a state of development that would correspond to about seventeen or eighteen so milk is not necessary and the She- Ancients are presented as being sexually unattractive and withered. This restates the description of the Ancients given earlier in the play. The first reference to the Ancients' lack of sexuality is as follows:

The Youth. You old fish! I believe you dont know the difference between a man and a woman. The Ancient. It has long ceased to interest me in the way it interests you. And when anything no longer interests us we no longer know it.

A She-Ancient is described in a stage direction as being "like the He- Ancient, equally bald, and equally without sexual charm...."

Their bowels are gone:

Just as the mammary glands have lost their function so the bowels have also lost their alimentary function and nutrition is accomplished through some means that is never specified within Back to Methuselah.

the very shapes of them are only ornaments

The bodies have become useless because they have no procreative function and are reduced to inspiration for artistic composition and sentimental lovemaking. for their children to admire and caress without understanding.

The children admire and caress each others' bodies without understanding the nature of the sexual act, partly because they are oviparous and partly because they do not seem to have sexual intercourse but only to engage in cuddling and non- sexual acts of affection.

Is this enough;

Is this evolutionary development enough, that is, is it satisfactory.

or shall I labour again?

Labour in this context has two possible meanings, both of which may be present. "Shall I work again. Shall I Lilith attempt to bring forth a new race of beings again by my effort." It can also mean "Shall I undergo labour, the pangs of a new birth in order to bring forth a new race." In this case the denotative usage of work and the connotative usage of the labour involved in birth co- exist.

Shall I bring forth something that will sweep them away

Lilith here implies that she has destructive capabilities as well as the procreative capabilities described above. She can bring forth on her own initiative as it were a race of beings that is capable of doing away with the ancients and their civilization.

and make an end of them

That the sweeping away will be total is suggested by the use of the word end. There will be no more men if Lilith chooses to bring forth a new race of beings.

as they have swept away the beasts of the garden,

The beasts of the garden must refer to the garden of Eden. No other garden has been mentioned in the play up until this moment so the reference of the beasts of the garden must refer not to a particular real garden but to a garden that stands as a symbol.

This is the garden of Eden. The beasts of the garden then becomes symbolic of all animals. The ancients have done away with all of the animals that formerly inhabited the garden of Eden.

*and made an end of the crawling things*

Among the animals that they have done away with are the crawling things, i.e., snakes and other animals that crawl along the ground.

*and the flying things*

*The have also killed off all of the birds.*

and of all them that refuse to live for ever?

The implication of this is that these creatures refused to live forever, they chose, in some fashion, to die, and therefore the ancients did away with them.

I had patience with them for many ages:

The tense has shifted to the past tense here. Is Lilith referring to the race of ancients or is she referring to some other race, the race that preceded the ancients perhaps?

*they tried me very sorely.*

The people, whoever they were, tried Lilith. Try is used here in the same way that it is used in the phrase "try my patience." Trying Lilith in this case means to test her, to bring her to the limit of her endurance. They did terrible things:

These people did things, things which will be enumerated in the next clause or series of clauses.

I stood amazed at the malice and destructiveness

Lilith is perplexed by the capacity for evil exhibited by these beings.

of the things I had made:

*She created them*

*Mars blushed*

Mars can be used in two senses that are widely known, as the next planet out from the sun and as the Roman god of war. The war god can also be associated with the planet as he is in astrology.

as he looked down on the shame of his sister planet:

The sense now becomes clear, the planet Mars is referred to but is their also a connotation of Mars the war god?

*cruelty and hypocrisy became so hideous*

At this point we still do not know whether Mars is merely an astronomical planet with no meaning beyond his closeness to the earth or whether it has some deeper significance.

that the face of the earth was pitted with the graves of little children

The fact that the earth is "pitted with the graves of little children" suggests that this is something which happened in the past and that this was in the nature of a catastrophe. The implication seems to be that it was the cruelty and hypocrisy that caused the earth to contain these graves.

*among which living skeletons crawled in search of horrible food.*

*Starvation and cannibalism are suggested here.*

*The pangs of another birth were already upon me*

*Lilith was ready to supersede the human race at this point.*

*when one man repented*

This one man who repented is Haslam, the minister of the second play and a major character in the third play of the cycle. The chain of reference that was started earlier, in fragment 18, has therefore shifted from the generation of ancients to the earlier race of men that was not long- lived. The reference to Mars now becomes clearer. The second play refers to events of the First World War and the Barnabas brothers developed their biological doctrine in response to the events of that war. The use of Mars is then a reference not only to the planet's proximity to earth but also its mythological associations as the planet of the war god.

However, since all of the things, the hypocrisy and cruelty, the First World War, in short all of the things referred to in 20-27 occur outside of the play these references are clearly exophoric and the reader/audience is expected to share, with Lilith, some of this knowledge.

*and lived three hundred years;*

The use of the word repented in 29 indicates that Haslam chose to live for three hundred years. The fact that Lilith says three hundred years refers back to the doctrine of the brothers Barnabas that three hundred years was the minimum amount of time necessary for a hum being to develop political capacity.

*and I waited to see what would come of that.*

Lilith stood aside as a silent witness to see the progress of mankind after a long life had been chosen and she decided not to supersede mankind. Here the that refers to the decision to live for three hundred years.

*And so much came of it*

Lilith, after a full stop, returns to the thought of what came about as a result of the decision to live for three hundred years. This sentence is therefore, in some sense, a continuation of the thought of the previous sentence. The and in this sentence differs from the and in the preceding sentence in that it comes after a full stop, indicated by the period, and represents a return to or a reply to the subject of the first sentence.

The and in fragment 31 is used as a simple conjunction between two clauses while in this case there is a different process going on than merely linking two clauses. And, used here as indicative of the consequence that followed upon an action is an additive conjunction that imposes a greater addition to the topic of fragment It would be at this point that the actress portraying Lilith would add stress to the utterance and thereby indicate the importance of the consequences of this action.

*that the horrors of that time seem now but an evil dream.*

The horrors of that time refers to either a specific period of time, such as the First World War or to the period when the short- lived race of men dominated the earth.

*They have redeemed themselves from their vileness,*

This cannot refer to the people of the past because it has already been established that they were marked by cruelty and hypocrisy. The tense has also shifted, however, and it has gone from the simple past tense of 18-33 back to the perfect tense of 1-17. The reference of the pronouns must also have shifted then and the reference is not to the past generations but to those living as Lilith speaks, that is to the ancients.

*and turned away from their sins.*

*Just as Haslam repented so also the race of ancients has repented.*

*Best of all,*

*There is more that is even better than the fact that they have repented and turned away from their sins.*

they are still not satisfied:

*The ancients are not fulfilled by what they have done.*

*The impulse I gave them*

Lilith gave them something but what it was and when she gave it to them are uncertain until the identification is made in fragment 39.

*in that day when I sundered myself in twain*

Lilith is not talking about the ancients now but the race of man as it was when it began. This is indicated by the shift back to the past tense in 38 and continued in 39 where the time is specifically indicated, the day when she divided herself into two. The time is therefore ancient and the reference of they refers not to the previous race of men or to the ancients alone but to mankind as a whole and thus includes both groups.

*and launched Man and Woman on the earth*

*Lilith's act of rendering herself brought sexual duality into being.*

still urges them:

*The impulse still exists.*

*after passing a million goals*

Here million is used not as a precise number but, because it is a round number, as one that is suggestive of an enormous number. The goals are what? not goals in soccer or rugby surely but goals of a personal or racial nature. They have passed all expectations might be another way of putting it.

*they press on to the goal of redemption from the flesh,*

They, again the ancients are referred to, have yet another goal in mind. To be redeemed from the flesh. Lilith again uses a form of the word redeem, which she used before in 34, just as she has earlier used the word repent when she referred to Haslam. Lilith has used the word repent in 29 and sins in 35. The repeated emphasis of words with explicitly religious meanings suggests that Lilith is linking biology and religion into one whole. The fact that men refuse to live for three hundred years or more is therefore a sin but one that can be remedied and redemption, of a kind, obtained by embracing eternal life.

*to the vortex freed from matter,*

Lilith now refers to an earlier dialogue between the two Ancients and the children in which the He- Ancient states that he wants to be a vortex.

*to the whirlpool in pure intelligence that,*

The nature of the vortex is stated. It is something that exists in pure intelligence.

*when the world began,*

The vortex existed from all time, or from the beginning of time when the world was created.

*was a whirlpool in pure force.*

The nature of the vortex was different then. It was a vortex in pure force, not a vortex in pure intelligence. Intelligence and force are different then but what is the nature of the difference between force and intelligence?

And though all that they have done seems but the first hour of the infinite work of creation,

The sentence begins with an and after a full stop but here Lilith does not return to the topic of 47 she goes on to a different topic which is what they have done but is the they to be understood as the ancients or as mankind in general. The fact that the tense is the same tense as in 34 would seem to indicate that it is the ancients that she is referring to but the use of the word all makes the implication seem more inclusive, all that they have done would seem to indicate that Lilith is referring not just to the race of ancients but to mankind in general.

*yet I will not supersede them*

The yet suggests that something would be proper but that it will not be done. The sentence now comes to mean that even though it would be proper and Lilith has the capability and the power to supersede them, in this case not the vanished race but the race of ancients, she will not do it.

*until they have forded this last stream*

The delay in supersession, however, is only temporary,

only until they have achieved what Lilith describes as fording the last stream.

*that lies between flesh and spirit,*

This last stream is that which separates flesh and spirit. The metaphor is drawn of l flesh and spirit as two shores or the two banks of a river that are separated by a current.

and disentangled their life from the matter that has always mocked it.

There is not a separate life of flesh and one of spirit but a single life as indicated by the use of their life (singular) instead of their lives (plural) and this life is entwined with matter. Matter, however, has always mocked it, the life of the flesh and the spirit. I can wait:

Lilith expresses her ability to wait and endure, but she pauses here, as if she expects to add a qualification to this statement. waiting and patience mean nothing to the eternal.

At this point Lilith qualifies the utterance in fragment 53 that she can wait by saying that she is eternal. At first glance this piece of information, which must, in this utterance, be classified as new, both on the grounds of stress, which would fall naturally on eternal and in terms of conventional description, seems ambiguous.

Lilith could be saying that she is one of a number of eternal beings and the utterance could be interpreted as meaning, "waiting and patience mean nothing to eternal beings, of whom I am one," or it could mean "waiting and patience mean nothing to the principal of eternity, which is myself."

This will not be clarified until fragment 74 and the utterances that follow it.

I gave the woman the greatest of gifts:

Lilith gave the woman a gift. In this case the woman is a substitutive usage that refers to Eve. We know this because the Serpent has told us earlier that Eve was born from Lilith's attempts to cleave herself in two and thus bring about a bisexual method of reproduction.

*curiosity.*

The gift of Lilith to Eve is identified as curiosity, in this case the ability to wonder and wait and see what will happen as the result of her actions.

*By that her seed has been saved from my wrath;*

The seed that Lilith mentions must in this context mean both the race of short- lived and the race of long- lived humans, both of which have Eve as their common ancestress. The word wrath is suggestive of more than passing anger and refers back to her earlier utterances beginning with fragment 12 about sweeping them away.

*for I also am curious;*

Lilith now gives a reason for her hesitation in sweeping away the human race, that she is curious as well. Instead of saying "I am curious also" she says "...I also am curious" which serves to shift the emphasis onto the fact that she, Lilith, is curious, as well as Eve. This intensifies her statement.

*and I have waited always*

The conventional way of phrasing this utterance would be "and I have always waited," the shift in position of the adverb always suggests that here the stress is placed on always as conveying new information. The fact that Lilith has waited has already been given earlier, what is now conveyed through the placement of the adverb is the duration of the waiting, this has been eternal, or nearly so and is conveyed by the shifted position of always.

*to see what they will do tomorrow.*

The purpose of her waiting is now stated, and that is to see what they will do in the future, tomorrow, in this case not representing a day which is the successor to the current day but rather an indefinite period of time in the future.

*Let them feed that appetite well for me.*

The them in this case follows the pattern that we have seen earlier in which the pronoun is used with the present or the perfect tense to refer to the current race of people or ancients and not to their short- lived predecessors. There is a shift in mood here from the indicative to the imperative. Lilith is now beginning to assume the aspect of a god who is capable of imposing orders upon her creatures.

*I say,*

The mood continues to be in the imperative mood begun in 61 but it now becomes more intense with the "I say," which is suggestive of of a moral commandment.

*let them dread,*

They, the beings who inhabit the earth are supposed to experience an emotion, the emotion of dread.

*of all things,*

This phrase carries the implication not only that there is a set of things which should cause them to experience this dread or which is related in some way to the dread which they are to experience but also that there is something, yet to be named, which is particularly dreadful.

*stagnation;*

The most dreadful thing is named, stagnation, or standing still.

*for from the moment I, Lilith,*

At this period Lilith will experience something which may cause her to make good the threat implied in fragment 12. This is intensified by using the pronoun I and then repeating her name, Lilith. We already know her name so the repetition immediately following the pronominal reference can only serve to intensify it, as if she were to point out not she is not merely a person but that she has a special identity and nature.

*lose hope and faith in them,*

Lilith will experience a loss of faith and hope in the creatures that live upon the earth if they stagnate. It is now clear that stagnation is linked in a causal way to a loss of faith and hope on the part of Lilith

*they are doomed.*

The race will be doomed to extinction and she will make good her earlier threat to sweep them away.

In that hope and faith I have let them live for a moment;

She returns to the idea of faith and hope but it is now clear that it is not the faith and hope of the creatures but the faith and hope that she has in them. It is as a consequence of this faith and hope that she has let them live. The period of time that they have lived is described as a moment, this contrasts sharply with Lilith's description of herself as eternal in fragment 54.

*and in that moment I have spared them many times.*

This fragment is linked with the preceding one by a simple and, which is used here purely to connect the two clauses, unlike the earlier usage in fragment 32. The repetition of moment emphasizes again the brevity of time but then is contrasted immediately by the fact that she has spared them, the people, "many times." In other words in a brief period of time which seems to an eternal being to be merely a moment she has spared mankind an indefinite number of times.

*But mightier creatures than they have killed hope and faith,*

The earlier usage of conjunctions after full pauses has been to use an additive conjunction, primarily and, now Lilith shifts from an additive to an adversative conjunction when she begins her next utterance with but. This indicates that it is still a possibility that they could be superseded and she makes this clear with "mightier creatures than they" which may indicate some larger and more ferocious creatures than human beings existed and vanished. These creatures have killed hope and faith, so what became of them?

*and perished from the earth;*

The question is answered, those beings that have killed hope and faith have become extinct.

*and I may not spare them for ever.*

Here she refers to the possibility of human extinction again and indicates that it is very possible that she may supersede the human race despite her curiosity and patience.

I am Lilith:

We already know that she is Lilith. Here the utterance must have the stress on the word Lilith, so what is new is not the fact that she is Lilith but that Lilith is a special person, one with a special identity.

*I brought life into the whirlpool of force,*

Lilith's identity is beginning to become clearer. She is not merely a proto- being who divided herself into two and created man and woman out of herself, she also has a cosmic identity in that she was capable of dealing with an abstract entity, life, and bringing it into a "whirlpool of force," which might be construed as energy as a physicist understands the concepts.

*and compelled my enemy,*

Enemy here is clearly new information. There is a brief pause, indicated by the comma and the stress of the line, when it is spoken, would seem to demand that enemy be stressed. Since we have had no previous indication that Lilith had any enemies this would seem to need immediate clarification.

*Matter,*

The enemy is identified as matter. The capitalization in the printed text would seem to indicate that this word is to be particularly stressed and is immediately recognized as new information. We have never before known that life was opposed by matter.

*to obey a living soul.*

Matter is organized, made organic, and forced to take orders from the spiritual entity which it envelops.

*But in enslaving Life's enemy I made him Life's master;*

Lilith again uses the adversative conjunction but after a full stop. The contrast started at the beginning of this fragment is carried through in the full fragment through the use of enemy and master. These two words connote an adversative relationship in and of themselves.

*for that is the end of all slavery;*

For is a causal marker and here the utterance states that the end of all slavery is for the slave to become the master's master.

*and now I shall see the slave set free*

Lilith returns to the additive conjunction and implies that she is certain to see at some time in the future, indicated by shall, the soul set free from the confines of matter.

*and the enemy reconciled,*

Matter and life will be reconciled and cease to be enemies once the two are separate from each other.

*the whirlpool become all life and no matter.*

She refers back to the whirlpool of force mentioned in fragment 75. This also refers back to the conversation between the two Ancients and the children in which the He- Ancient expresses the wish to be a vortex.

And because these infants that call themselves ancients are reaching out towards that,

Lilith, after a full stop, refers to the older members of the long- lived race and calls them infants. This is contrastive, she is contrasting those individuals who live for even as long as eight hundred years with the eternal being, Lilith and saying that they are mere infants compared with her. The fact that they aspire to be vortices is, however, given by the fact that they are "reaching out towards that," where that is understood as the whirlpool referred to in the preceding fragment.

*I will have patience with them still;*

Despite all of her threats she will have patience with them. This is emphasized by the placement of still, the final position in the clause, coming as it does at the pause indicated by the semicolon would seem to show that it is to be stressed and that the still is new information. She will have patience with these creatures now and for an indefinite period of time seems to be the implicature of the word still in this fragment.

*though I know well that when they attain it they shall become one with me and supersede me,*

Lilith again switches to an adversative formation with though and it becomes not a question of whether or not the human race can attain this goal but a question of time, as shown by when. The attainment of the goal is certain then but this will have consequences for both the race and Lilith in that they will become one with her and supersede her. The supersession will be because no one is around to remember her.

*and Lilith will be only a legend and a lay that has lost its meaning.*

Lilith continues and adds the information that she will be a legend and a lay, which is used here as a synonym for song, in this case a song on an heroic or epic theme, but that it will have no meaning because no one will exist in a material form and understand sexual duality and material existence.

*Of Life only is there no end;*

In the printed text life is capitalized, this would again seem to indicate that a greater stress is to be placed here, so life is effectively new information and the fact that it is the only thing that has no end is emphasized by the placement of end before a major pause as indicated by the semicolon. Life and end are therefore marked as new information, but if life is the only thing that has no end or finality then the inference to be made is that everything else has an end.

*and though of its million starry mansions many are empty and many still unbuilt,*

The most important point to be gotten from this fragment is the allusive nature of the word mansions. This is an exophoric reference to the scriptural verse where Jesus says "In my father's house are many mansions."

*and though its vast domain is as yet unbearably desert,*

The domain is that of life and Lilith states by implication that despite all of the time that has passed and all of the people that have lived the house of life is as yet unfilled, hence the domain is a desert.

*my seed shall one day fill it and master its matter to its uttermost confines.*

Mankind is now identified not as the seed of Eve but as the seed or progeny of Lilith. Further the universe shall be filled and the matter that composes it shall be controlled or mastered by mankind until the farthest reaches of the universe are brought under the control of mankind.

*And for what may be beyond,*

Once again there is a full stop and Lilith continues with the additive conjunction and. She has evidently paused and then gone on to say that there is the possibility of something beyond even this.

*the eyesight of Lilith is too short.*

Eyesight is used as a symbol of thought, the usage here is similar to the usage of foresight in which knowledge and vision are implicitly related. The fact that her eyesight is too short is used as a substitution for near- sightedness, or myopia in which objects that are near to the eyes are seen in focus and those that are distant are blurred. The utterance then means that her intellectual knowledge or vision cannot focus beyond a certain point and so she cannot perceive or know what lies beyond this point, that of becoming a vortex or disembodied spirit.

It is enough that there is a beyond.

This does not matter, however, the fact that there is an eternity in which all of this can take place and that there is something beyond even the furthest point that she can see is itself sufficient.

## Chapter 4

# "Arms and the Man"- An Analysis of the Social Context

George Bernard Shaw wrote Arms and the Man in 1893 during the Victorian era when most plays were lighter dramas or comedies in the vein of The Importance of Being Earnest, which was a play about manners and other Victorian conventions. Still, in many ways, Arms and the Man, despite some of its themes, is a perfect example of Victorian literature. The play opened to the British public in 1894 to mixed reviews and was one of the plays included in the Plays Pleasant Volume which included a few of Shaw's other, less popular works including "You Never Can Tell."

What is most interesting about *Arms and the Man* is that, although it is a comedy, it deals with several political and social themes covertly. Ideas such as the idealism behind war and the romanticism of love are attacked through satire and even more importantly, issues of class are brought to the forefront. Shaw was an avid socialist and had a number of beliefs about class that are appropriate to the historical situation in Europe. At the time the play was performed, Britain was experiencing a number of significant social and political changes as issues of class were coming to the forefront of national debates.

The idea of class struggle is at the heart of "Arms and the Man" by George Bernard Shaw but instead of making the reader or viewer keenly aware of them, he slips in a number of thought-provoking lines and makes one think about these issues after the laughter has faded. Unlike other plays of the time, *Arms and the Man* did not seek to merely entertain an audience with polite humour. Instead, it sought to expose some of the most pressing issues of the day in a palatable format—the comedy.

This is a trademark feature of Shaw's plays and he once wrote, "What is the use of writing plays, what is the use of writing anything, if there is not a will which finally moulds chaos itself into a race of gods" (Peters 109). In other words, George Bernard Shaw thought that there was no sense in writing something for mere entertainment, what he wrote had to serve a higher purpose and encourage people to think rather to sit and be content to be entertained.

At the time George Bernard Shaw wrote the Arms and the Man there were a number of class struggles taking place in Britain as a new wave of socialist ideology was taking hold. Up until this point, workers in Britain were often paid low wages and offered little security as their country became even further industrialized. In response there were several workers movements that rose up across the nation and this drew the attention of artists and writers such as Shaw.

Issues of class struggle were coming to the forefront of both political and debates in Europe and Shaw began working with the socialist cause. His feelings that the British workers were not advocating their interests enough and that the political structure in England was making it impossible for them to have any success led him to speak out publicly, often at the risk of some of his personal friendships. In addition to writing plays, Shaw became a full-time advocate of socialism and joined the Fabian Society where he wrote a number of socialist documents. He also traveled to Russia, met with Stalin, and came home to declare how wonderfully he believed socialism was going in that country.

In "Arms and the Man" George Bernard Shaw chose to set his place in the midst of a foreign war, in part so that he could offer some commentary about war. The lead female in the play, much like English audiences of the time, is sucked into the idea of the war hero and finds it difficult to think that war is anything except not glamorous.

Notions of love and war as well as class are turned upside down and the reader is forced to confront them just as British playgoers of the time would eventually have to face these issues when the First World War finally came around over a decade later. At this time though, war was still a vague enough notion that it could be romanticized and this is part of the criticism George Bernard Shaw offers in the play Arms and the Man.

In addition to this is his commentary about class which is the most important in terms of the social context of this play. "Arms and the Man" by George Bernard Shaw occurs during the Serbo-Bulgarian War in 1885.

She is supposed to marry one of the heroes of the war who she thinks of in terms of the idealized version of soldiers many British held during this pre-World War I era. The peace of the beginning scenes is interrupted with the arrival of a Swiss soldier in Raina's bedroom asking for a safe place to hide.

Raina offers him refuge and laughs because he does not carry guns or ammunition but chocolate instead. As the play progresses, Raina eventually begins to understand that her betrothed does not fit into the same heroic image she has always had and instead begins to fall in love with the Swiss soldier. By the end of the play "Arms and the Man" by George Bernard Shaw she finally declares her love for the soldier and the story ends happily for nearly everyone.

What is missing from this short synopsis is the way that George Bernard Shaw addresses the important social issue of class during this time. Throughout "Arms and the Man" George Bernard Shaw he constantly but with subtlety makes a number of important statements about his political and social beliefs about society and class that make reference to the social context of this play—Victorian England.

Throughout "Arms and the Man" by George Bernard Shaw, slight variances are used in the speech of the characters to indicate class distinctions. It is clear that Shaw, a noted socialist, has a great deal of concern about class issues and instead of making the reader keenly aware of these notions through any direct mention, he uses their dialogue as well as cues within the setting to reveal these elements. "Despite the prominence of debate and speechmaking in his plays, one sometimes forgets that before Shaw-the-playwright came Shaw-the-debater and public speaker.

All were platform spellbinders". Part of the reason it is so easy to forget that there a number of encoded social messages within the text is because is remarkably deft at conveying injustices and problems through characterization and language. His writing style is thus very critical of the Victorian-era society yet instead of doing this overtly, he relies on gestures, dialogue, and setting to set the stage for the debate. His "public speaking" would, in this sense be limited to the voices of his characters who come from variable class backgrounds and have a system of language that is suitable for their class. Only through this mode can Shaw open a platform for class debates.

At the very beginning of "Arms and the Man" by George Bernard Shaw, the reader is already cued into the class differences that will plague the text until the end. For instance, the introduction of Raina in "Arms and the Man" by George Bernard Shaw is not one that values her inner life, but those of outer appearances, something that is of great importance to her and her family. Without dialogue, she is introduced in one of the important quotes from Arms and the Man by George Bernard Shaw, "On the balcony, a young lady, intensely conscious of the romantic beauty of the night, and of the fact that her own youth and beauty is a part of it, is on the balcony, gazing at the snowy Balkans.

She is covered by a long mantle of furs, worth, on a moderate estimate, about three times the furniture of the room". Here, it is not important who she is or what she thinks about her class position, but rather it is made clear that she is within an upper class and strives to maintain the outward appearances through her luxurious clothing while the representative items of her "inner life" (in this case her bedroom) are shoddy and unremarkable. Without being told the first thing about this character's thoughts, it is clear that reader should be immediately attentive to class distinctions through outward appearances. It should also be noted that this setting is beautiful, but we are not expected to focus on the beauty in a traditional way, but rather to pay attention to the social statement—that there is a woman who obviously pays more for her clothes than the upkeep of her living quarters.

In the mind of one critic, "The world, as he [Shaw] looks out upon it, is a painful spectacle to his eyes. Pity and indignation move him. He is not sentimental, as some writers are, but the facts grind his soul... in a word, art has an end beyond itself; and the object of Shaw's art in particular is to make men think, to make them uncomfortable, to convict them of sin".

This is an especially succinct observation in this scene since there is opportunity for sentimentality and romanticism (since she is framed by a lovely setting) but this is not enough for Shaw; he must shift the object of the reader's gaze away from physical beauty to the darker world of class and character. Descriptions go beyond setting as well in "Arms and the Man" by George Bernard Shaw. The class of characters is not only revealed and critiqued by the setting itself, but by the narrated actions and stage directions for particular characters.

For instance, consider the graceful language and the almost fairy-tale nature of the "dance" of Raina and her fiancée as they simply sit down for dinner. The narrator states in one of the important quotes from "Arms and the Man" by George Bernard Shaw, "Sergius leads Raina forward with splendid gallantry, as if she were a queen. When they come to the table, she turns to him with a bend of the head; he bows; and thus they separate, he coming to his place, and she going behind her father's chair". This is a very detailed and complex routine these characters act out and is representative of the codified ideals of chivalric behaviour typically associated with the elite.

This stands in sharp constant to the plodding nature of the exchanges between Nicola and Louka, whose settings and stage directions are not filled with the same dreamy interludes. While Sergius and Raina literally appear to dance in the aforementioned scene, the lower class scenes of the two servants are much less stunning, the narrator only stating where they are in physical space and their language being stunted and free from the dramatic connotations and Byron-like feel of the upper class characters.

This same shift in possibilities, from the potential sentimentality to the social critique, is apparent in terms of language as well as setting descriptions. According to one scholar, "Characters whose impulses are conventional or traditional will use language reflecting their mechanical responses and will be satirized accordingly, while characters who posses a Shavian vitality will express that spontaneity through a freedom not only from moral and ethical formulas but from verbal convention as well" (Weintraub 215).

This is apparent when contrasting two particular classes represented in the play. First of all, it should be noted that those of the lower class, especially the solider who enters Raina's room and the servant girl Nicola are all exciting and interesting characters. They posses the "Shavian vitality" and their language is free from the ornament and needless over-romanticized talk of the upper classes. Consider, as a comparison, the meaning that is compressed, while remaining vital when Louka scolds her servant friend, saying with "searching scorn" no less, "You have the soul of a servant, Nicola".

Some of the most powerful emotion in the text is present in these short but potent thesis statements. Another example of this would be when the solider tells Raina, "I've no ammunition. What use are cartridges in battle? I always carry chocolate instead; and I finished the last cake of that yesterday". In many ways, it seems as though these characters with clipped but highly powerful statements are much like Shaw. They are making massive overarching statements about their world without seeming to do it, as if any implied social critique might have been incidental.

These short bursts of meaning for much farther to reveal genuine sentiment than Raina's long winded proclamations of love when she confesses, breathlessly and dramatically, Well, it came into my head just as he was holding me in his arms and looking into my eyes, that perhaps we only had our heroic idea because we are so find of reading Byron and Pushkin, and because we were so delighted with the opera that season at Bucharest. Real life is so seldom like that—indeed never, as far as I knew it then" (Shaw 10).

While at the end she makes a powerful statement, she is too caught up in the class-driven notions of how a lady should speak to be able to make a direct and succinct statement that has the gravity of the aforementioned quotes from the lower class characters. In sum, Shaw is not overt in his social critiques in this play.

His style requires that the reader interpret not only the varied language of his characters, but of the deeper meanings behind the settings and speech. While a particular scene's description might seem, on first glance, to offer a beautiful setting or something simple, underneath these images are deeper layers of meaning that are geared towards society. In terms of dialogue and *Arms and the Man,* Shaw writes his characters as complete individuals whose class and deep thoughts lay masked behind relatively simple-sounding speeches.

The ultimate effect of this writing style is that the reader becomes implicated in class debates (as well as other equally prominent debates about the nature of war as well) and is left with a moving story as well as something more to consider. In more broad terms, the play, *Arms and the Man* by George Bernard Shaw reflects some of the intense class conflicts of the day and addresses several of Shaw's ideas about society and politics as well.

# Chapter 5

# George Bernard Shaw's Reception of Mozart's *Don Giovanni*

The two major cultural figures of Mozart and Shaw appear at first glance to be an unlikely pairing: One an eighteenth-century composer of music mainly for the aristocracy; the other a twentieth-century socialist. Wolfgang Amadeus Mozart, born in 1756, represents the apogee of the Viennese Classical style and composed works in practically all musical genres including such unforgettable operas as *The Marriage of Figaro, The Magic Flute,* and of course, *Don Giovanni.*

George Bernard Shaw was born exactly a hundred years later than Mozart in 1856. He enjoyed an enormous reputation as a prolific dramatist through such plays as *Joan of Arc, Pygmalion, Caesar and Cleopatra, Heartbreak House* and *Man and Superman*. He was active in the Fabian Society advocating democratic socialism and was well-known as a social and political iconoclast. He enjoyed world-wide fame, won the Nobel Prize for Literature in 1925, was offered a knighthood which he declined, and refused the Order of Merit stating in typically brusque Shavian fashion that he had already awarded it to himself.

Shaw was also music critic until 1876 of the London papers, *The Hornet, The Star,* and *The World*. Although he knew a great deal about music, he confessed that he did not know as much as one would suppose from his articles but, as he said, "in the kingdom of the deaf the one-eared is king" [Shaw, II, 808] and he never ceased using his position of influence as music critic to encourage the public to demand better standards and the musicians to produce them. As William Irvine states, "Shaw was by no means content to tell composers how to compose, musicians how to play, stage managers how to produce, and audiences how to feel.

He also told financiers of music how to venture and manage, and the government how to legislate with reference to musical problems. In his critical pages the English, a placid and political people, discovered with amazement that music was a burning political issue, and might at any moment explode into social revolution". [Irvine, 324] He wrote under the pseudonym *Corno di Bassetto* as he felt that he had no name worth signing: G.B.S. meant nothing to the public at the time and he chose *Corno di Bassetto* because a) he felt it sounded like a European title and b) because nobody knew what a Corno di Bassetto actually was. [Shaw, I, 30] He was later to say though that, "if I had ever heard a note of it [then] I should not have selected it for a character which I intended to be sparkling.

The devil himself could not make a basset horn sparkle". [Ibid., 31] These subjective, trenchant and inimitably Shavian reviews reveal a portrait of musical life in London during the late Victorian Era and beyond and were collected and published by the Shaw scholar Dan Lawrence in three volumes in 1981 under the title *Shaw's Music*.

Mozart's music did not enjoy the same enormous popularity during the late nineteenth century as it does today. In London the most important musical events were the great Choir Festivals at which works by Bach, Handel, and particularly Mendelssohn were presented in performances with gigantic forces of singers. There was an over-exaggerated sense of the importance of Italian opera and many English composers actually had to have their operas first performed in Italian translations in order to be taken seriously (the first performance of Wagner's *Der Fliegende Holländer* was sung in Italian translation); in fact Wagner was rarely heard at all, and as Shaw wrote in 1890, "a man who has seen *Die Walküre* on the stage is a much greater curiosity than one who has explored the Congo". [Ibid., 924] Indeed, most of the concert-goers only wanted to hear the popular operettas of Gilbert and Sullivan. Shaw was famous for his championing of both Wagner and Mozart: In 1891, the year of the Mozart Centenary, Shaw wrote in an article in *The Illustrated London News* that "at present his music is hardly known in England except to those who study it in private.

Public performances of it are few and far between, and, until Richter conducted the E flat Symphony here, nobody could have gathered from the vapid, hasty, trivial readings which were customary in our concert rooms that Mozart, judged by 18th century standards, had any serious claim to his old-fashioned reputation". [Shaw, II, 488]

The Centenary was celebrated nonetheless, although Shaw was scathing about how journalists were prepared to cover it with "likenesses of Mozart at all ages; view of Salzburg; portrait of Marie Antoinette [...] to whom he proposed marriage at an early age" etc. [Ibid., 478] He pitied the unfortunate singers, players and conductors most because they would have to actually make the public hear the wonders which the newspapers were describing so lavishly.

Of the performance of Mozart's music he writes that "nothing but the finest execution - beautiful, expressive, and intelligent - will serve [...] whilst, at the same time, your work is so obvious, that everyone thinks it must be easy, and puts you down remorselessly as a duffer for botching it". [Ibid., 482f.] He goes on to say that "there was no way of getting out of the centenary: something had to be done. Accordingly, the Crystal Palace committed itself to the *Jupiter Symphony* and the *Requiem*; and the Albert Hall, by way of varying the entertainment, announced the *Requiem* and the *Jupiter Symphony*". [Ibid., 483]

The main part of this talk will deal with Shaw's reception of Mozart's opera *Don Giovanni*. Firstly though, for those who either do not know the opera or need a refresher, I offer a brief synopsis of the important parts of the work, omitting the sub-plots, and playing you a few musical excerpts.

*Don Giovanni* is based on the story of the legendary Spanish nobleman and philanderer Don Juan as immortalised by Molière and Byron. The opera takes place in Seville in the eighteenth century and was first performed in Prague in 1787. The libretto was by Lorenzo da Ponte.

Mus. Ex.: *Overture.* The nobleman Don Giovanni is attempting to seduce Donna Anna the daughter of Don Pedro (the Commendatore of Seville). Don Giovanni, according to Leporello his manservant, has had many conquests and lists them off: 640 in Italy, 231 in Germany etc, but 1003 in Spain, so far. Don Pedro enters and challenges Don Giovanni to a duel, but is killed. Donna Anna and her fiancé Don Ottavio vow to avenge her father's death.

Giovanni continues his philandering with other women and gets into various scrapes, for example with the peasant girl Zerlina for whom Mozart wrote one of his most famous duets: Mus. Ex.: "Là ci darem la mano". Later Don Giovanni is recognized by Donna Anna as being her father's killer and she proclaims her love for Don Ottavio in a beautiful aria: Mus. Ex.: "Non Mi Dir" The opera gets quite complicated in typically Mozartian fashion with various changes of identities. During one of these escapades in a graveyard, Giovanni is addressed by the statue of the dead Commendatore whereupon he laughingly invites him to supper. Later at supper the statue appears dramatically: Mus. Ex.: "Statue Music": *Finale,* bars 379-62. The Commendatore orders Don Giovanni to repent of his ways, but Giovanni, blasé as ever, refuses and is dragged down to hell by devils.

Shaw has stated in his writings that the piece by Mozart that influenced him most was the opera *Don Giovanni.* He began his self-tuition, not with Czerny's five-finger exercises, but with the overture to *Don Giovanni* as he wanted to start with something he knew well enough so that he would at least know whether the notes were right or wrong. [Shaw, I, 55] Later he was to say that he considered learning *Don Giovanni* so early was the most important part of his musical education. [Shaw, II, 482] He described it as the greatest of all operas and he mentions it the most frequently in his writings. He castigated a performance of it in *The Pall Mall Gazette* in 1887 describing it as "little more than a rehearsal of the orchestral parts" [Shaw, I, 509] and in 1891 in *The World* in an article entitled "A Non-Mozartian Don", he criticised the acting ability of the then world-famous baritone, Viktor Maurel who was not sufficiently terrified by the entrance of the statue during his meal, but rather reacted very much as "if his uncle had dropped in unexpectedly in the middle of a bachelor's supper party". [Shaw, II, 339]

Shaw first used the Don Juan story in a novel entitled *The Unsocial Socialist* in 1883 but, four years later in 1887, a hundred years after the first performance of *Don Giovanni* in Prague, Shaw wrote a short story, *Don Giovanni Explains*. In this he relates the story from a Shavian point of view. The action takes place on a train as a young attractive girl is on her way home from a performance of *Don Giovanni*. In the girl's description of the performance, one can hear all the frustration of Shaw who often had to endure third-rate productions of the opera:

*The Don was a conceited Frenchman, with a toneless, dark nasal voice, and such a tremolo that he never held a note steady long enough to let us hear whether it was in tune or not. Leporello was a podgy, vulgar Italian buffo who quacked instead of singing. The tenor, a reedy creature, left out Dalla sua pace because he couldn't trust himself to get through it. The parts of Masetto and the Commendatore were doubled, I think, by the call-boy [...] The orchestra was reinforced by local amateurs, the brass parts being played on things from the band of the 10th Hussars. Everybody was delighted; and when I said I wasn't, they said, "Oh! you're so critical and so hard to please. Don't you think you'd enjoy yourself far more if you were not so particular." The idea of throwing away music like Mozart's on such idiots! When the call-boy and the Frenchman sank into a pit of red fire to the blaring of the 10th Hussars and the quacking of the podgy creature under the table, I got up to go....* [Shaw, 1934, 170f.]

A man appears opposite the girl in the carriage and explains that he is the ghost of Don Giovanni. She asks him, why as a ghost he is travelling by train when he could project himself from place to place if he so wished, but he replies that, having eternity at his disposal, he is in no hurry. He explains that his reputation as a philanderer has always been exaggerated and misunderstood, whereas he was always pursued by women and forced into love affairs.

Actually he was only looking for tranquillity and leisure for study. He relates how his relationship with Donna Elvira developed and explains the "true story" of what happened on that fateful night at Donna Anna's house, namely that he went to visit her because she was engaged to a friend of his. In the twilight, she mistook him for a friend and embraced him, the alarm was raised, and the Commendatore, without waiting for an explanation tried to kill him. He retaliated and ran his sword through her father in self-defence. The story continues with Don Giovanni explaining the opera from his point of view and he eventually leaves through the glass and wood of the carriage bidding her farewell with the words, "We shall meet again, within eternity". [Ibid., 190] He does indeed appear again, namely in the drama *Man and Superman*.

Shaw was challenged by the critic Arthur Bingham Walkley to write a new version of the Don Juan mythos. This he did only with grave misgivings. In a letter to Walkley he asked "have they not Molière and Mozart, upon whose art no human hand can improve?" [Shaw, 1903, 13] Nevertheless, in 1903 Shaw published what was to become one of his best-known works, the drama *Man and Superman: A Comedy and a Philosophy*, a four-act play with a dream-interlude interpolated as the third act.

It is a comical love story, the plot consisting of the flight of the protagonist John Tanner from his ward, Ann Whitefield and his eventual capitulation and marriage to her. The third act, the dream interlude, constitutes a continuation of the *Don Giovanni* story. It begins where the opera ends, namely when Don Giovanni descends into hell, and it is sometimes performed separately under the title of *Don Juan in Hell*. The main characters in the play are presented as dead characters from the opera: Ann Whitefield as Donna Anna, Ramsden her father, as Don Pedro the Commendatore, Mendoza, the bandit who captures Tanner, as the Devil, and Tanner himself as Don Juan.

John Tanner, a prosperous and loquacious intellectual,

author of *The Revolutionist's Handbook* printed at the back of the play (containing the famous quote on Education "He who can, does. He who cannot, teaches" [Ibid., 253]), is a reluctant guardian of Ann Whitefield. He sees Ann as an unscrupulous young woman who always gets her own way. Octavius (Don Ottavio) is in love with Ann and proposes a couple of times to her, but she is only interested in Tanner. Tanner flees to Spain to escape her and is attacked by bandits near Granada. The beginning of Act III (the dream interlude) takes place in the bandit's camp in the Sierra Nevada. Tanner dreams and descends into Hell:

*Stillness settles on the Sierra and the darkness deepens* [...] *Instead of the Sierra there is nothing: omnipresent nothing. No sky, no peaks, no light, no sound, no time nor space, utter void. Then somewhere the beginning of a pallor, and with it a faint throbbing buzz as of a ghostly violoncello palpitating on the same note endlessly. A couple of ghostly violins presently take advantage of this bass* Mus. Ex.: *Overture*, bars 31ff. *and therewith the pallor reveals a man in the void, an incorporeal but visible man, seated, absurdly enough, on nothing. For a moment he raises his head as the music passes him by. Then, with a heavy sigh, he drops in utter dejection; and the violins, discouraged, retrace their melody in despair and at last give it up, extinguished by wailings from uncanny wind instruments, thus:* Mus. Ex.: *Overture*, bars 40ff. *It is all very odd. One recognizes the Mozartian strain; and on this hint, and by the aid of certain sparkles of violet light in the pallor, the man's costume explains itself as that of a Spanish nobleman of the XV-XVI century. Don Juan, of course; but where? why? how?* [...] *Another pallor in the void, this time not violet, but a disagreeable smoky yellow. With it, the whisper of a ghostly clarinet turning this tune into infinite sadness:* Mus. Ex.: "Non mi dir", bars 1ff. *The yellowish pallor moves: there is an old crone wandering in the void, bent and toothless; draped, as well as one can guess, in the coarse brown frock of some religious order. She wanders and wanders in her slow hopeless way, much as a wasp flies in its rapid busy way, until she blunders against the thing she seeks: companionship.* [Ibid., 123ff]

There follows a dialogue between Don Juan and this old woman. After the transformation of the old woman into a young, magnificently attired young woman, Don Giovanni of course recognizes the young Donna Anna. Suddenly, "two great chords rolling on syncopated waves of sound break forth. D minor and its dominant: a sound of dreadful joy to all musicians". [Ibid., 131] Mus. Ex.: *Finale,* bars 433f. "Ha", says Don Juan, "Mozart's statue music. It is your father. From the void comes a living statue of white marble, designed to represent a majestic old man". [Ibid., 131] It is, of course, Don Pedro, the Commendatore, Donna Anna's father.

He is usually to be found in heaven but drops by into hell from time to time because he finds heaven so boring. He is on the best possible terms with Don Juan and insists that he was the better swordsman and would have killed him but for his foot slipping (this excuse is also mentioned in the short story).

The action continues in this parodic fashion with everyone reflecting on their previous lives. The devil enters (preceded by distorted statue chords) and a discussion ensues with a debate on democracy, morality, and the nature and respective virtues of heaven and hell. Dispelling the notion of heaven and hell as places of reward and retribution [Grene, 60], Don Juan complains that "hell is full of amateur musicians.

Music is the brandy of the dammed". [Shaw, 1903, 135]. For Shaw, a hedonistic approach to life leads to damnation; as the Shaw biographer, Michael Holroyd puts it, "Man's quest for knowledge and understanding has set him off on the great adventure of transforming his environment and mastering the universe. He may not stop the world and go off on a perpetual holiday." [Holroyd, 76]

The *raison d'etre* of this interlude, however, is to give Shaw the opportunity through dramatic rhetoric to debate teleological and mechanistic philosophies which strive to explain the development of mankind. He rejects a Darwinistic approach of natural selection in favour of a biological and intellectual evolution in which a creative Life-Force ultimately leads mankind by trial and error to the goal of a God-like Superman who will solve the world's social and political problems. Don Juan (representing Shaw's optimism) states that the Life-Force is "the force that ever strives to attain greater power of contemplating itself" [Shaw, 1903, 141] whereas the Devil (representing Shaw's pessimism) replies that "the power which governs the earth is not the power of Life but of Death [...] because man measures his strength by his destructiveness: Man the inventor of the rack, the stake, the gallows, the electric chair, of sword and gun and poison gas: above all, of justice, duty, patriotism, and all the other isms by which even those who are clever enough to be humanely disposed are persuaded to become the most destructive of all the destroyers." [Ibid., 144].

The Life-Force also influences the woman in her choice of partners for procreation ("a woman seeking a husband is the most unscrupulous of all the beasts of prey." [Ibid., 156]) Mozart's theme of seduction has been replaced by a debate on eugenics, in this case a synthesis of various philosophies ranging from Schopenhauer and Nietzsche (*Übermensch)* to the later concept of the *élan vital* of Henri Bergson. (Shaw continued this theme in *Back to Methuselah* (1923), a play in which elements of *The Magic Flute* are introduced.)

The scene ends with Donna Anna, having being told by the Devil that the Superman has not yet been created, crying that she believes in the Life to come, and goes to look for "A father - a father for the Superman". [Ibid., 173] In Act IV, the rest of the party catches up with Tanner and they all proceed to Granada where Tanner eventually capitulates to the triumphant Ann. Tanner declares that "Ann looks happy, but she is only triumphant [...] That is not happiness but the price for which the strong sell their happiness. What we have done this afternoon is to renounce happiness, renounce freedom, renounce tranquillity, above all, renounce the romantic possibilities of an unknown future, for the cares of a household and a family". [Shaw, 1903, 208]

Shaw employs the *Don Giovanni* libretto "almost wholly for purposes of parody, comic relief [and] a series of running gags based on anticlimactic inversion of the characters and attitudes of the opera [...] serv[e] as comic counterpoint to the Shavian dialectic." [Grene, 59] But, the major dramaturgical problem that confronted Shaw in this interlude was how to sustain interest in a long interlude devoid of action (and indeed perhaps even unactable). He solved this by employing a series of literary solos, duets, trios and quartets analogous to the first act of the opera *Don Giovanni*: a duet/ dialogue - Don Juan and Donna Anna; a trio - Don Juan, Donna Anna and the Commendatore; a quartet - all three and the devil interpolated with rhetorical monologues or solos.

One could further debate the influence of *Shaw* on *Mozart* in that we cannot hear Mozart's *Don Giovanni* objectively today without recalling Shaw's continuation of it; *Man and Superman* has irretrievably influenced our reception of the opera because we are now aware of a possible sequel. However, I will instead conclude by reading you an abridged version of a letter that Shaw wrote to *The Times* in July 1905 after attending a performance of *Don Giovanni* at Covent Garden starring the great tenor, Enrico Caruso. Even though Shaw was not active as a music critic at this stage of his career, it did not deter him from expressing his opinions on the evening in general:

*Sir, - The opera management at Covent garden regulates the dress of its male patrons. When is it going to do the same to the women? On Saturday night I went to the Opera. I wore the costume imposed on me by the regulations of the house [...] Not only was I in evening dress by compulsion, but I voluntarily added many graces of conduct as to which the management made no stipulation whatever. I was in my seat in time for the first chord of the overture. I did not chatter during the music not raise my voice when the opera was too loud for normal conversation. I did not get up and go out when the statue music began.*

*My language was fairly moderate considering the number and nature of the improvements on Mozart volunteered by Signor Caruso, and the respectful ignorance of the dramatic parts of the score exhibited by the conductor and the stage manager - if there is such a functionary at Covent Garden. In short, my behaviour was exemplary. At 9 o'clock (the Opera began at 8) a lady came in and sat down very conspicuously in my line of sight. She remained there until the beginning of the last act. I do not complain of her coming late and going early; on the contrary, I wish she had come later and gone earlier. For this lady, who had very black hair, had stuck over her right ear the pitiable corpse of a large white bird, which looked exactly as if someone had killed it by stamping on its breast, and then nailed it to the lady's temple, which was presumably of sufficient solidity to bear the operation.*

*I am not, I hope, a morbidly squeamish person, but the spectacle sickened me. I presume that if I had presented myself at the doors with a dead snake around my neck, a collection of blackbeetles pinned to my shirtfront, and a grouse in my hair, I should have been refused admission. Why then is a woman to be allowed to commit such a public outrage? [...] I suggest to the Covent Garden authorities that, if they feel bound to protect their subscribers against the danger of my shocking them with a blue tie, they are at least equally bound to protect me against the danger of a woman shocking me with a dead bird. [Shaw, III, 585ff.]*

# Chapter 6

# Shaw's Pygmalion: Play and Film

Bert Cardullo (after Pygmalion credits): Well, it's nice to be back in a place where we speak American English after watching the perils of British English up and down the class scale in a marvelous film. And there's a lot to talk about because this is a film of significance, based on a major play from a major twentieth-century artist.

I'm happy to say that, to speak with me, I have a man who's been referred to as the "dean" of American film criticism, Stanley Kauffmann. Known to many readers for his years of film criticism for The New Republic, he's also a distinguished critic of the theater, an author (of novels and plays) in his own right, and a professor who has taught at Yale, the CUNY Graduate Centre, and is currently teaching at Hunter College in Manhattan. Stanley, here as we sit in the twentyfirst century, I think it is well worth beginning by recalling just what a towering figure George Bernard Shaw was, and is, for English-language theater. You told me you'd fallen in love with his work as a young man.

Cardullo: So what is it about Shaw as an artist that's kept your interest for all these years? Because you have taught him at the undergraduate as well as at the highest graduate level, written about him, lectured on his work, and so on.

Kauffmann: What's kept my interest is that every time I read him, I discover him. Which is true, of course, of any great artist. You think you know something about him and you find out that you 've only begun to investigate him. It's hard for me to talk calmly about Shaw.

Cardullo: Don't! Go wild.

Kauffmann: Because I think he is a titan. I think that there can be very little question that he 's the second greatest playwright in the English language. he is also the greatest comic dramatist after Molière. Those judgments can be argued with a bit, but not decisively against. Those, for me, are data from the world of play writing. In addition, talking about his reputation during the twentieth century-remember that one?

Cardullo: Yeah, I remember that one!

Kauffmann: He was, you could almost say, through the first half of that century, omnipresent. Whenever anything happened-a flood in Johnstown, Ohio, a revolution somewhere in South America-the first thing, it seemed to me, that any newspaper did was to find out what Shaw had to say about it. There's a newspaper in Belgium, I was told, that for many years every day in a corner of its front page, where the New York Times ran the weather, this paper had a quotation from Bernard Shaw-every day!

The man was inexhaustible in two senses: as a source and as a figure of energy. His work in the theater just went on and on, but it began quite late. He didn't write his first play until well into his thirties, in 1892. He was thirty-six. He'd done mostly novels and criticism before then. Before he wrote a play, he was a famous music critic-a great music critic. When I talk about Shaw in seminars, it takes me three or four weeks just to get to his plays. Because first you have to deal with the fact that he was a fine music critic, who has the respect of every reasonably serious music critic I have ever read on the subject of Shaw. And second, he is the greatest theater critic-critic!-who ever wrote in the English language. I don't need anyone else's opinion on that; I know that! And, again, that's before you get to his plays.

As a matter of fact, you can demonstrate-I've tried to-that the three books he wrote before he began writing plays are the source of a lot of the material in his plays. Books on Wagner and other subjects as well. You can see that this man devoured ideas. He got a reputation-misleading-as a "brain-box" playwright, when, as a matter of fact, he is one of the most sensitive-you see it in this film-most humane writers ever. He couldn't be a great playwright if he were just a merchant of ideas. If there 's anything that drives me nuts-and I suppose I am nuts on this subject-it is to hear the stale, false comment that all Shaw 's characters are voices expressing different ideas of his. Nothing could be more false. If you want proof of that, ask any actor who's ever been in a Shaw play. Actors-finally-are those who keep plays alive. Not critics. Actors want to do plays or not, and they want to do Shaw.

Cardullo: There's a wonderful anecdote about that: Shaw sent a copy of one of his plays to the great actress Ellen Terry. And Terry was very busy in her dressing room, so she had her attendant simply read it to her. And somewhere through the first act, the attendant just stopped and said, "Madam, this is you, this is you. This has been written for you." And thus the recognition that Shaw's plays are not just about ideas, they consist of characters who have been gracefully molded with this or that actor in mind.

Kauffmann: That leads to one more of the ten thousand things we could be saying about Shaw. He was his era's greatest casting agent. He knew the work of every available actor in Britain. And if you read his letters-which are fascinating in themselves-he was also a great letter writer. You could read his advice, comments, and suggestions to the people who were going to do his plays. For example, apropos of a sad passing very recently, he said in one of his letters around 1940, I think it was, "I suggest that you"-to whomever he was writing-"take a look at a young actor named Alec Guinness." That occurs as a passing note in one of his letters-it's fantastic! You can't talk about Shaw without beginning to sound hyperbolic. Because he was a living hyperbole and remains a hyperbole today.

Cardullo: So here we have someone of such a high level of professional accomplishment in so many different fields, but who also is one of the great creations-and manipulators-of celebrity culture in the twentieth century.

Kauffmann: He often said, "My greatest creation is G. B. S." And it wasn't an entirely beneficial one, as he knew. Because the fact that he made this public persona-he himself said-a little too facetious, a little too omniscient, interfered a bit with the appreciation of Shaw as a serious artist. People began to think of him as a jokester-as unthinking and superficial. He knew he himself was responsible for that. But he was one of the first of the twentieth century's infamous public personne. You know Daniel Boorstein's definition of celebrity: someone who's famous for being famous. (Both laugh.) Shaw, in a certain sense, instigated that definition. He was famous for something, but he added too much to his fame.

Cardullo: Right. In a second, we are going to turn to Pygmalion the play and the film, but it is interesting to note that, if it were now 1935, [if] you were to be anywhere in the world, and I were to name two people in the entertainment world known everywhere, they would be Charlie Chaplin and George Bernard Shaw.

Kauffmann: I think that's a very fair statement. They're quite comparable in terms of fame. There was a time until maybe the last decade of the last century when you could say-in fact, I did say, and I bet someone a dollar on it once!-that at any given moment of any day in any year, somewhere on this globe, a Bernard Shaw play was being performed. It might be an amateur performance in Korea, but somewhere someone was doing Shaw. he was almost as omnipresent as Shakespeare.

Cardullo: That's interesting because we think, you know, of "globalization" as the buzzword of today, but it's important to recover the degree to which an artist like Shaw had a fully global penetration in his time. Shaw would have been at the top of any list of "quantity of translations, and performances, from English into another language."

Kauffmann: Additionally, the first books about Shaw's work were written in foreign languages. I think I'm correct in saying that the first book about him was written in Spanish; I once noted that in one of the many bibliographies of the writings about Shaw.

Cardullo: This makes for a good transition into our discussion of Pygmalion. I want our readers to know that we have just seen the third film version of this play.

Kauffmann: That's quite true. The first was a Dutch one, the second German.

Cardullo: Right. Have you seen those other two?

Kauffmann: No. The only person I know, or know of, who has seen them is a man named Bernard Dukore, who has done a good deal of work in the field of Shaw scholarship and has also edited a collection of Shaw's screenplays. And he wrote a long, detailed introduction to that collection. Moreover, he went to see what he was talking about. Just to add one more item. Henry Higgins in the German film is played by Gustaf Grundgens, who, you may remember, is the leader of the crooks and thieves in Fritz, Lang's M.

Cardullo: Small world, as they say. (Both laugh.) Let's move to the play Pygmalion and talk a bit about where it stands in Shaw's overall trajectory. How do you evaluate it among all his plays, and where does it stand in our collective imagination today?

Kauffmann: Its first production was in London in 1912. Shaw wrote it with a woman named Mrs. Patrick Campbell in mind as Eliza, and she did play it in this production, which he directed. Higgins was written for a then-famous actor named Herbert Beerbohm Tree-whose grandson, David Tree, plays Freddy Hill in the film! And, incidentally, Esme Percy, who plays the Hungarian expert at the ball, played Higgins himself three times in revivals of the play in London.

Pygmalion comes in Shaw's career at a peculiar juncture, if you look at the whole line of that long career. he began in the 1890s as a playwright who took relatively accepted forms and used them in brand-new, explosive ways. I won't go into details because there isn't time. After the turn of the century, he began to experiment with innovative dramatic forms, as in Man and Superman, Getting Married, and Misalliance. But by the time he got to Pygmalion, he had some kind of hankering to go back to the 189Os state of mind that he had already experienced, and to take a familiar form, refurbish it, and make it new-renovate it. He had already done this, after the turn of the century, in something called Fanny's First

Play. He did it again, I think in part, because of his infatuation with Mrs. Campbell.

He had precedents for this play. W. S. Gilbert of Gilbert and Sullivan had written a play in blank verse called Pygmalion and Galatea, I think. But Shaw had his own Impetus for doing a Pygmalion, which was first of all to use the theater to dramatize and titivate a social subject. One of the many things I haven't done, which I'd like to do, is to write an essay on the subject of class in Shaw's plays. It runs all through much of his work, including this play, this film. And here is a play, Pygmalion, in which he says, "The only thing that keeps this girl in the gutter is the fact that she doesn't speak like someone of a better class. And I will show you how brains and education can burrow through and explode that false barrier." There's not a difference in humanity, not a difference in character, between Eliza and other people; there's a difference caused simply by the manifestation of class. One that still applies in Britain, to some degree.

Cardullo: And even in New York, in certain neighborhoods.

Kauffmann: I know that's true. I could give you examples. In any event, class was one aspect of the play. The other was that Shaw always liked to lean toward classical antecedents, and what could be more classical than the legend of Pygmalion and Galatea? He once said, "I standen the shoulders of Shakespeare and Moliere." And now he was also standing on the shoulders of Hellenic civilization. So these factors, plus his desire to do something for Mrs. Campbell, plus his ambition as a director-what they used to call "producer" in England-produced Pygmalion.

He wrote a very interesting pamphlet once, by the way, called "The Art of Rehearsal," about directing. There's an anecdote connected with the subject of directing or rehearsal and Pygmalion. It's well known that Shaw was a vegetarian; one might say a passionate vegetarian if that weren't an oxymoron. (Laughs.) He was directing a rehearsal of Pygmalion, the story goes, and really working on Mrs.

Campbell-working on her and working on her to frazzle her nerves. He was in the auditorium of the theater; she was on the stage. She came down to the footlights and said, "George Bernard Shaw, some day you are going to eat a lamb chop, and then God help every actress in London." (Both laugh.)

Cardullo: If he could have that effect with vegetables, one can imagine...

Kauffmann: The play was a success. But this production closed after a while, and one of the things that helped to close it was the approach of the First World War. When Pygmalion was first revived, about 1920, Mrs. Campbell continued as Eliza and Higgins was played by C. Aubrey Smith, who became quite an English figure in American films.

Cardullo: Quite so. Let's make a transition now to the film itself. The film of Pygmalion pleased Shaw, and it was a worldwide success, deservedly so. Not only did it win Academy Awards, have a large box office, and garner critical praise, but it's also revived with some frequency,

Kauffmann: More than that. Courtesy of the tape you gave me, I saw it again the other day for the first time in, maybe, twenty years. I was bowled over by it as film: it is a very fine piece of filmmaking.

Cardullo: Absolutely.

Kauffmann: Leslie Howard, I think, had much to do with the excellence of the acting. Anthony Asquith-the only film director who was the son of a Prime Minister (Laughs.)-had great skills, and he did wonders with the picture. But, after all, David Lean was the editor.

Cardullo: Arthur Honegger is the

Kauffmann: Composer, my next point. This is one of the prime film scores, an extraordinarily fine piece of film-music writing. And it has been overlooked completely. When people talk about-as they should-Prokofiev and Nino Rota and Bernard Herrmann, wonderful film composers, what about what Arthur Honegger did for Pygmalion? He wrote a lot of other film scores, which I can't recall at the moment. But this is a very fine piece of writing.

About the screenplay: you know there was a good deal

of argy-bargy back and forth about how it was to end. Shaw wanted to keep the ending unromantic: he was more interested-and you can see it in a number of his plays-in the teacher-student relationship. In Caesar and Cleopatra, for example, he subverted history. In point of fact, Caesar and Cleopatra had a child, but they 're father and daughter, so to speak, in Shaw's play about them. We won't go into some thirty-second psychoanalytical explanation about why it was true that Shaw was more interested in the teacher-student or parent-child relationship; it was true of him. And he fought a sentimental ending-a romantic ending-to Pygmalion. There were three endings filmed for this picture, as I'm sure you know.

Cardullo: Before we go into that, let's remind people of what the ending of the play as written is.

Kauffmann: The ending of the play as written is that Eliza goes off to meet Freddy Hill, and Higgins-left alone on stage at the end-doubles up with laughter at "Freddy! Freddy!! Ha ha ha ha ha!!!!!" But I must add that that's in the film, too. This is, I think, the best Shaw film. Not only because of the cast, but because, relatively speaking, most of the play has been retained. Only some of it has been taken out. The Doolittle scene in the first act, for instance, is so drastically condensed in the film that you never quite understand why he got all that money for being a great moralist. But what the filmmakers kept almost pristine is that last scene between Eliza and Higgins in his mother's house, a very beautiful scene. "You devil, you know how to twist..."-in the middle of a quarrel, Higgins says something that turns her heart around. Anyone who thinks that Shaw didn't know how to write about human beings, just take a look at that scene in the film. It's wonderful.

Shaw wanted Eliza and Higgins to part as satisfied, and yet not quite satisfied, with each other. And one of the three endings that he supplied for the film was that she does marry Freddy, he has a flower shop in South Kensington or somewhere, and he has muttonchop whiskers as he waits on a customer in the last shot. But the ending of the picture, as filmed, is, as far as I can remember, almost exactly like the ending of My Fair Lady, the musical, which of course, was made from the play. There's an interesting point to make here. Harry Stradling was the cinematographer for Pygmalion; he was also the cinematographer on My Fair Lady about twenty-five years later.

Cardullo: There's a whole progression from the play through this film to the stage once again as My Fair Lady.

Kauffmann: Poor film, I think, My Fair Lady. I believe it's one of George Cukor's weakest pieces of direction.

Cardullo: It's one of those instances where a director seems overwhelmed by the phenomenon surrounding him.

Kauffmann: Yes. There's no congeniality between him and the idea of making this picture. Whereas there's nearly absolute synchronicity between the codirectors or comakers of the film of Pygmalion and the work itself.

Cardullo: Well, that brings us back to the central character of Eliza. Because while I am a deep admirer of many of Audrey Hepburn's performances, this seems to be one of her weakest ones. I mean, Cukor's using of all her features as if she were a model, whereas Wendy Hiller fully characterized the woman.

Kauffmann: Wendy Hiller-whom I never saw on the stage, but I would have died just for a glance from her in the theater-had played Eliza in the stage production at the Malvern Festival in Britain, just before the film was made. And when Shaw saw it, he was simply captivated. He said, "If ever a film gets made of this"-in English, that is; there had been the other two-"you are Eliza." A lot of actresses wanted to play the film part. Marion Davies appealed to Shaw-a very big star at the time with some money behind her in the person of Mr. Hearst-but she didn't get it. It's interesting apropos of this subject of casting to remark that, in order to ensure there was no romance, no romantic hint, between Higgins and Eliza, Shaw's original choice for Higgins in the film was Charles Laughton-so that there would be a father/daughter relationship established right from the start.

Cardullo: Well, that casting would have changed the male-female chemistry altogether.

Kauffmann: Right.

Cardullo: But the casting of Leslie Howard puts a very different spin on the matter: it adds a romantic element. Yet, as manipulated in the film, his casting maintains a tension as well.

Kauffmann: Shaw admired Leslie Howard as an actor, but he thought that Howard would add too much of a romantic flavour to the picture. just a year or so before the film of Pygmalion, Howard had played Romeo in the film of Romeo and Juliet with Norma Shearer. And Shaw was afraid that that particular effluvium would carry over into the film. It does, to an extent.

Cardullo: Yes, absolutely. If there's one aspect of this film you would say you admire most, what is it?

Kauffmann: My chief admiration for the film of Pygmalion is that, in somewhat distilled form, it gives me the genius of Shaw as incarnated by some very fine acting.

Cardullo: Great, and that's a great place for us to end. Stanley, I can't tell you how much I appreciate your having talked with me today.

Kauffmann: I loved seeing you, and I loved talking about Shaw.

Cardullo: Well, Mr. Kauffmann, we now know one button to push in any conversation with you.

Kauffmann: Indeed, my chief button.

## PLACED IN PERSPECTIVE

Critic, translator, and playwright Eric Bentley conversed Saturday with New York Post theater columnist Michael Riedel about George Bernard Shaw at the New York Public Library for the Performing Arts. The programme was part of a celebration marking the centennial of various Shaw achievements, such as the first performance of "Major Barbara" and "Man and Superman." Introducing the talk, Alan Pally acknowledged another lesser known anniversary, and said he hoped to make amends to Shaw. "A hundred years ago," he said, "the New York Public Library restricted access to 'Man and Superman,'" considering its content too inflammatory. "We're not like that anymore," he said to audience laughter.

Mr. Riedel commented on how rarely one sees Shaw produced, and mused whether Shaw's public persona as a witty jester had overshadowed his reputation as a profound playwright. "When I ask people about Shaw, it's not so much the plays people talk about. It's the one-liners people remember: 'Youth is wasted on the young,' 'a government that robs Peter to pay Paul can always count on the support of Paul,' and my faviurite, 'hell is full of musical amateurs.'"

Mr. Bentley praised Shaw as a thinking playwright - and an incredibly sexual writer - whose dialogues were "erotic flirtation, even when not openly so." He described Shaw as a dramatist who could be serious without abandoning the light touch, perfectly capable of being trivial and naughty like Noel Coward while at the same time writing tragedy like Goethe or Shakespeare. He had a rare combination of philosophic and histrionic personality, with both a lively and dialectical mind.

Mr. Bentley recalled seeing Shaw performed while in high school. On a trip to London, he saw "Man and Superman," which had such "charm and cogency" that it could take hold of a 15 year-old who was interested in things such as "Does God exist, and if not, why not?"

Shaw's energy extended beyond playwriting to musical criticism and political reform. For four years in the 1890s, the Dublin-born figure wrote drama criticism that rejected the conventional Victorian theater of the time. Mr. Bentley, who too was a theater critic for four years ("I copied him"), said that in a way his own drama criticism in the 1950s likewise was a rejection of Broadway theater in New York.

Shaw found a counterforce to the West End theater in championing Ibsen from abroad, whose plays were "the equivalent of off-off Broadway." Shaw also harbored an animus against Shakespeare for elbowing out other important playwrights: "It was hard for a serious playwright to get a word in edgewise."

Mr. Riedel asked about Shaw's later years, when he

expressed despair over the world not taking his advice. Mr. Bentley cautioned against taking Shaw literally, as Shaw was an ironist, after all. Shaw played a role in the development of English politics, as a lot of people learned socialism from him. Mr. Bentley referred to a one-volume edition of Shaw's collected plays, in which Shaw wrote that no one paid attention to him, also suggesting that the "dear reader" read through Shaw's collected works twice a year

An audience member asked about the prefaces Shaw wrote. Mr. Bentley said Shaw's 100-page essay introducing "Androcles and the Lion," a play about early Christianity, was the playwright's only pronouncement on the New Testament. In it "he has to tell the life of Jesus and gives his opinions on the Four Gospels. He remarks, for example, that St. Luke was obviously a French novelist."

The voluble Shaw even performed a preface himself once. He filmed it in 1940 for American audiences of the film "Major Barbara." Mr. Bentley said Shaw practically stole the show "by making a few simple remarks about the play and the occasion." Filmed in London during the Battle of Britain, Shaw addressed the American people, saying "a bomb may crash through this roof and blow me to atoms."

An audience member asked which was Shaw's faviurite of his own plays. Mr. Bentley said "Heartbreak House," which was also his most pessimistic. Mr. Bentley described Shaw's daily schedule at his house in the country, about an hour's drive from London. Each day Shaw, who lived modestly, would write all morning, sitting in a little wooden hut in the garden. After dinner with his wife in the evening, he would ask for the bag of mail. "Shaw never let anybody else open his mail," Mr. Bentley said. He would answer any letters that interested him and discard the others.

Mr. Bentley said these letters, some of which are collected in four volumes, are so interesting that he sometimes dips into them when he's awake late at night with insomnia.

An audience member inquired what Shaw read when he couldn't sleep at night. Mr. Bentley paused. Mr. Riedel interjected, "Shaw, I imagine."

## Chapter 7

# The Promethean Passion for Improving the Race

In 1913, Shaw published Pygmalion, a satire on snobbery and a participation to educational theory. It is a play about education, a subject with which Shaw was more than concerned. In Pygmalion, Eliza, through whom Shaw's conception of education is revealed, learns not only upper-class sounds but also self-reliance and self-sufficiency. Yet, the central theme of the play remains :"the contrast between the Promethean passion for improving the race and the ordinary human desire for the comforts and consolations of the domestic hearth". It is a contrast between the vital and the mechanical, between the living person and his artificial social role.

In Pygmalion, Shaw dramatizes the whole world in which "people play roles that have often been artificially, and cruelly, forced upon them". Hence, much of the play deals with role-playing. Elisa is trained for a role of a lady in a flower shop, like an actress; her father, Alfred Doolittle, becomes a performer and a lecturer for Wannafeller Moral Reform World League; Henry Higgins lacks social manners and is accordingly a bad actor in a play within a play. The two major characters through whose fates the message of the play is expressed are Alfred Doolittle and his daughter, Eliza Doolittle. By the end of the play, both achieve a new social role through two different means: Eliza through education and Doolittle through money, as the following sketch of the events of the play illustrates.

Tempted by Colonel Pickering's financial support, Henry

Higgins, a celebrated phonetician, undertakes the responsibility of changing Eliza Doolittle, a common flower girl, into a duchess within six months in an ambassador's party by teaching her proper English pronunciation. Being interested only in his bet and in showing his talent to the world, Higgins continually abuses Eliza while teaching her without taking into account her feelings and future, in an attempt to get her ready to win the bet for him in the ambassador's party.

In the same time, Higgins, for the sake of fun, writes a letter to one American millionaire that Alfred Doolittle, Eliza's father, a poor dustman, is the most original moralist in England and is fit for a lecturer for that millonaire's Moral Reform World League. He does it without Doolittle's consent. The first trying-out of Eliza takes place at Mrs. Higgins's at-home day, and it is successful because nobody among the guests can identify her as Eliza the flower girl.

The real test, however, remains the one at the ambassador's party. It is similarly successful, and it is Eliza's public debut in society. Though she wins the bet for him, Higgins does not condescend to utter the slightest word of congratulation to Eliza. On the contrary, he continues abusing her and ordering her to fetch him his slippers, which will incite Eliza to revolt against him as she makes sure that Higgins does not care for her.

In the same time, Alfred Doolittle, who has inherited a bequest worth three thousand pounds a year, comes to blame Higgins for having turned him into a gentleman, for he likes his old status as a dustman, in which he was happy. In the same fashion, Eliza reproaches Higgins for his having turned her into a good-for-nothing lady, unable to earn even her living. The play ends with Eliza's going to marry Freddy. As for Doolittle, he is going to church to celebrate his wedding ceremony as a middle-class man.

Higgins, creator of all these transformations, is quite satisfied with his achievement. The end in Pygmalion echoes the one in Ibsen's A Doll's House, with Nora slamming the door on Helmer. Like A Doll's House, Pygmalion, has no definite resolution. Maurice Valency sums up the difference between the two plays in what follows:

"Ibsen framed his play along the lines of conventional domestic drama, so that his final situation seemed both unusual and shocking, Pygmalion, on the other hand, was based on a fairy tale... It is difficult to imagine anything artistically more inept than a rationalistic conclusion of the Cindrella story").

Shaw, therefore, gives the most popular fairy-tale story a quite rationalistic conclusion in order to emphasize the invalidity of idle feelings and romantic thinking. In this fashion, Shaw brings in the focus the inevitability and omnipresence of reason. For this reason, Shaw reverses the Cindrella story and disappoints the audience's expectation of a happy marriage between Higgins and Eliza, and the reconciliation of the other characters; by making Eliza refuse Higgins.

Such a reversal of happy ending of the Cindrella story on the level of dramatic techniques is accompanied, on the level of thought, by a reversal of the social conventions, beliefs, values and ideals. This is best shown in Pygmalion through the continuous contrast between the established order and the ideal order: Between the capitalist system imposed on society with all its hypercritical, exploiting and class nature, and the shavian order in which society, people, morality, social manners are unified and seen as indivisible entities/ realities.

In this respect, Bernard Shaw writes that reality is the result of many factors that cannot be simplified but considered as they are: Because simplification entails dividing facts into positive and negative, deeds into right and wrong, people into heroes and villains, society into high and low classes. All such divisions aim at stratifying society, and at giving authority to some class of people and bestowing validity to their pretension to dignity, which will only strenghthen the class reality.

By considering things as entities, society will be classeless, not as a gathering of disparate classes; people will be mere human beings, not as gentlemen and common men; women will be as human as man; morality will be based on real humanity, not on right and wrong; manners will be the same for all situations and with all people; speech will be standardized and will no longer refer the speaker's class or origin... It is in such unification of social and moral concepts that the problem of "equality" in Pygmalion finds his way towards solution.

## EQUALITY AT THE LEVEL OF SOCIAL CLASSES

Shaw's opening scene sets a group of prolitarians -some timidly deferential, some sarcastically impolite- along with an impoverished middle-class family with genteel pretensions, and two gentlemen –all under a church portico. It is quite plain from such a class distinction as it is revealed through Eliza's actions that the society which Bernard Shaw is dealing with is a class society. Eliza Doolittle is quite aware of the class system and the class values and she exploits them to her own interest by using flatters as a medium in order to win Pickreing's and Higgins's favours and pity, and make them buy her flowers.

*"... So cheer up, Captain; and by a flower off a poor girl" (P.18).*

*"... By a flower, kind gentlemen. I'm short for my lodging" (P.28).*

Eliza avails herself of her low-class situation and attracts customers and make them buy her flowers. She even can make Mrs. Eynsford Hill pay for the flowers Freddy has spoilt, profitting from the Eynsford Hills' snobery and gentility. Eliza is class-conscious. She knows that lower-class girls talking with gentlemen are accused of prostitution. That is the reason why Eliza reacts hysterically when she hears that a police-informer is copying down her words.

*"I'm a respectable girl: So help me, I never spoke to him except to ask him to buy a flower off me" (PP. 19-20).*

*"... He's no right to take away my character. My character is the same to me as any lady's" (P.26).*

She reacts so because she believes herself to belong to a class that cannot afford lawyers, and –accordingly- she has to be loud and vigorous in her protestations of virtue. Louis

Crompton considers vulgarity as, specifically, a class trait. Eliza is vulgarly familiar with customers, vulgarly hysterical in fear of offence, and vulgarly keen on calling people "gentlemen" and "lady".

Clara is another example of vulgarity. She is even worse than Eliza. Clara is suspicious and as quick to take offence as the flower-girl. She quickly rebukes Higgins, who tries to localize her from her speech: "Don't dare to speak to me". Vulgarity is a trait of the lower classes as opposed to the formalities of the upper classes: Throughout the play, Mrs. Higgins, for example, is shown to be self-controlled, phlegmatic, formal... etc. The contrast between social classes, however, is better revealed through Doollittle's and Eliza's journey upward in the social hierarchy. In Mrs. Higgins' at-home day, Eliza says:

"When he [her father] was out of work, my mother used to give him four pence and tell him to go out and not come back until he'd drunk himself cheerful and loving-like. Theres lots of women has to make their husbands drunk to make them fit to live with... If a man has a bit of conscience, it always takes him when he is sobre; and then it makes him low-spirited. A drop of booze just takes that off and makes him happy" (P.77).

Alfred Doolittle, in Act Two, comes for five-pound note:

"I don't eat less hearty than him [deserving man]; and I drink a lot more. I want a bit of amusement... I want cheerfulness and a song and a band when I feel low" (P.58).

He continues:

"Don't be afraid that I'll save it and spare it [five-pound note] and live idle on it. There wont be a penny of it left by Monday: I'll have to work same as if I never had it" (P.59).

Doolittle refuses Higgins's ten-pound note and takes only five pounds:

"Ten pounds is a lot of money: It makes a man feel prudent-like; and then goodbye to happiness" (P.59).

When Doolittle rises in the world, the values of the middle class are revealed to us through his situation:

*"I was happy. I was free. I touched pretty nigh everybody for*

*money when I wanted it, same as I touched you Enry Iggins. Now I am worrited... and everybody thouches me for money... A year ago I hadnt a relative in the world except two or three that wouldnt speak to me. Now Ive fifty... I have to live for others not for myself" (P. 116).*

He continues:

"Happier men than me will call for my dust, and touch me for their tip: and I'll look on helpless, and envy them" (P.117).

As for Mrs. Doolittle, Eliza's formerly-wicked stepmother, she has completely changed with the rise of her social situation:

"She never comes to words with any one now, poor woman! Respectability has broke all the spirit out of her" (P.124).

From the contrast between these two stages of Doolittle's social status –first, as an undeserving poor; then, as a middle-class man- society is disclosed as highly stratified to the extent that Margery Morgan has been able to distinguish between two distinct values of two disparate classes: The values of the under-privileged are characterized by idleness, open-handedness, high spirits, festive eating and drinking, happiness, freedom from care, hedonism and a form of serial polygamy; whereas the values of capitalism are work, thrift, responsibility, abstinence, respectability, prudence, puritanism and chaste monogamy. Higgins himself is aware of the class system. Hence, when Eliza comes to his laboratory to have lessons in phonetics, and offered to pay one shilling per hour for learning English, Higgins accepts the cost as he draws a comparison between the sum that Eliza offers to pay and that a millionaire can do:

"You know, Pickering, if you consider a shilling, not as a simple shilling, but as a percentage of this girl's income, it works out as fully equivalent to sixty or seventy guineas from a millionaire" (P.39).

He continues:

"She offers me two-fifths of her day's income for a day would be somewhere about £.60. It's handsome. By George, it's enormous! It's the biggest offer I ever had" (P.40).

By comparing Eliza's offer to that of a millionaire, Higgins alludes to the class nature of society. Yet, the most important in that comparison is the fact the Higgins does not accept the offer as Eliza offers it but as a millionaire would. The equation of Eliza to a millionaire shows Higgins transcendence of the conventional thinking which cannot grasp reality unless simplified. Higgins sees society as indivisible whole, and need not divide it into classes. He believes that his job is "filling the gap that separates class from class and soul from soul" (P.82). Because "there are no third-class carriages, and one soul is as good as another" (P.126).

Yet, out of the desire to unify society, there grows a need to strike at poverty, being the heart of all social splits and divisions. Shaw is influenced by Samuel Butler's "poverty is the worst of all crimes". Following the same tradition, Shaw believes that poverty is the source of all evils; and putting an end to evil means abolishing, first and foremost, poverty. In this way, Bernard Shaw, by presenting Alfred Doolittle as a blackmailer and as a man who sells his daughter for the sake of drinking, aims as a socialist to abolish the poor as a class from existence since such people are dangerous and contemptible. Hence, the necessity of obliterating class distinctions for the sake of a future class-less society.

For this purpose, Shaw believes that individuals should take their proper places in the social hierarchy regardless of the class into which they were born:

"For Shaw caste is essentially a matter of character and ability, not of birth, so that once the individual is cut free of the restrictions of class, he tends to find his own level in the human hierarchy. Social mobility is indispensable to the evolutionary process"

In Pygmalion, in the light of this citation, Eliza and her father are highly evolved individuals whose potentialities would normally be stifled by the limitations of a rigidly social environment. Eliza is emancipated by education, and Doolittle by money. After her development, Eliza has given up her former vulgarity and commonness and she has grown a typical petite bourgeoise who is no longer fit for "gutter" jobs, and who judges the world wholly in relation to herself. That is, unlike Higgins's interest in humanity and his scientific passion for reform, Eliza Doolittle sees life and personal relations in commercial terms, as Higgins observes.

As for Doolittle, he joins the middle class and is haunted with the care for respectability all the rest of his life. Yet, Eliza and Doolittle show disapproval of the change in their situation. Doolittle, in Act Five, comes to blame Higgins: "It's making a gentleman of me that I object to. Who asked hím to make a gentleman of me? I was happy. I was free". In the same fashion, Eliza rebukes Higgins for having changed her: "Why didnt you leave me where you picked me out of? –in the gutter". She continues lamenting: "I sold flowers. I didnt sell myself. Now you've made a lady of me I'm not fit to sell anything else. I wish you left me where you found me".

Eliza's and Doolittle disapprobation of the change of their situation shows that social mobility can be both perilous and uncomfortable though it is indispensable to the evolution of society. Yet, Shaw does not consider personal happiness as the end of human existence. He believes that "we must not think about and concern ourselves but lose ourselves in what is greater than and external to the self". This quotation is parroted by Higgins: "Eliza... think of other people's futures; but never think of your own". Maurice Valency resumes this philosophy as follows:

"The evolutionary principle involves a constant displacement of individuals within the class structure. The result is doubtless of benefit to the species, but it is not uniformly pleasant for the individual".

Evolution, therefore, is all that matters; and life continues its own development indifferent to individual suffering. That is the reason why Alfred Doolittle, who is ignorant of the "universal law " feels "intimidated" into evolution. Doolittle does not want to change his situation: "I'm undeserving; and I mean to go on being undeserving. I like it; and thats the truth". In Pygmalion, Henry Higgins symbolizes Life: he identifies with nobody; he is inhuman; and all his attention is focused on getting Eliza "out of the gutter" and preparing her to win his "own" bet. Besides, Higgins is the one who has changed both Eliza's and Doolittle's situation without checking their consent.

Life, then, is aware of its purpose and need not bother about the individual protests. It is perhaps for this reason that Doolittle is dragged out of the lower classes. Doolittle as a lower-class man, was spent-thrift, hedonist, drunkard, and he would beat his wives. With the social mobility he has undergone, the slightest standards of decency that Doolittle acquires is a positive gain if we take into consideration the immoral values he had.

By inserting Doolittle and Eliza into the upper classes, the norms of social classes are violated and class restrictions are shattered, and the classless society is clearer. It is on the basis of this classless society that "equality" will be established. Shaw, here, seems to have developed a gradualistic approach in advocating "equality". This is most evident in his stressing the importance of education and the inevitability of establishing new social values as repudiation of the capitalist values which are based on class distinctions.

## EQUALITY AT THE LEVEL OF SOCIAL VALUES

In Pygmalion, George Bernard Shaw deals with various aspects of the dominant social values under capitalism. His main concern is to correct those values in such a fashion as to make them go with the classless society and the "equality" he preaches in his philosophy. He attacks the dominant capitalist values through exposing their conventional and outdated role that reinforce the class system and the class restrictions laid upon the individual. The first major theme which Shaw develops for this purpose is the relationship between speech and class status.

### *Speech*

In the portico of St. Paul's Church, through Henry Higgins's detecting people's speeches, many accents which are different from the standard pronunciation comes to the surface. This reflects the class society that the play depicts. Hence, from their own words and accents, Higgins can identify:

Eliza as native of Lisson Grove,
*Pickering of Cambridge,*
*Mrs. Eynsford Hill of Epson,*
*The bystander of Selsey,*
*The sarcastic bystander of Hoxton,*
*Alfred Doolittle as brought up in Hounslow...s*

Shaw even uses phonetic alphabet to highlight this idea of "multi-accent". In Act One, after Freddy throws her flower-basket down when rushing out of the portico, Eliza shouts in her own accent: "Nah then, Freddy: look wh' y' gowin, deah". Shaw transcribes it phonetically to clarify the idea of the relationship between speech and class status though he is able to write Eliza's words in normal spelling –probably as the following: "Now then, Freddy; look where you are going, dear".

Such an accent is likely to attract the attention of a phonetician in the size of Henry Higgins, he remarks:

"A woman who utters such depressing and disgusting sounds has no right to live. Remember that you are a human being with a soul and the divine gift of articulate speech: that your native language is the language of Shakespeare and Milton and the Bible; and dont sit there crooning like a bilious pigeon" (P.27).

Here, Higgins compares Eliza's sounds with those of Shakespeare and Milton in order to shock her into awareness of "lower-class" accent. Later, Higgins even will undertake to teach Eliza proper English pronunciation. It may sound queer that a low, common girl like Eliza should talk like a lady; but Shaw's aim is the estrangement of the girl from class restrictions embodied here at the level of speech.

In this respect, Shaw, in his preface to Pygmalion, applauds the new scientific approach to language by phoneticians because it raises pronunciation above the intense self-consciousness and class snobbery. Accordingly, Higgins teaches Eliza proper English pronunciation in order to emancipate her of her class status. He tells his mother, Mrs. Higgins: "she talks English almost as you talk French". Even Nepommuck, famous translator at the ambassador's party, is cheated by Eliza's speech owing to the violation of the relationship between speech and class status. He believes Eliza to be a Hungarian princess because she speaks English "too perfectly. Can you show me any English woman who speaks English as it should be spoken? Only foreigners who have been taught to speak it speak it well".

By Eliza's success in speaking in an alien accent, the relationship between speech and class status is broken. The main point here is that dialects have no intrinsic dramatic or social significance and that the real basis of our reaction to anyone's dialect is our association of particular kind of speech with particular classes and particular manners". Shaw's attempt to free the individual from class restrictions is carried at the level of social manners.

### *Social Manners*:

In Pygmalion, manners are best discussed and focused on at Mrs. Higgins's at-home day, which starts with Mrs. Higgins asking her son, Henry Higgins, out because he spoils her parties with his lack of manners. This is Shown in action when the Hills have come: Higgins does not shake hands with the guests or entertain them with a small talk. Instead of answering Clara's: "How do you do?" he stares at her:

"Ive seen you before somewhere. I havent the ghost of a notionwhere; but Ive heard your voice. [drearily] It doesnt matter. You better sit down" (P.70).

Higgins uses no form of politeness: no "please", no "would you mind setting down?", nor any other form. He uses a quasi-imperative word to show his lack of social manners and his inexperience with societies. Higgins even leaves the guests and "goes to the central window, through which, with his back to the company, he contemplates the river...".

Similarly, when Freddy comes in to join the party, Higgins, instead of answering back Freddy's greeting, says, looking at Freddy "as if he were a pickpocket": "I'll take my oath Ive met you before somewhere. Where was it?" Then he "shakes Freddy's hand and almost slings him on to the ottoman". Higgins comes from the window and sits with the society and almost brutally says: "And now, what the devil are we going to talk about until Eliza comes?"Having no small talks, he stars:

*"You see we're all savages, more or less, we're supposed to be civilized and cultured –to know all about poetry and philosophy and art and science, and so on; but how many of us know even the meaning of these names? [to Miss. Hill] What do you know of poetry? [to Mrs. Hill] What do you know of science? [indicating Freddy] What does he know of art or science or anything else? What the devil do you imagine I know of philosophy" (P.73).*

As the diction and the topic of the citation indicate, Shaw's Prometheus of phonetics is without manners.Yet, he is neither a snob like Clara, nor a vulgar like Eliza, nor even a gentleman like Pickering. At home, he takes his boots off and wipes his hands on his dressing gown, etc. As far as Eliza is concerned, when Mrs. Higgins asks her if it will rain, she says:

*"The* shallow *depression in the west of these islands is likely to move slowly in an easterly direction. There are no indications of any great change in the barometrical situation" (P.75).*

Eliza is Higgins's creation and is, accordingly, his device to violate conventions, here, embodied in social manners. So, in the quotation Eliza's reciting the weather forecast gives two scientific informations to be an answer for Mrs. Higgins's conventional question. Another instance of the violation of social manners is Eliza's small talk: she uses very formal language where the subject is quite low. That is, she expresses gutter ideas in aristocratic diction. The third instance of Eliza's violation of social manners takes place when Freddy asks her if she will walk across the park, to which she reacts instantly: "Walk! Not bloody likely". The violation here is due to Eliza's use of a taboo word in so decent a situation. These instances of violation of social manners cause some of the characters in Pygmalion to reconsider their conception of social manners:

Pickering:... Ive been away in India for several years; and manners have changed so much that I sometimes dont know whether I'm at a respectable dinner-table or in a forecastle.

Clara Hill: It's all a matter of habit. Theres no right or wrong in it. Nobody means anything by it (P.79).

Manners, therefore, are in constant change with habits, and there is no use judging them as good or bad, right or wrong. Such a deduction is drawing nearer to Higgins's motto in the play, which forms the final definition of social manners. He tells Eliza in Act Five:

"The great secret, Eliza, is not having bad or good manners or any other particular sort of manners, but having the same manner for all human souls: in short, behaving as if you were in Heaven, where there are no third-class carriages, and one soul is as good as another" (P.126).

By unifying social manners and considering them as reality, the relationship between manners and class status is already dissolved. Yet, the issue of manners is continued at the level of social titles and the care for appearance and behaviour like a lady or a gentleman. This leads to a perusal of the concept of "lady" as a social title, in Pygmalion.

**The concept of lady:**

In Act Two, Mrs. Pearce introduces Eliza to Higgins as "quite a common girl... Very common indeed" (P.36). Mrs. Pearce very clearly judges common girls, as opposed to ladies, in terms of clothes, speech and manners. Eliza agrees to this conception after her transformation in Act Five:

*"It was from you [Pickering] that I learnt really nice manners; and that is what makes one a lady, isnt it?" (P.121)*

Then, Eliza believes in the conventional interpretation of "lady", which stand for excelling in social manners. Yet, she comes back to tell Pickering:

*"The difference between a lady and a flower girl is not how she behaves, but how she is treated. I shall always be a flower girl to Professor Higgins, because he always treats me as a flower girl, and always will; but I knew I can be a lady to you, because you always treat me as a lady, and always will" (P.122).*

Here, Eliza shifts from the belief that a lady equals her excellence at performing social manners to the belief that a lady depends on the consideration which the others owe to her. This is a positive turning-point in Eliza's attitude towards the issue of "lady", as a social title. On defending himself before Eliza's accusation of his ill-treatment of her as a lady, Higgins insists on the fact that he treats duchess and flower- girl alike: "one soul is as good as an other", which is –as Martin Meisel observes- a radical attack on the very concept of "lady", on the social and economic structure it presupposes, and is the dialectical destination of the play.

By introducing a common girl to the upper-class society as a lady, Higgins violates the conventional distinction between a lady and a flower girl. Hence, Eliza the lady speaks like a lady and uses taboo words: "bloody"; comes from the lower classes: "the gutter"; loves a low, common, foolish, young man: Freddy Hill; goes out to work for her living: techer of phonetics.

Such a violation aims at abolishing the signs of class distinctions perpetuated by the concept of "lady" or "gentleman". Hence, the importance of looking at people as they are, without any social connotation to load them with. The relationship between man and woman is included here, and seriously emphasized.

Gender relationship:

In Act Two, Doolittle comes to sell his daughter for the sake of "boozing". He even tries to convince Higgins to by Eliza from him: "I can see youre one of the straight sort, Governor. Well, whats a five-pound note to you? And whats Eliza to me?" Eliza is as cheap to Doolittle as five-pound note is to Higgins. Such a comparison clearly reveals the status of woman under the patriarchal, hierarchical and capitalist society. Doolittle goes as far as to advise Pickering to marry Eliza:

"Take my advice, Governor –marry Eliza while she is young and dont know no better. If you dont youll sorry for it after. If you do, she'll be sorry for it after; but better her than you, because youre a man, and she is only a woman and dont know to be happy anyhow" (P.60).

Doolittle is expressing his vision that woman is inferior

to man and, accordingly, her feelings and rights are unimportant. He even tells Higgins: "If you want Eliza's mind improved, Governor, you do it yourself with a strap". The inferiority of woman here is reinforced with the Nietzscheistic logic –the logic of the strap. Doolittle protests that he likes a little "ginger" in his life. For Doolittle, "ginger" to his mind is the privilege of beating his female paramours and changing them at will.

As for the relationship between Higgins and Eliza, it supplies another model of gender relationship in the play. It is a relationship between exploiter and exploited. Higgins takes Eliza, tames her and teaches her proper English pronunciation just in order to win his bet for him and show his talent to the world. To achieve his goal, Higgins acts with the girl as if she were an object or a slave, careless of her emotions and her future. Eliza wins him his bet, fetches him his slippers... Yet, in reward, he abuses and insults her, calling her "Monkey Brand" "infamous creature" "heartless guttersnipe", "unfortunate animal".

The struggle between male and female is highlighted in the play, with male characters like Doolittle and Pickering siding with Higgins; and female characters like Mrs. Pearce and Mrs. Higgins siding with Eliza. Accordingly, while Doolittle advises Higgins to wallop Eliza in teaching her, and while Pickering supports Higgins financially in order to prove his genius by transforming Eliza into a duchess, the females in the persons of Mrs. Pearce and Mrs. Higgins reproach Pickering and Higgins for playing with Eliza's life. Mrs. Pearce tells Higgins: "... You cant take a girl up like that as if you were picking up a pebble on the beach". She continues:

"Mr. Higgins, I want to know on what terms the girl is to be here... And what is to become of her when you have finished your teaching? You must look ahead a little" (P.44).

Mrs. Pearce is urging Higgins to treat Eliza as a human being, as an equal. Similarly, Mrs. Higgins wants Higgins to tell her what will happen to Eliza after her education because Higgins is teaching Eliza "the manners and habits that disqualify a fine lady from earning her own living without giving her a fine lady's income". Mrs. Higgins even shows her contempt of Henry and Pickering in their faces: "You have no more sense, either of you, than two children". Yet, the sex-antagonism is better revealed when Higgins and Pickering leaves her flat by the end of Act Three with Mrs. Higgins shouting: "Oh, men! men!! men!"

Before all these gender conflicts, Eliza finally throws slippers at her "master" as a revolt against Higgins's ill-treatment of her as well as against the patriarchal society which submits Eliza to male authority, deprives her of her rights and wastes her potential. She refuses the gender distinctions deepened in society. These distinctions are shown in Pygmalion to be invalid. Hence, Freddy, as a man, is shown to be incompetent and good-for-nothing. Even Eliza is shown to be more practical and hard-working. She will marry Ferddy and work for him; "Freddy loves me: that makes him king enough for me. I dont want him to work: he wasnt brought up to it as I was. I'll go and be a teacher". She even says: "Perhaps I could make something of him", just like Higgins made a lady of her.

In this way, man and woman are no longer judged by their gender distinctions but as human beings. Throughout the play, Eliza struggles to show Higgins that she is a human being, that she has feelings, and that she needs kindness. She tells Higgins:

*"I want a little kindness... I'm not dirt under your feet" (P.130).*

*"I got my feelings same as anyone else" (P.45).*

The equality between man and woman advocated here is based on real humanity, not on conventions, since it ignores the gender differences between the two sexes. It is only through "equality" that the talents and energies of all people, of both sexes, are utilized. Yet, conventional morality remains a wall before evolution and "equality", with its ready-made laws and good-evil complications: a reinforcement of the dominant values.

*Morality*:

Morality in Pygmalion goes hand-in-hand with the other issues concerned with Shaw's social reform: speech, manners, etc. Morality is shown to affect characters very much. Thus, in the portico, in the opening scene, Eliza is afraid of the supposed police informer to charge her with prostitution because she is coaxing money out of a gentleman. Accordingly, she reacts hysterically to save her honour: "I'm a respectable girl: so help me, I never spoke to him except to ask him to buy a flower off me" (PP.19-20).

Similarly, when Eliza goes to Higgins' laboratory in Act One, she is determined not to be cheated. She is suspicious of being drugged and seduced, as the impetuous professor bullies and tempts her. She keeps saying: "I'm a good girl, I am" in order to show Higgins that she is not a call-girl, but a respectable one who comes on business: to have lessons and pay for them: "... and if my money's not good enough I can go else-where". This is to show that Eliza has honourable purposes, and that she cannot yield to -what she suspects- Higgins's sexual desire.

Alfred Doolittle first appears in Wimpole Street in the hypocritical role of the virtuous, with the intention to blackmail the two have taken up Eliza. He menaces Higgins: "I want my daughter: that's what I want, see". By this menace, Doolittle probably thinks that allying with morality will put him in a position of power in order to dictate his orders on Higgins. Yet, ironically, Higgins allows him to take his daughter away. Doolittle, shocked in his goal, tries to convince Higgins, entreating him, that he has not come to take away Eliza:

"All I ask is my right as a father; and youre the last man alive to expect me to let her go for nothing; for I can see youre one of the straight sort, Governor. Well, whats a five-pound note to you? And whats Eliza to me?" (P.57).

Doolittle even continues that if he had known Higgins's intentions are not honourable, he would have asked Higgins for fifty pounds. After selling his daughter, Doolittle does not only throw morality aside, but –what is more- he argues for consideration as an undeserving poor man done out of his natural right to happiness by the narrow-minded prejudices of middle-class morality. Doolittle even clearly claims that he is victim of the morality that classifies people into deserving and undeserving according to the moral value of their deeds, and punishes Doolittle as undeserving because of his "immoral" behaviour. Doolittle refuses such a distinction:

*"My need is as great as the most deserving widow's... I dont need less than a deserving man: I need more. I dont eat less hearty than him; and I drink a lot more" (P.58).*

*Doolittle even goes as far as to strike at the foundation on which the dominant morality is based;*

*"Higgins:... Doolittle: either youre an honest man or a rogue.*

Doolittle [tolerantly]: A little of both, Henry, like the rest of us; a little of both" (P.117).

By being honest and dishonest at the same time, Doolittle suggests the alternative morality and shatters away the conventional duality (good/evil) on which ready-made moral judgements is based. According to Shaw, morals cannot be simplified into right and wrong deeds, but considered as one reality/entity. Thus, even in Shaw's problem plays, there is no conflict between good and evil, and the villain is as conscientious as the hero; there are even no heroes or villains at all, they are only human beings.

By dividing morals into good and evil, hypocrits are given the life-time chance to enter public life pretending dignity and virtue in order to win the consideration of the masses and exploit them better. It is for this reason that Doolittle wonders: "What is middle-class morality? Just an excuse for never giving me anything". Yet, through the process of evolution, Shaw predicts that the morality based on virtue and evil will be repudiated by a morality based on real humanity. It is only through such humanist morality that all mankind –men and women, rich and poor- are considered as equal human being without the interference of any moral prejudice to praise or despise them, for people are what they are.

Pygmalion is a play about Class Society and a class culture shown to be omnipresent in social values, human relationships, language... The Shavian alternative has been to detach those values and habits from their class connotations as a preliminary step towards more individual freedom and wider prospects of social equality. In Pygmalion, such a claim is echoed by the American millionaire Ezra D. Wannafeller's desire to found "Moral Reform Societies" all over the World and to have a "Universal" language invented for him by Higgins, "author of Higgins's Universal Alphabet".

Therefore, reform for "equality" has not been only Shaw's goal but also his characters'. It has in been made clear in this present study that Shaw's religion is Evolution, a will to which the individual is a mere device to promote its own process of development. Yet, with that individual rigidly succumbing under class restrictions, his talents and capacities die down unprofitted. Only social equality can emancipate the individual and set free his energies to contribute in furthering the process of Evolution: his first and ultimate role in existence. It is through Evolution that Equality is achieved: Equality takes its shape through "gradualness". Evolution and Equality, in this study, are two faces of just one Shavian conception of Existence: improving the human race.

## Chapter 8

# The Playwright in Spite of Himself

Nobody called him "George." It was his father's name, and George Bernard Shaw hated his father. Disrespect for authority became the theme of his life, along with the complementary certainty that he had better answers to life's questions than anyone else. Usually, such a personality merely annoys a small circle of friends, family, and associates, but Shaw had an unusual talent—he was one of the most brilliant of British playwrights.

He annoyed just about everybody and still does. With the passion of a Puritan minister dispensing hellfire sermons, Shaw preached through his plays his vision of How Things Ought to Be. This included, at various times, such harmless beliefs as vegetarianism and abstention from alcohol, but they also included such vile beliefs as the endorsement of fascism and a blind devotion to Stalinism. All had a cynical edge to them, of disdain for lesser folk.

George Bernard Shaw was born in Dublin, Ireland, on July 26, 1856, to a Scottish-Protestant family. His father, George Carr Shaw, was a grain wholesaler who suffered from a serious squint, which Oscar Wilde's father, a famous Dublin ophthalmologic surgeon, operated on. But squinting wasn't his worst problem—alcoholism was. George Shaw's wife, Lucinda "Bessie" (Gurley) Shaw, came to have contempt for his weakness, even though they remained sufficiently well off to have their children reared by servants.

In a letter to Ellen Terry (June 11, 1897), Shaw describes how his sudden recognition of his father's alcoholism converted him into a cynical teetotaler: "The first moral lesson

I can remember as a tiny child was the lesson of teetotalism, instilled by my father, a futile person you would have thought him. One night, when I was about as tall as his boots, he took me out for a walk. In the course of it, I conceived a monstrous, incredible suspicion. When I got home, I stole to my mother and in an awestruck whisper said to her, 'Mamma, I think Papa's drunk.'

She turned away with impatient disgust, and said, 'When is he ever anything else?' I have never believed anything since: then the scoffer began.... Oh, a devil of a childhood, Ellen, rich only in dreams, frightful in realities." Bessie Shaw brought her children up to loathe George Shaw so much that, when he died in 1885, neither she nor they attended his funeral.

Although Bessie was an affectionate mother to her daughters, she remained emotionally distant from George, her only son and youngest child. A singer who taught music to her daughters, Bessie made no effort to teach "Sonny" music, nor to send the obviously bright boy to university. What Shaw became was by dint of his own efforts. He never knew encouragement or praise from his mother. "Fortunately I have a heart of stone," the playwright would write as an adult, "else my relations would have broken it long ago."

George Shaw was not the only George whose influence prompted the playwright to eschew his first name. Bessie, who was sixteen years younger than her husband, studied voice under the tutelage of a man who called himself Vandeleur Lee. Lee, also known as George Lee, George John Lee, and George Vandeleur Lee, developed a passionate relationship with Bessie. In 1866, he moved in with the Shaws, in a ménage à trois, which may or may not have been consummated. In 1876, Bessie, Lee, and Shaw's elder sister, Lucy, moved away together to London. Shaw left his father and followed soon after. It would be almost thirty years before he would return to Ireland.

To pay his bills, Shaw ghostwrote a music column for Vandeleur Lee, for the London newspaper the *Hornet*. He also produced several novels but was unable to get any published.

Shaw supported himself by expanding his repertoire of critical writing to include art, literary, and drama criticism for magazines such as the *Dramatic Review, Our Corner,* the *Pall Mall Gazette,* the *World,* and the *Star.*

He wrote for this last under the pen name Como di Bassetto, which is Italian for a type of high-pitched clarinet, poking fun at the timbre of his own voice. In 1895, Shaw became the drama critic for the *Saturday Review,* where he startled readers by revealing his contempt for Shakespeare. The turning point in Shaw's career was his discovery of socialism, the religion in which he found his life's calling. Of this conversion, he remarked, "I became a man with some business in the world." In 1882, Shaw heard political economist Henry George lecture and was intrigued by George's theory that if government owned the land, while individuals owned their labour, poverty could be alleviated without destroying individual incentive.

This made sense to Shaw, and, in search of like-minded men, he joined the Social Democratic Federation, where he became friends with such figures as William Morris, Eleanor Marx, and Annie Besant. He read Karl Marx but recognized that Marxism would not be embraced by ordinary workers. As Shaw observed, "Marx never got hold of [the working man] for a moment.... The middle and upper classes are the revolutionary element in society; the proletariat is the conservative element."

Shaw believed that the change to socialism must come gradually, "by prosaic installments of public regulation and public administration enacted by ordinary parliaments, vestries, municipalities, parish councils, school boards, etc." Shaw became one of the earliest members of the Fabian Society, a group of middle-class socialists, which was named after the Roman general Quintus Fabius Maximus, famous for advocating a war of attrition over direct confrontation with Hannibal. The Fabian Society was founded in May 1884, and Shaw served on the executive committee from 1885 until 1911.

The organization believed in "the inevitability of gradualism" and emphasized a gradual replacement of capitalism with socialism. The Fabian Society also endowed government with the quasi-religious role of the development of individual character, believing that society could be rebuilt "in accordance with the highest moral possibilities." Shaw's own description of socialism reflects his cold perspective on humanity: "Socialism is not charity nor loving-kindness, nor sympathy with the poor, nor popular philanthropy... but the economist's hatred of waste and disorder, the aesthete's hatred of ugliness and dirt, the lawyer's hatred of injustice, the doctor's hatred of disease, the saint's hatred of the seven deadly sins."

Basing society on hatred fit well with Shaw's disdainful character. Although socialism promised future benefits for the masses, it had a more immediate benefit for Shaw. It was a fashionable belief. Shaw's interest in socialism, and the networking it afforded with some of England's most wealthy and powerful people, paid off nicely for him. His fifth attempt to publish a novel, *The Unsocial Socialist,* was accepted for serialized publication in 1884.

As a member of the Fabian Society, he produced pamphlets such as The Fabian Manifesto (1884), *The True Radical Programme* (1887), *The Impossibilities of Anarchism* (1893), *Fabianism and the Empire* (1900), and *Socialism for Millionaires* (1901). He briefly translated his ideas into action and, from 1897 to 1903, served as councillor for the London borough of St. Pancras. This bit of authority produced no revolution. His most significant achievement was establishing the borough's first public ladies' room. In Shaw's time, as now, social progressives out to improve human character were drawn to ideological micromanagement.

Even their clothing was employed as a billboard for their belief in progress through "scientific" knowledge, which is more theory than examined and proven fact. The trendy Dr. Jaeger, professor of zoology at Stuttgart, proclaimed wool the most healthful fabric, which he recommended wearing from the skin out; the suits Jaeger designed became the politically correct fashion statement of the 1880s. In 1885, along with William Morris and Oscar Wilde, Shaw started wearing garments designed by Jaeger—two suits, one brown, the other silver gray. He rigidly adhered to this sartorial correctness, long after the fashion had passed. About Shaw's choice of garments, G.K. Chesterton observed (1910), "His costume has become part of his personality: one can come to think of the reddish-brown Jaeger suit as if it were a sort of reddish brown fur.... His brown woolen clothes, at once artistic and hygienic, completed the appeal for which he stood; which might be defined as an eccentric healthy-mindedness." Although Shaw professed interest in helping laborers, like many socialists today, he confined his personal relationships to the intellectual and social elite. What friends he did make were primarily political allies within his socialist circles. He was profoundly uncomfortable around ordinary people, preferring words over actions and ideas over human contact when it came to helping the poor.

It is when we look at Shaw in love, however, that his lack of any interest in or ability to form normal attachments becomes most apparent. His cool relationship with his mother, contempt for his father, and awareness of the curious trilateral arrangement between his parents and Vandeleur Lee convinced him that a permanent, loving commitment within marriage was sustainable only in fiction. Shaw remained a virgin until the age of twenty-nine, when he surrendered to the charms of Jenny Patterson, a widow who was one of his mother's friends.

At the same time, however, he pursued actress Florence Farr (who was also Yeats' mistress), with whom he would spend the evenings reading Walt Whitman. On one memorable evening, Patterson, who had been in Italy, returned unexpectedly and discovered Shaw and Farr involved in a fairly unusual means of interpreting Whitman's verse. In a scene straight out of a bad play, Patterson screamed at Farr that she couldn't have Shaw. The next morning, at Shaw's urging, Patterson sent an apology to Farr, giving her note to May Morris Sparling to deliver—unaware that this young woman, the married daughter of Shaw's friend William Morris, was yet another object of his seductions. When Shaw heartlessly turned the embarrassing catfight between his two mistresses into a scene in *The Philanderer*, the outraged Farr wrote a novel, *The Dancing Faun*, in which an angry woman gets away with murdering her lover.

Melodramatics were, however, largely uncharacteristic of Shaw's own philandering. It seemed that unconsummated seductions were more appealing to him than consummated relationships, that he derived more pleasure from the romantic conquest than from the spoils of love's war. While this might seem an exercise in chaste romance, it was more a game of dominance and withheld self.

Generally, Shaw's loveless love was channeled into mere flirtations with young actresses, so much so that biographer Frank Harris deemed him "the first man to have cut a swathe through the theatre and left it strewn with virgins." In a peculiar iteration of his parents' relationship with Vandeleur Lee, Shaw repeatedly entered into chaste manages trois with married women. This pattern was evident in his relationships with Edith Nesbit (Mrs. Hubert) Bland, May Morris (Mrs. Henry) Sparling (the aforementioned messenger), and actress (Alice) Ellen Terry (1847—1928), who was involved in a long-term relationship with Henry Irving. Shaw each time positioned himself as an innocent pursued by an unavailable but ardent woman.

The fear of death finally inspired him to involve himself with a woman free to accept his proposal. In 1898, mistakenly believing himself near death, Shaw married the wealthy Charlotte Payne-Townsend, a fellow member of the Fabian Society. Though the couple had engaged in sexual relations prior to marriage, the marriage itself remained unconsummated for its forty-five-year duration.

This was as much Charlotte's wish as Shaw's, as she wanted to ensure that she did not have children—a wish he seems to have shared. Among the most passionate of Shaw's amours was with the actress Mrs. Patrick Campbell (Beatrice Stella Tanner, 1865—1940), with whom he became obsessed while reviewing plays in which she appeared. Shaw wrote *Pygmalion* for her, including its determinedly unhappy ending, where the lovers nearly merge, then part, presumably forever. "The quantity of Love that an ordinary person can stand without serious damage," claimed Shaw, "is about ten minutes in fifty years."

When Stella came upon hard times, she asked Shaw if she might publish his love letters to her to make some money. Shaw refused to give her permission, responding, "I will not, dear Stella, at my time of life, play the horse to your Lady Godiva." Shaw's affection for her did, however, last the rest of her life—indeed, beyond it. When she died in poverty in the south of France in 1940, Shaw secretly paid for her funeral, and when her family tried to repay him, he accepted their checks but never cashed them.

The one true love of Shaw's life was socialism. Shaw did not start out to be a playwright. He decided to become one, after he realized the propaganda possibilities of the drama, which occurred to him while reading the translations of Ibsen done by his friend William Archer. Ibsen's plays deal compellingly with social and moral problems. Shaw studied his technique and, in 1891, published "The Quintessence of Ibsenism," one of the most important essays in modern drama criticism. In this essay, Shaw explains that man is a philistine (a category to which he relegates most of us), an idealist (intellectual revolutionaries), or a Great Man, the rare, Nietzschean leader characterized by great personal force.

Greatness, for Shaw, meant power—and the men he deemed great would, unfortunately, include fascists and Stalinists. Shaw's early attempts to use plays to promote socialism were thinly veiled lectures on social and moral problems, in which capitalism plays the top-hatted, mustachioed villain. In *Widowers' Houses* (1892), the capitalist evildoers were slum landlords.

His next effort, Mrs. Warren's Profession (1894), was banned, as *Mrs. Warren's Profession* turned out to be the oldest one. Shaw classified these early efforts as "Plays Unpleasant," as they focus on unpleasant ideas, though he could have called them with equal accuracy "Plays Unsuccessful." In part, this was because he conceived of characters not as flesh-and-blood human beings but as mouthpieces for conflicting political and social points of view.

If he were to have any influence, Shaw realized, he would have to write plays people were willing to watch. He had greater success with his comedy *Candida,* about a woman who must choose between remaining with her contented, if dull, clergyman husband and running off with an 18-year-old poet who wants to rescue her from respectability. Candida is considered a wise and strong woman, except by feminist critics, who are contemptuous of her choice to remain with the man who needs her, rather than to embrace short-lived pleasure with a flattering naîf.

Similarly, *Arms and the Man* (1894) balances serious themes with a plot that evokes interest and sympathy—in this case, contrasting a romantic with a realistic view of war—and culminates in a happy, romantic ending. Shaw recognized that another means of expanding his influence was to print his plays with detailed introductions and stage directions articulating his views, thus fusing two genres, the polemical essay with the drama. *Man and Superman* (1903), for example, offers a discussion of his Great Man theory, particularly in the famous dream sequence, "Don Juan in Hell."

The play that really launched Shaw's career as a playwright, however, was *John Bull's Other Island* (1904), which Yeats commissioned for the Abbey Theatre, then rejected. The plot concerns an Anglo-Irish plan to transform worthless land into a garden city. Shaw presents Irish concerns about independence unsentimentally but with a recognition of the importance of home rule to Ireland, as evidenced by comments such as this: "A healthy nation is as unconscious of its nationality as a healthy man of his bones. But if you break a nation's nationality it will think of nothing else but getting it set again."

Though making many serious points, the comedy was so successful that British King Edward VII fell off his chair, laughing. Among Shaw's most popular plays is *Major Barbara* (1905), which focuses on an idealistic heiress who joins the Salvation Army, hoping to help the poor by saving their souls. She rejects the capitalism of her father, the arms manufacturer Undershaft, until she visits the village in which his contented workers lead happy lives and comes to recognize the importance of financial stability to spiritual and social growth.

"I am a Millionaire," explains Undershaft when his daughter offers to save his soul. "That is my religion." Major Barbara comes to see that people desperate for bread are not in a position to make fine distinctions about theology. "Spiritual values," asserted Shaw, "do not and cannot exist for hungry, roofless and naked people. Any religion that puts spiritual values before physical necessities is what Marx meant by opium and Nietzsche called a slave morality."

Of all Shaw's plays, his greatest commercial success was *Pygmalion* (1912), despite the unhappy, unromantic ending, which Beerbohm Tree, who played the male lead, tried to persuade Shaw to change. *Pygmalion* articulates one of Shaw's theories about language—that the poor lack social mobility, at least in part, because of their inability to pronounce or use English well.

Being almost entirely self-taught, Shaw sympathized with those who tried to teach themselves by reading. He believed that the unphonetic nature of English was a serious obstacle to economic and social advancement. In the preface to *Pygmalion*, Shaw writes, "No man can teach himself what [English] should sound like from reading it; and it is impossible for an Englishman to open his mouth without making some other Englishman despise him."

In *Pygmalion*, through intensive tutoring in pronunciation, language use, and manners, Professor Henry Higgins transforms Cockney flower girl Eliza Doolittle into a lady—and in the course of the transformation, the two develop an intense mutual attraction. Shaw keeps the two determinedly apart at the end of his play, but in the two movies made of *Pygmalion* and the musical comedy *My Fair Lady*, the conclusion is revised to unite the lovers.

Though *Pygmalion* was an enormous success, Shaw soon fell out of favour with the public, on account of his insensitive and unpatriotic antiwar newspaper commentaries called "Common Sense About the War" (1914). As a socialist, Shaw felt no special allegiance to England; he saw the war as merely the crumbling of a corrupt capitalist system he had no wish to repair. Shaw's countrymen, who often had little or no intellectual distance between themselves and the brutalities of war, responded to his flip condescension with contempt, and he became something of a pariah for several years.

He would, however, regain his standing, as postwar cynicism became fashionable. Shaw would go on to write many more plays, including *Androcles and the Lion* (1913); *Heartbreak House* (1919), a scornful view of the Bloomsbury circle in the days before World War I that was a critical but not a popular success; *Back to Methuselah* (1921), a kind of fusion of metaphysics and Darwin, which Shaw considered his *Ring* cycle; and St. Joan (1923), startling for its sympathetic portrayal of Joan's judges. Shaw's Joan is bloodless and sexless, more pigheaded than ecstatic. T.S. Eliot described Shaw's Joan as "a great middle-class reformer... [whose] place is little higher than Mrs. Pankhurst's." Whatever its weaknesses, *St. Joan* captured for Shaw the Nobel Prize in literature in 1925. Shaw donated the prize money to support the translation of Strindberg's drama into English.

After Charlotte died in 1943, Shaw continued to lead an active life on his property at Ayot St. Lawrence in Hertfordshire. (Like most socialists, he had no objection to owning property himself.) He continued to write until very shortly before his death. He had written some sixty-five plays and dozens of pamphlets, on subjects as varied as feminism, marriage, vivisection, the Soviet Union, natural selection, and capital punishment. His ironic wit endowed the language with the adjective *Shavian*, to refer to such clever observations as "England and America are two countries divided by a common language."

While trimming a tree at the age of 94, he fell off a ladder, dying a few days later, on November 2, 1950, from complications. Shaw was cremated, and, at his request, his ashes were mixed with his wife's. His memorial ceremony was not religious, though Sydney Cockerall read, ironically, from *The Pilgrim's Progress,* a religious allegory most popular among fundamentalist Christians. Among the greatest beneficiaries of Shaw's will was a project to revise the English alphabet to make it more phonetic—with at least forty letters—a project that failed utterly.

Shaw's values have either puzzled critics or prompted them to ignore or whitewash his attraction to and ultimate embrace of evil. The Shaw who objected to World War I may, indeed, have been a genuine, if undiplomatic, pacifist: "I regard war as wasteful," he wrote, "demoralizing, unnecessary, and ludicrously and sordidly inglorious in its reality. This is my unconditional opinion. I *don't* mean war in a bad cause, or war against liberty, or war with any other qualification whatever: I mean war. I recognize no right of the good man to kill the bad man or to govern the bad man."

As the years passed, however, he grew impatient that the world was not turning socialist fast enough to suit him. Shaw came to see value in brutality. As the old saying goes, you can't make an omelette without breaking eggs, and Shaw wanted his omelette. He found a new hero in Oswald Mosley, the founder of the British Union of Fascists. Shaw would describe Mosley admiringly, as "the only striking personality in British politics." He also admired the Italian fascist Mussolini and, even more, the communist Stalin.

Shaw visited Stalin in Moscow, in 1931, and found nothing disconcerting about Stalin's mass murders: "Our question is not to kill or not to kill, but to select the right people to kill... [T]he essential difference between the Russian liquidator with his pistol (or whatever his humane killer may be) and the British hangman is that they do not operate on the same sort of person." The playwright famous for inventing Shavian irony would, without irony, recommend Joseph Stalin for the Nobel Peace Prize.

Some readers rationalize Shaw's attraction to fascism and communism—two philosophies he knew to be responsible for the murderous oppression of millions of people—as a puzzling aberration, or, yet more bizarrely, as evidence of his determination to believe in human perfectability. This attraction is, however, fully consistent with Shaw's cold-blooded calculus in human relationships. His relationships with women consisted mainly of intellectual masturbation. His marriage to Charlotte was a marriage in name only.

His friendships were more political alliances than true friendships—as Wilde quipped, "Mr. Bernard Shaw has no enemies, but is intensely disliked by all his friends." Individual human beings were of no consequence to Shaw—he sympathized with men only in the aggregate—and he found human passions uncompelling. He spent his last half-century nearly celibate and without the pleasures of a slice of roast beef, a glass of cognac, or even a good cigar. Worse, he possessed an unrelenting and unquiet passion to convert others to his joyless, jackbooted asceticism.

As Benjamin de Casseres observed, "Shaw is a Puritan who missed the *Mayflower* by minutes." Shaw's writing is amusing but brittle. It is far more brittle than that of Oscar Wilde, who, for all his shortcomings, at least had a heart to be broken. Indeed, everything about Shaw himself and Shavian drama is cold, sterile, calculated. It is brilliant; it is clever; it contains some truth; but there is no heart to it, and what flame burns is an icy one. What limits Shaw as both man and artist is his unwillingness to acknowledge the difference between idea and flesh; to see that people, in both art and life, are meant to be more than mere mouthpieces for ideology.

In his vanity, he refused to recognize fascism and communism as evil, or to acknowledge that he was a fool for being deluded by them. Shaw's political pontificating transformed the literary giant into a Lilliputian, whose socialism mutated, unapologetically, into a worship of murder, of force in its most raw and ugly form. Shaw's plays should, then, be read because they pose important questions in an interesting way. His life should be read as a cautionary tale, illustrating the unintended consequences of playing with grand plans to order others' lives. But Shaw must be read in the context of Shaw.

As one is delighted by the sparkling wit and charmed by characters engaged in adolescent rebellion against a world that does not live up to their expectations and desires, one must remain mindful that the hand which created *Major Barbara* penned, with equal fervor, defenses of Stalin's vilest practices.

Had Shaw set out to be merely a playwright who wished to amuse, we could hold him to a lower standard; but he considered his plays a means of seducing others to his ideology, which, like himself, ends in sterile darkness. For Shaw, it was all about his being the only way. Everything was simple to him: One only need do what he believed correct. Like a socialist version of Ross Perot, he evinced a blustery self-confidence that was self-indulgent and intellectually dishonest.

While Perot embraced simpleminded "common sense," Shaw went to the opposite extreme, proclaiming intellectuals as the true masters of mankind and setting himself up as the foremost intellectual. It is indeed curious that a man who hated his father would come to see himself as a father figure to all mankind.

## Chapter 9

# Debate between G.K. Chesterton and Bernard Shaw

In justice to all concerned I feel it to be my duty to state frankly that this account of a public discussion between Mr. Chesterton and Mr. Shaw is something less than a verbatim report. But with some assistance from the debaters it has been possible to save enough from oblivion to justify publication.

Mr. Belloc: I am here to take the chair in the debate between two men whom you desire to hear more than you could possibly desire to hear me. They will debate whether they agree or do not agree. From what I know of attempts at agreement between human beings there is a prospect of a very pretty fight. When men debate agreement between nations then you may be certain a disastrous war is on the horizon. I make an exception for the League of Nations, of which I know nothing.

If the League of Nations could make a war it would be the only thing it ever has made. I do not know what Mr. Chesterton is going to say. I do not know what Mr. Shaw is going to say. If I did I would not say it for them. I vaguely gather from what I have heard that they are going to try to discover a principle: whether men should be free to possess private means, as is Mr. Shaw, as is Mr. Chesterton; or should be, like myself, an embarrassed person, a publishers' hack. I could tell them; but my mouth is shut. I am not allowed to say what I think. At any rate, they are going to debate this sort of thing. I know not what more to say They are about to debate. You are about to listen. I am about to sneer.

Mr. Shaw: Mr. Belloc, and Ladies and Gentlemen. Our subject this evening, "Do We Agree?" was an inspiration of Mr. Chesterton's. Some of you might reasonably wonder, if we agree, what we are going to debate about. But I suspect that you do not really care much what we debate about provided we entertain you by talking in our characteristic manners.

The reason for this, though you may not know it—and it is my business to tell you—is that Mr. Chesterton and I are two madmen. Instead of doing honest and respectable work and behaving ourselves as ordinary citizens. We go about the world possessed by a strange gift of tongues— in my own case almost exclusively confined to the English language—uttering all sorts of extraordinary opinions for no reason whatever.

Mr. Chesterton tells and prints the most extravagant lies. He takes ordinary incidents of human life—commonplace middle-class life— and gives them a monstrous and strange and gigantic outline. He fills suburban gardens with the most impossible murders, and not only does he invent the murders but also succeeds in discovering the murderer who never committed the murders.

I do very much the same sort of thing. I promulgate lies in the shape of plays; but whereas Mr. Chesterton takes events which you think ordinary and makes them gigantic and colossal to reveal their essential miraculousness, I am rather inclined to take these things in their utter commonplaceness, and yet to introduce among them outrageous ideas which scandalize the ordinary play-goer and send him away wondering whether he has been standing on his head all his life or whether I am standing on mine.

A man goes to see one of my plays and sits by his wife. Some apparently ordinary thing is said on the stage, and his wife says to him: "Aha! What do you think of that?" Two minutes later another apparently ordinary thing is said and the man turns to his wife and says to her: "Aha! What do you think of that?" Curious, is it not, that we should go about doing these things and be tolerated and even largely admired for doing them? Of late years I might say that I have almost been reverenced for doing these things. Obviously we are mad; and in the East we should be reverenced as madmen.

The wisdom of the East says: "Let us listen to these men carefully; but let us not forget that they are madmen." In this country they say "Let us listen to these amusing chaps. They are perfectly sane, which we obviously are not." Now there must be some reason for shewing us all this consideration. There must be some force in nature which... (At this point the debate was interrupted by persistent knocking at the doors by ticket-holders who had, through some misunderstanding, been locked out. On the chairman's intervention the doors were opened, and order was restored Mr. Shaw then proceeded.)

Ladies and Gentlemen, I must go on because, as you see, if I don't begin to talk everybody else does. Now I was speaking of the curious respect in which mad people are held in the East and in this country. What I was leading up to is this, that it matters very little on what points they differ: they have all kinds of aberrations which rise out of their personal circumstances, out of their training out of their knowledge or ignorance.

But if you listen to them carefully and find that at certain points they agree, then you have some reason for supposing that here the spirit of the age is coming through, and giving you an inspired message. Reject all the contradictory things they say and concentrate your attention on the things upon which they agree, and you may be listening to the voice of revelation. You will do well to-night to listen attentively, because probably what is urging us to these utterances is not personal to ourselves but some conclusion to which all mankind is moving either by reason or by inspiration.

The mere fact that Mr. Chesterton and 1 may agree upon any point may not at all prevent us from debating it passionately. I find that the people who fight me generally hold the very ideas I am trying to express. I do not know if it is because they resent the liberty I am taking or because they do not like the words I use or the twist of my mind; but they are the people who quarrel most with me. You have at this moment a typical debate raging in the Press. You have a very pretty controversy going on in the Church of England between the Archbishop of Canterbury and the Bishop of Birmingham. I hope you have all read the admirable letter of the Archbishop of Canterbury. Everybody is pleased with that letter. It has the enormous virtue of being entirely good-humoured, of trying to make peace, of avoiding making mischief: a popular English virtue which is a credit to the English race.

But it has another English quality which is a little more questionable, and that is the quality of being entirely anti-intellectual. The letter is a heartfelt appeal for ambiguity. You can imagine the Archbishop of Canterbury, if he were continuing the controversy in private, saying to the Bishop of Birmingham: "Now, my dear Barnes, let me recommend you to read that wonderful book, the Pilgrim's Progress. Read the history of the hero, Christian, no doubt a very splendid fellow, and from the literary point of view the only hero of romantic fiction resembling a real man. But he is always fighting. He is out of one trouble into another. He is leading a terrible life.

How different to that great Peacemaker, Mr. Facing-Both-Ways! Mr. Facing-Both-Ways has no history. Happy is the country that has no history; and happy, you may say, is the man who has no history; and Mr. Facing-Both-Ways in The Pilgrim's Progress is that man." Bunyan, by the way, does not even mention Mr. Facing-Both Ways' extraordinary historical feat of drafting the Twenty-seventh Article of the Church of England.

There being some very troublesome people for Elizabeth to deal with—Catholics and Puritans, for instance, quarrelling about Transubstantiation—Mr. Facing-Both Ways drafted an Article in two paragraphs. The first paragraph affirmed the doctrine of Transubstantiation. The second paragraph said it was an idle superstition. Then Queen Elizabeth was able to say "Now you are all satisfied; and you must all attend the Church of England. If you don't I will send you to prison."

But I am not for one moment going to debate the doctrine of Transubstantiation. I mention it only to shew, by the controversy between the Archbishop and the Bishop, that in most debates you will find two types of mind playing with the same subject. There is one sort of mind that 1 think is my own sort. I sometimes call it the Irish mind, as distinct from the English mind. But that is only to make the English and Irish sit up and listen.

Spengler talks not of Irish and English minds, but of the Greek, or Grecian mind, and the Gothic mind—the Faustian mind as he, being a German, calls it. And in this controversy you find that what is moving Bishop Barnes is a Grecian dislike of not knowing what it is he believes, and on the other side a Gothic instinctive feeling that it is perhaps just as well not to know too distinctly. I am not saying which is the better type of mind. I think on the whole both of them are pretty useful. But I always like to know what it is I am preaching. It gets me into trouble in England, where people say, "Why go into these matters?

Why do you want to think so accurately and sharply?" I can only say that my head is built that way; but I protest that I do not claim any moral superiority because when I know what I mean the other people do not know what they mean, and very often do not know what I mean. And one subject on which I know what I mean is the opinion which has inevitably been growing up for the last hundred years or so, not so much an opinion as a revolt against the mis-distribution, the obviously monstrous and anomalous mis-distribution of wealth under what we call the capitalist system.

I have always, since I got clear on the subject of Socialism said, Don't put in the foreground the nationalisation of the means of production, distribution, and exchange: you will never get there if you begin with them. You have to begin with the question of the distribution of wealth. The other day a man died and the Government took four and a half million pounds as death duty on his property.

That man made all his money by the labour of men who received twenty-six shillings a week after years of qualifying for their work. Was that a reasonable distribution of wealth between them? We are all coming to the opinion that it was not reasonable. What does Mr. Chester ton think about it? I want to know, not only because of the public importance of his opinions, but because I have always followed Mr. Chesterton with extraordinary interest and enjoyment, and his assent to any view of mine is a great personal pleasure, because I am very fond of Mr. Chesterton. Mr. Chesterton has rejected Socialism nominally, probably because it is a rather stupid word. But he is a distributist, which means today a Redistributist.

He has arrived by his own path at my own position. (Laughter.) I do not see why you should laugh: I cannot imagine anything more natural. But now comes the question upon which I will ask Mr. Chesterton whether he agrees with me or not.

The moment I made up my mind that the present distribution of wealth was wrong, the peculiar constitution of my brain obliged me to find out exactly how far it was wrong and what is the right distribution. I went through all the proposals ever made and through the arguments used in justification of the existing distribution; and I found they were utterly insensate and grotesque. Eventually I was convinced that we ought to be tolerant of any sort of crime except unequal distribution of income.

In organized society the question always arises at what point are we justified in killing for the good of the community. I should answer in this way. If you take two shillings as your share and another man wants two shillings and sixpence, kill him. Similarly, if a man accepts two shillings while you have two shillings and sixpence, kill him. On the stroke of the hour, I ask Mr. Chesterton: "Do you agree with that?"

Mr. Chesterton: Ladies and gentlemen. The answer is in the negative. I don't agree with it. Nor does Mr. Shaw. He does not think, any more than I do, that all the people in this hall, who have already created some confusion, should increase the confusion by killing each other and searching each other's pockets to see whether there is half-a-crown or two shillings in them. As regards the general question, what I want to say is this: I should like to say to begin with that I have no intention of following Mr. Shaw into a discussion which would be very improper on my part on the condition of the Church of England. But since he has definitely challenged me on the point I will say—he will not agree—that Mr. Shaw is indeed a peacemaker and has reconciled both sides. For if the Arch bishop is anti-intellectual there will be nobody to pretend that the Bishop is intellectual.

Voice: Yes he is.

Mr. Chesterton: Now as to the much more interesting question, about a much more interesting person than Bishop Barnes—I mean Mr. Shaw—I should like to say that in a sense I can agree with him, in which case he can claim a complete victory. This is not a real controversy or debate. It is an enquiry, and I hope a profitable and interesting enquiry. Up to a point I quite agree with him, because I did start entirely by agreeing with him, as many years ago I began by being a Socialist, just as he was a Socialist. Barring some difference of age we were in the same position. We grew in beauty side by side. I will not say literally we filled one home with glee: but I do believe we have filled a fair number of homes with glee.

Whether those homes included our own personal households it is for others to say. But up to a point I agreed with Mr. Shaw by being a Socialist, and I agreed upon grounds he has laid down with critical justice and lucidity, grounds which I can imagine nobody being such a fool as to deny: the distribution of property in the modern world is a monstrosity and a blasphemy.

Thus I come to the important stage of the proceedings. I claim that I might agree with Mr. Shaw a step farther. I have heard from nearly all the Socialists I have known, the phrase which Mr. Shaw has with characteristic artfulness avoided, a phrase which I think everyone will agree is common to collectivist philosophy, and the phrase is this: "that the means of production should be owned by the community." I ask you to note that phrase because it is really upon that that the whole question turns. Now there is a sense in which I do agree with Mr. Bernard Shaw.

There is a point up to which I would agree with that formula. So far as is possible under human conditions I should desire the community—or, as we used to call it in the old English language, The Commons—to own the means of production. So far, I say, you have Mr. Bernard Shaw and me walking in fact side by side in the flowery meads... But after that, alas! a change takes place. The change is owing to Mr. Shaw's vast superiority, to his powerful intellect. It is not my fault if he has remained young, while I have grown in comparison wrinkled and haggard, old and experienced, and acquainted with the elementary facts of human life. Now the first thing I want to note is this. When you say the community ought to own the means of production, what do you mean? That is the whole point.

There was a time when Mr. Shaw would probably have said in all sincerity that anything possessed by the State or the Government would be in fact possessed by the Commons: in other words, by the community. I do not wish to challenge Mr. Shaw about later remarks of his, but I doubt whether Mr. Shaw, in his eternal youth, still believes in democracy in that sense.

I quite admit he has a more hopeful and hearty outlook in some respects, and he has even gone to the length of saying that if democracy will not do for mankind, perhaps it will do for some other creature different from mankind. He has almost proposed to invent a new animal, which might be supposed to live for 300 years. I am inclined to think that if Mr. Shaw lived for 300 years— and I heartily hope he will—I never knew a man more likely to do it— he would certainly agree with me. I would even undertake to prove it from the actual history of the last 300 years, but though I think it is probable I will not insist upon it. As a very profound philosopher has said, "You never can tell."

And it may be that Mr. Shaw's immortal power of talking nonsense would survive even that 300 years and he would still be fixed in his unnatural theories in the matter. Now I do not believe myself that Mr. Shaw thinks that the community, in the sense of that state which owns and rules, the thing that issues postage stamps and provides policemen, I do not believe he thinks that that community is now, at this moment, identical with the Commons, and I do not believe he ready thinks that in his own socialistic state it would be identical.

I am glad therefore that he has sufficient disordered common sense to perceive that, as a matter of fact, when you have vast systems, however just and however reasonably controlled, indirectly, by elaborate machinery of officials and other things, you do in fact find that those who rule are the few. It may be a good thing or a bad thing, but it is not true that all the people directly control. Collectivism has put all their eggs in one basket. I do not think that

Mr. Shaw believes, or that anybody believes, that 12,000,000 men, say, carry the basket, or look after the basket, or have any real distributed control over the eggs in the basket. I believe that it is controlled from the centre by a few people. They may be quite right or quite necessary. A certain limit to that sort of control any sane man will recognise as necessary: it is not the same as the Commons controlling the means of production.

It is a few oligarchs or a few officials who do in fact control all the means of production. What Mr. Shaw means is not that all the people should control the means of production, but that the product should be distributed among the vast mass of the Commons, and that is guide a different thing. It is not controlling the means of production at all. If all the citizens had simply an equal share of the income of the State they would not have any control of the capital.

That is where G. K. Chesterton differs from George Bernard Shaw. I begin at the other end. I do not think that a community arranged on the principles of Distributism and on nothing else would be a perfect community. All admit that the society that we propose is more a matter of proportion and arrangement than a perfectly clear system in which all production is pooled and the result given out in wages. But what I say is this: Let us, so far as is possible in the complicated affairs of humanity, put into the hands of the Commons the control of the means of production—and real control. The man who owns a piece of land controls it in a direct and real sense.

He really owns the means of production. It is the same with a man who owns a piece of machinery. He can use it or not use it. Even a man who owns his own tools or works in his own workshop, to that extent owns and controls the means of production. But if you establish right in the middle of the State one enormous machine, if you turn the handle of that machine, and somebody, who must be an official, and therefore a ruler, distributes to everybody equally the food or whatever else is produced by that machine, no single one of any of these people receiving more than any other single person, but all equal fragments: that fulfils a definite ideal of equality, yet no single one of those citizens has any control over the means of production.

They have no control whatever—unless you think that the prospect of voting about once every five years for Mr. Vanboodle— then a Socialist member—with the prospect that he will or will not make a promise to a political assembly or that he will or will not promise to ask a certain question which may or may not be answered— unless you think that by this means they possess control. I have used the metaphor of the Collectivists of having all your eggs in one basket. Now there are men whom we are pleased to call bad eggs.

They are not all of them in politics. On the other hand there are men who deserve the encomium of "good egg." There are, in other words, a number of good men and a number of bad men scattered among the commonwealth. To put the matter shortly, I might say that all this theory of absolutely equal mechanical distribution depends upon a sort of use of the passive mood. It is easy enough to say Property should be distributed, but who is, as it were, the subject of the verb? Who or what is to distribute? Now it is based on the idea that the central power which condescends to distribute will be permanently just, wise, sane, and representative of the conscience of the community which has created it. That is what we doubt. We say there ought to be in the world a great mass of scattered powers, privileges, limits, points of resistance, so that the mass of the Commons may resist tyranny. And we say that there is a permanent possibility of that central direction, however much it may have been appointed to distribute money equally, becoming a tyranny. I do not think it would be difficult to suggest a way in which it could happen.

As soon as any particular mob of people are behaving in some way which the governing group chooses to regard as anti-civic, supplies could be cut off easily with the approval of this governing group. You have only to call someone by some name like Bolshevist or Papist. You have only to tie some label on a set of people and the community will contentedly see these people starved into surrender. We say the method to be adopted is the other method. We admit, frankly, that our method is in a sense imperfect, and only in that sense illogical.

It is imperfect, or illogical, because it corresponds to the variety and differences of human life. Mr. Shaw is making abstract diagrams of triangles, squares. and circles; we are trying to paint a portrait, the portrait of a man. We are trying to make our lines and colours follow the characteristics of the real object. Man desires certain things. He likes a certain amount of liberty, certain kinds of ownership, certain kinds of local affection, and won't be happy without them. There are a great many other things that might be said, but I think it will be clearer if I repeat some of the things we have already said. I do in that sense accept the propositions that the community should own the means of production, but I say that the Commons should own the means of production, and the only way to do that is to keep actual hold upon land. Mr. Bernard Shaw proposes to distribute wealth. We propose to distribute power.

Mr. Shaw: I cannot say that Mr. Chesterton has succeeded in forcing a difference of opinion on me. There are, I suppose, at least some people in this room who have heard me orating on this platform at lectures of the Fabian Society, and they must have been considerably amused at Mr. Chesterton's attempt to impress upon me what income is. My main activity as an economist of late has been to try to concentrate the attention of my party on the fact not only that they must distribute income, but that there is nothing else to distribute.

We must be perfectly clear as to what capital is. I will tell you. Capital is spare money. And, of course, spare money means spare food. If I happen to have more of the means of subsistence than I can use, I may take that part that is unconsumed, and say to another man: "Let me feed you whilst you produce some kind of contraption that will facilitate my work in future."

But when the man has produced it for me, the capital has all gone: there is nothing left for me or him to eat. If he has made me a spade I cannot eat that spade. I have said I may employ my spare subsistence in this way; but I must employ it so because it will not keep: if nobody eats it, it will go rotten. The only thing to be done with it is to have it promptly consumed. All that remains of it then is a figure in a ledger. Some of my capital was employed in the late war; and this country has still my name written down as the proprietor of the capital they blew to pieces in that war. Having said that for your instruction, let us come down to facts. Mr. Chesterton has formed the Distributist League which organized this meeting.

What was the very first thing the League said must be done? It said the coal-mines must be nationalized. Instead of saying that the miner's means of production must he made his own property, it was forced to advocate making national property of the coal mines. These coal-mines, when nationalized, will not be managed by the House of Commons: if they were you would very soon have no coal. But neither will they be managed by the miners. If you ask the man working in the mine to manage the mine he will say, "Not me, governor!

That is your job." I would like Mr. Chesterton to consider what he understands by the means of production. He has spoken of them in rather a nineteenth-century manner. He has been talking as though the means of production were machines. I submit to you that the real means of production in this country are men and women, and that consequently you always have the maximum control of the individual over the means of production, because it means self-control over his own person. But he must surrender that control to the manager of the mine because he does not know how to manage it himself.

Under the present capitalistic system he has to surrender it to the manager appointed by the proprietors of the mine. Under Socialism he would have to surrender it to the manager appointed by the Coalmaster-General. That would not prevent the product of the mine being equally distributed among the people. There is no difficulty here.

In a sense Mr. Chesterton really does not disagree with me in this matter, since he does see that in the matter of fuel in this country you have to come to nationalization. Fuel must be controlled equally for the benefit of all the people. Since we agreed upon that, I am not disposed to argue the matter further. Now that Mr. Chesterton agreed that the coal-mines will have to be nationalized he will be led by the same pressure of facts to agree to the nationalization of everything else.

I have to allow for the pressure of facts because, as a playwright, I think of all problems in terms of actual men and women. Mr. Chesterton lets himself idealize them sometimes as virtuous peasant proprietors and self-managing petty capitalists. The capitalist and the landlord have their own particular ways of robbing the poor; but their legal rights are quite different. It is a very direct way on the part of the landlord.

He may do exactly what he likes with the land he owns. If I own a large part of Scotland I can turn the people off the land practically into the sea, or across the sea. I can take women in child-bearing and throw them into the snow and leave them there. That has been done. I can do it for no better reason than I think it is better to shoot deer on the land than allow people to live on it. They might frighten the deer. But now compare that with the ownership of my umbrella. As a matter of fact the umbrella I have to-night belongs to my wife; but I think she will permit me to call it mine for the purpose of the debate. Now I have a very limited legal right to the use of that umbrella.

I cannot do as I like with it. For instance, certain passages in Mr. Chesterton's speech tempted me to get up and smite him over the head with my umbrella. I may presently feel inclined to smite Mr. Belloc. But should I abuse my right to do what I like with my property—with my umbrella—in this way I should soon be made aware— possibly by Mr. Belloc's fist—that I cannot treat my umbrella as my own property in the way in which a landlord can treat his land. I want to destroy ownership in order that possession and enjoyment may be raised to the highest point in every section of the community. That, I think, is perfectly simple. There are points on which a landlord, even a Scottish landlord, and his tenant the crofter entirely agree. The landlord objects to being shot at sight. The Irish landlord used to object.

His tenants sometimes took no notice of his objection, but all the same they had a very strong objection to being shot themselves. You have no objection to a State law being carried out vigorously that people shall not shoot one another. There is no difficulty in modern civilized States in having it carried out. If you could once convince the people that inequality of income is a greater social danger than murder, very few people would want to continue to commit it; and the State could suppress it with the assent of the community generally.

We are always adding fresh crimes to the calendar. Why not enact that no person shall live in this community without pulling his weight in the social boat, without producing more than he consumes—because you have to provide for the accumulation of spare money as capital—who does not replace by his own labour what he takes out of the community, who attempts to live idly, as men are proud to live nowadays. Is there any greater difficulty in treating such a parasite as a malefactor, than in treating a murderer as a malefactor? Having said that much about the property part of the business, 1 think I have succeeded in establishing that Mr. Chesterton does not disagree with me.

I should like to say I do not believe in Democracy. I do believe in Catholicism; but I hold that the Irish Episcopal Protestant Church, of which I was baptized a member, takes the name of Catholicism in vain; that the Roman Church has also taken it in vain; and so with the Greek Church and the rest. My Catholicism is really catholic Catholicism: that is what I believe in, as apart from this voting business and democracy. Does Mr. Chesterton agree with me on that?

Mr. Chesterton: Among the bewildering welter of fallacies which Mr. Shaw has just given us, I prefer to deal first with the simplest. When Mr. Shaw refrains from hitting me over the head with his umbrella, the real reason—apart from his real kindness of heart, which makes him tolerant of the humblest of the creatures of God—is not because he does not own his umbrella, but because he does not own my head. As I am still in possession of that imperfect organ, I will proceed to use it to the confutation of some of his other fallacies. I should like to say now what I ought perhaps to have said earlier in the evening, that we are enormously grateful to Mr. Shaw for his characteristic generosity in consenting to debate with a humble movement like our own. I am so conscious of that condescension on his part that I should feel it a very unfair return to ask him to read any of our potty little literature or cast his eye over our little weekly paper or become conscious of the facts we have stated a thousand times.

One of these facts, with which every person who knows us is familiar, is our position with regard to the coal question. We have said again and again that in our human state of society there must be a class of things called exceptions. We admit that upon the whole in the very peculiar case of coal it is desirable and about the best way out of the difficulty that it should be controlled by the officials of the State, just in the same way as postage stamps are controlled. No one says anything else about postage stamps. I cannot imagine that anyone wants to have his own postage stamps, of perhaps more picturesque design and varied colours. I can assure you that Distributists are perfectly sensible and sane people, and they have always recognized that there are institutions in the State in which it is very difficult to apply the principle of individual property, and that one of these cases is the discovery under the earth of valuable minerals.

Socialists are not alone in believing this. Charles I, who, I suppose, could not be called a Socialist, pointed out that certain kinds of minerals ought to belong to the State, that is, to the Commons. We have said over and over again that we support the nationalization of the coal-mines, not as a general example of Distribution but as a common-sense admission of an exception. The reason why we make it an exception is because it is not very easy to see how the healthy principle of personal ownership can be applied. If it could we should apply it with the greatest pleasure. We consider personal ownership infinitely more healthy. If there were a way in which a miner could mark out one particular piece of coal and say, "This is mine, and I am proud of it," we should have made an enormous improvement upon State management.

There are cases in which it is very difficult to apply the principle, and that is one of them. It is the reverse of the truth for Mr. Shaw to say that the logic of that fact will lead me to the application of the same principle to other cases, like the ownership of the land. One could not illustrate it better than by the case of coal. It may be true for all I know that if you ask a miner if he would like to manage the mine he would say, "I do not want to manage it; it is for my betters to manage it." I had not noticed that meek and simple manner among miners.

I have even heard complaints of the opposite temper in that body. I defy Mr. Shaw to say if you went to the Irish farmers, or the French farmers, or the Serbian or the Dutch farmers, or any of the millions of peasant owners throughout the world, I defy him to say if you went to the farmer and said, "Who controls these farms?'" he would say, "It is not for the likes of me to control a farm." Mr. Shaw knows perfectly well it is nonsense to suggest that peasants would talk that way anywhere. It is part of his complaints against peasants that they claim personal possessions. I am not likely to be led to the denial of property in land, for I know ordinary normal people who feel property in land to be normal. I fully agree with Mr. Shaw, and speak as strongly as he would speak, of the abomination and detestable foulness and sin of landlords who drove poor people from their land in Scotland and elsewhere. It is quite true that men in possession of land have committed these crimes; but I do not see why wicked officials under a socialistic state could not commit these crimes.

But that has nothing to do with the principle of ownership in land. In fact these very Highland crofters, these very people thus abominably outraged and oppressed, if you asked them what they want would probably say, "I want to own my own croft; I want to own my own land." Mr. Shaw's dislike of the landlord is not so much a denial of the right to private property. not so much that he owns the land, but that the landlord has swallowed up private property.

In the face of these facts of millions and millions of ordinary human beings who have private property, who know what it is like to own property, I must confess that I am not overwhelmed and crushed by Mr. Shaw's claim that he knows all about men and women as they really are. I think Mr. Shaw knows something about certain kinds of men and women; though he sometimes makes them a little more amusing than they really are. But I cannot agree with his discovery that peasants do not like peasant property, because I know the reverse is the fact.

Then we come to the general point he raised about the State. He raised a very interesting question. He said that after all the State does command respect, that we all do accept laws even though they are issued by an official group. Up to a point I willingly accept his argument. The Distributist is certainly not an anarchist. He does not believe it would be a good thing if there were no such laws. But the reason why most of these laws are accepted is because they correspond with the common conscience of mankind. Mr. Shaw and

Bishop Barnes might think it would be an inadequate way of explaining it, but we might call attention to an Hebraic code called the Ten Commandments. They do, I think, correspond pretty roughly to the moral code of every religion that is at all sane.

These all reverence certain ideas about "Thou shalt not kill." They all have a reverence for the commandment which says, "Thou shalt not covet thy neighbour's goods." They reverence the idea that you must not covet his house or his ox or his ass. It should be noted, too, that besides forbidding us to covet our neighbour's property, this commandment also implies that every man has a right to own some property.

Mr. Shaw: I now want to ask Mr. Chesterton why he insists, on the point about the nationalization of the coal-mines—on which he agrees with me—that they are an exception. Are they an exception? In what way are the coal-mines an exception? What is the fundamental reason why you must nationalize your coal-mine?

The reason is this. If you will go up to the constituency of Mr. Sidney Webb, to the Sunderland coast, you will be able to pick up coal for nothing, absolutely nothing at all. You see people doing it there. You take a perambulator, or barrow, or simple sack, and when the tide goes out you go out on the foreshore and pick up excellent coal. If you go to other parts of England, like Whitehaven, you will find you have to go through workings driven out under the sea, which took 20 years to make, 20 years continual expenditure of capital before coal could be touched, where men going down the shaft have to travel sometimes two or three miles to their work. That is the reason at bottom why you cannot distribute your coal mine. The reason you have to pay such monstrous prices for your coal is they are fixed by the cost of making the submarine mines. People who have mines like the Sunderland foreshore naturally make colossal fortunes.

Everyone can see at once that in order to have any kind of equable dealing in coal, the only way is to charge the citizens the average cost for the total national supply. You cannot average the cost by putting your eggs into different baskets.

Now this is not the exception: it is the rule. You have exactly the same difference in the case of the land. You have land worth absolutely nothing at all and land worth a million an acre or more. And the acre worth more than a million and the acre worth nothing are within half-an-hour's drive in a taxi.

You cannot say that the coal-mine is an exception. The coal-mine is only one instance. Mr. Chesterton in arriving at the necessity for the nationalization of the coal-mines has started on his journey towards the nationalization of all the industries. If he goes on to the land, and from the land to the factory, and from there to every other industrial department, he will find that every successive case is an exception; and eventually he will have to say to himself: "I think it will be better to call nationalization the rule rather than the exception." I must deny that I ever said that the coal-miner says he wants to be ruled by his betters. I may not be a democrat; but I am not a snob. Intellectually I am a snob, and you will admit that I have good ground for that. Socially I am not a snob.

There is no question of betters at all in the matter. The manager is not better than the executant, nor the executant better than the manager. Both are equally necessary and equally honourable. But if you ask the executant to manage he will refuse on the ground that it is not his job; and vice versa. Mr. Chesterton says he does not see why State officials under a system which recognises nationalization of land should not act as the old landlords acted. I should say, in the first place, they won't have the power. A State official does what he is instructed to do and paid to do, just as a landlord's agent does; and there is no more danger of the official making himself a landlord than there is now of the agent making himself one.

As to the instinct of owning—and you have it widely in the country—you have not got it in the towns. People are content to live in houses they do not own: when they possess them they often find them a great nuisance. But you must not conclude that because a miner would refuse to manage a mine a farmer will refuse to manage his farm. The farmer is himself a manager. How does this wonderful system of peasant proprietorship work? Do you realise that it has to be broken up every day?

The reason is that when a man owning a farm has a family, each son, when the farmer dies, has a right to an equal part of the land. They find that this arrangement is entirely impossible, and they have to make some other arrangement, and some of the sons have to go off into the towns to work. It is unthinkable that all could remain on the land: you cannot split up the land and give every person a bit of property. I have stolen two minutes from Mr. Chesterton, and I apologise.

Mr. Chesterton: I am sure Mr. Shaw is very welcome to as many minutes as I can offer him, or anything else, for his kindness in entertaining us this evening. It is rather late now and there is not much time left for me. He has been rather slow in discovering what Distributism is and what the whole question is about. If this were the beginning of the discussion I could do over our system completely.

I could tell him exactly what we think about property in towns. It is absurd to say it does not exist. In rural ownership different problems have to be faced. We are not cutting a thing up into mathematical squares. We are trying to deal with human beings, creatures quite outside the purview of Mr. Shaw and his political philosophy.

We know town people are a little different from country people; business of one kind is different from business of another kind; difficulties arise about family, and all the rest of it. We show man's irrepressible desire to own property and because some landlords have been cruel, it is no use talking of abolishing, denying, and destroying property, saying no one shall have any property at all. It is characteristic of his school, of his age. The morality he represents is above all the morality of negations. Just as it says you must not drink wine at all as the only solution to a few people drinking too much: just as it would say you must not touch meat or smoke tobacco at all!. Let us always remember, therefore, that when Mr. Shaw says he can persuade all men to give up the sentiment of private property, it is in exactly the same hopeful spirit that he says he will get all of you to give up meat, tobacco, beer, and a vast number of other things.

He will not do anything of the sort and I suspect he himself suspects by this time that he will not do it. It is quite false to say you must have a centralised machinery, even in towns. It is quite false to say that all forces must be used, as they are in monopolies, from the centre. It is absurd to say that because the wind is a central thing you cannot separate windmills.

How am I to explain all that in five minutes? I could go through a vast number of fallacies into which he has fallen. He said, ironically, he would like to see me go down a mine. I have no difficulty in imagining myself sinking in such a fashion in any geological deposit. I really should like to see him doing work on a farm, because he would find out about five hundred pieces of nonsense he has been speaking to be the nonsense they are. It is absolutely fallacious to suggest that there is some sort of difficulty in peasantries whereby they are bound to disappear.

The answer to that is that they have not disappeared. It is part of the very case against peasantry, among those who do not like them, that they are antiquated, covered with hoary superstition. Why have they remained through all these centuries, if they must immediately break up and become impossible? There is an answer to all that and I am quite prepared to give it at some greater length than five minutes. But at no time did I say that we must make the whole community a community of agricultural peasants.

It is absurd. What I said was that a desire for property which is universal, everywhere, does appear in a perfect and working example in the ownership of land. It only remains for me to say one thing. Mr. Shaw said, in reference to the State owning the means of production, that men and women are the only means of production. I quite accept the parallel of the phrase. His proposition is that the government, the officials of the State, should own the men and women: in other words that the men and women should be slaves.

MR. BELLOC: I was told when I accepted this onerous office that I was to sum up. I shall do nothing of the sort. In a very few years from now this debate will be antiquated. I will now recite you a poem:

*"Our civilization*
*Is built upon coal.*
*Let us chant in rotation*
*Our civilization*
*That lump of damnation*
*Without any soul,*
*Our civilization*
*Is built upon coal.*
*"In a very few years,*
*It will float upon oil.*
*Then give three hearty cheers,*
*In a very few years*
*We shall mop up our tears*
*And have done with our toil.*
*In a very few years*
*It will float upon oil."*

In I do not know how many years—five, ten, twenty—this debate will be as antiquated as crinolines are. I am surprised that neither of the two speakers pointed out that one of three things is going to happen. One of three things: not one of two. It is always one of three things. This industrial civilization which, thank God, oppresses only the small part of the world in which we are most inextricably bound up, will break down and therefore end from its monstrous wickedness, folly, ineptitude, leading to a restoration of sane, ordinary human affairs, complicated but based as a whole upon the freedom of the citizens.

Or it will break down and lead to nothing but a desert. Or it will lead the mass of men to become contented slaves, with a few rich men controlling them. Take your choice. You will all be dead before any of the three things comes off. One of the three things is going to happen, or a mixture of two, or possibly a mixture of the three combined.

# Chapter 10

# Send for Shaw, not Shakespeare

When I was invited to write the authorized biography of Bernard Shaw in the early 1970s, he was still accepted as a great force in the world, an influence on the young, a bearded prophet from a past age warning us provocatively, uncomfortably, of the dangers in our contemporary world. He did of course acclaim some social changes that had taken place, such as the National Health Service. But his role was mainly to challenge rather than to celebrate.

His plays were quite regularly performed at the National Theatre and politicians such as Tony Benn and Robin Cook made no secret of having read him attentively and of having been influenced by his writings – nor did that legendary insurgent on his prison island, Nelson Mandela. American and Canadian academics in particular were devoting their careers to studying his work – his letters, his diaries, his music and drama criticism as well as his prefaces, political essays and plays. He was so prolific, so voluminous, so various, that there seemed plenty to keep them busy well into this century.

But now that we are half a dozen years into it, Shaw seems to have gone largely out of fashion – presented more as a matinee playwright than an exciting, revolutionary dramatist. In the age of Beckett and Pinter those plays of his seemed increasingly wordy and windy. There was so much of him, too much of him. People took against him. He was no longer a stimulus to radical progressive thought but an insensitive supporter of dictators – particularly Stalin. In fact he was seen as an enemy of democracy itself, a fifth column agent in our society. We appear to have more need these days of villains than of guides, philosophers and friends, more need of cautionary than exemplary tales.

And there was something else that counted very strongly against him: he lacked what was once called sex appeal and appeared to have ink rather than blood in his veins. Was there not something rather inhuman about him, something seriously lacking? Of course you could not wholly discount his writings; he was not altogether off the page as it were, but he had been marginalized, he was no longer centre stage – he was somewhere in the wings. That, it seems, is where he stands today, in this, the 150th anniversary of his birth on July 26, 1856. And the questions I want to ask are: Does it matter? Is it just?

I can hear his voice mocking these questions. To hear his voice is of course poetic licence, or rather a prose writer's licence, claimed on the strength of having lived and worked so long among his published and unpublished writings. It is a conceit, like St Joan's gift for hearing voices, which enables me to speak his lines with an air of confidence. So what do I hear him say? Something very unsettling: that there is no such thing as natural justice unless it be red in tooth and claw. Spin the coin and one man's justice is another man's revenge.

Look through the history of the human race, that mixture of all our races, and it is often the acts of justice that most horrify us in retrospect – acts performed in cold blood with pomp and circumstantial evidence that exceed the crimes of lesser breeds without the law. Justice is fickle, blown hither and thither by the winds of fashion and climate of ideology, instigated by fear (what we have recently learnt to call "terror") and dictated by those who win their wars – or think they have won them. Shaw, it must be remembered, opposed the Nuremberg trials – or rather the punishments handed out by the trial judges because he believed that an ideal justice contained no element of punishment. I can hear his voice years later pointing out the awful fate of Rudolf Hess and challenging us to call this just.

By the same token Shaw believed that the only revolutions which would not lead to counter-revolutions, landing us back to approximately where we had begun, were bloodless revolutions, revolutions that arose through changing the mind of a country by its writers, philosophers, thinkers, men and women of imagination. If you are bombed, for heaven's sake, do not go blindly bombing back – unless you actually want more bombing, more deaths, indiscriminately all over the place. The way to judge people's motives is to look at the results of their actions: that is the pragmatist's philosophy. One of the ironies of history is that in most wars both sides eventually come to resemble each other and impose defeat on themselves. Or as Shaw succinctly put it: "A victory for anybody is a victory for war".

What would Shaw be telling us today? Would he, for example, have supported suicide bombing? I hear him answer this with a resounding No! But then he would never have been so stupid, so uncomprehending, as to label suicide bombers "cowardly" – that really is the voice of terror. Early in the twentieth century, Shaw proposed giving all Irishmen guns so that they could enjoy the privilege of a civil war without the intervention of the English. Such a man would not have hesitated to advocate the elimination of suicide bombing by giving Palestine an army equal in strength to that of Israel.

He would, however, have castigated a Palestinian culture that encouraged young people to throw away their lives and be applauded for doing so by their parents and grandparents. It would have been far more honourable, I hear him saying, for old people to volunteer – indeed he had recommended calling up seventy- and eighty-year-olds for military service before turning to the young in time of war. In short: send Shaw out to the Middle East and he would unite all enemies in opposition to himself. Send Shaw today round the world and he would be called mad for recommending publishers in every country to put all sacred texts, from the Bible to the Koran, on their backlists and find new sacred works from contemporary writing.

Two or three years ago, the Lincoln Centre Theater in New York staged an updated version of Aristophanes' The Frogs. In the original version, Dionysos brings back Euripides from the underworld. In the new version, he has to choose either Shakespeare or Shaw to visit the post-9/11 world. Which would be the more useful?

At the beginning he thinks it will be Shaw, but finally he returns with Shakespeare. I argued that this was the wrong choice because Shaw exercised his democratic right to be unpopular in time of war, which is especially valuable. "You'll never have a quiet world till you knock the patriotism out of the human race", he wrote, in his recruiting play, O'Flaherty V. C. Shakespeare's poetry often touches war with glamour; Shaw's headlong, fantastical wit never does this. He asked no favours from those in power. As W. B. Yeats acknowledged: "He could hit my enemies, and the enemies of those I loved, as I could never hit, as no living author who was dear to me could hit". Surely this was the man Dionysos needed – the man we need today.

The case against Shaw, which may well have persuaded Dionysos not to retrieve him from the underworld, is partly based on the number of newspaper articles and prefaces to plays he wrote, mainly during the 1930s, that were favourable to Hitler and Stalin. He did not do this because he liked either of them – the world, he thought, would have been a far better place without them. But they existed. They had to be dealt with. Shaw's articles were written in the hope of modifying British foreign policy – a policy that was full of strong words and weak initiatives.

People were to blame Neville Chamberlain for appeasing Hitler. Shaw blamed the Versailles Treaty for humiliating Germany and making Germans feel they were the enemies of humankind. Was it any surprise they chose others to replace them as objects of such loathing? Was it any surprise that, robbed of their self-esteem, they should have chosen a man such as Hitler to be their leader – a leader who set out to regain self-esteem by embarking on a policy of revenge (revenge that initially seemed so much like a search for justice)? In

1919 Shaw had predicted that there would be another World War in his lifetime, and his writings between the wars must be read in that rather desperate context. It might surprise anyone reading these writings to learn that Stalin thought him an awful man and that Hitler banned some of his plays – in particular Geneva, his satire on Fascist dictators, as well as the preface to The Millionairess, in which he speculates on Hitler's Semitic forebears.

In my opinion Shaw wrote one serious tragedy and that was his Saint Joan. In the preface to this play he likens Joan to the Prophet Mahomet, both conquerors, prophets, saints who, like Mary Baker Eddy, the naive founder of Christian Science, were "always ready with a private revelation from God to settle every question and fit every occasion". God, it seems, was an accomplished ventriloquist.

For almost every religion is a blasphemy or insult in the face of every other religion, Shaw argued, which is one reason why he would have eliminated all faith schools – in the interests, that is, of social unity. In his play it is Cauchon, the Bishop of Beauvais, the most lenient of Joan's judges, who asks what would become of the world when every girl thinks herself a Joan and every man a Mahomet. "I shudder to the very marrow of my bones when I think of it", he says.

It is extraordinary how often the Prophet Mahomet appears to force his way into Shaw's prefaces and plays. In the preface to his political comedy On the Rocks, we see him ruling the Arabs by means of "promises of a paradise and threats of a hell the details of which he must have known to be his own invention even if he did believe generally in a post mortem life of rewards and punishments for conduct in this world". Shaw likens him to a nurse disciplining and coaxing a group of small children so that they might behave well.

For as he explains in the preface to The Simpleton of the Unexpected Isles, the Prophet could not trust his followers to behave correctly when his back was turned. It was for this reason that he was obliged to invent the most disgusting penances awaiting those who behaved badly and all sorts of sensual delights for those who behaved well. To inspire credulity he allowed his followers to believe that the angel Gabriel acted as a celestial postman between him and Allah. In short, like Moses and John Smith the Mormon, he had to plead divine revelation in order to gain authority.

And there was something else that did not wholly escape Shaw's attention. Like Henry VIII, he reminds us, Mahomet had a good many wives. When writing his Fable Play, Androcles and the Lion, Shaw conjured up a spectacle of the great Prophet "lying distracted on the floor of his harem whilst his wives stormed and squabbled and henpecked round him". This picture brings to mind the interlude from his political extravaganza The Apple Cart, which takes place in Orinthia's bedroom – though it would have been a far more crowded extravaganza had he actually written a play about Mahomet.

The reason why the Prophet keeps turning up on his pages is that he had "long desired to dramatize" his life, he tells us. His drama, which was to be set in a slave market, would, he claimed, rescue the Prophet from Voltaire, whose play Mahomet was an outrage. In the 1890s the novelist Hall Caine had written a drama called The Prophet for Henry Irving. It could not be produced, however, because the censor forbade this on the grounds that any play dealing with the founder of Islam "would give offence to many of Her Majesty's subjects". Shaw described this "restriction of the historical drama" as an "absurdity". But when the Queen died the embargo lived on. All his life Shaw campaigned against theatre censorship – and only won this battle posthumously.

So where are we now? In December 2004, the dramatist Gurpreet Kaur Bhatti had her play called Behzti (meaning dishonour), which was produced by the Birmingham Repertory Theatre as an alternative to the season of pantomimes, removed from the stage because of fears for her safety and that of the cast and theatre staff after violent protests by members of the Sikh community. The Arts Minister at that time, Estelle Morris, was reported as having issued a surprising statement. "Although today is a sad day for freedom of speech," she said, "I think the Rep has done the right thing." It is certainly a sad day when a government minister, appointed to represent the art of drama, can so easily turn back the clock more than one hundred years by supporting the removal of a play that, like Hall Caine's The Prophet, might "give offence to many of Her Majesty's subjects".

In such a climate of terrified legislation, we have need of Bernard Shaw – need of his stimulating incorrectitudes, need of his ability to show where dishonour truly lies and of his power to ridicule such absurdities out of court. It is time for Dionysos to go back and find him for us. A puzzlingly long queue greeted the manager of WH Smith in Baker Street as he arrived for work exactly 60 years ago yesterday. At first he thought the buses were running late, but it turned out that people were queuing up to mark George Bernard Shaw's 90th birthday by buying his books. Penguin had the audacious idea of celebrating the occasion by publishing the "Shaw million" - 10 works in editions of 100,000 copies each. They sold out in six weeks.

There is much less fanfare today, on the 150th anniversary of Shaw's birth. He has long been out of fashion. But while his plays may be absent from the London stage, they still divide the critics. Michael Billington of this parish, a keen Shavian, wonders how "the idea has got about that Shaw is a dated, didactic old windbag with little to offer us today, when in fact he anticipated every theatrical trend of the 20th century". His Independent counterpart, Paul Taylor, however, hails Nicholas Hytner as a "great and unsung humanitarian" for not programming a Shaw revival at the National Theatre. But the National does mark the anniversary tonight, with a Platform debate on a subject considerably more neglected than the plays themselves: Shaw as a political thinker.

The politics are part of the case against the plays. "There will be nothing but talk, talk, talk, talk, talk - Shaw talk... an eternity of brain-racking dullness," complained a Telegraph preview for one. In fact, Shaw had written the piece himself, having invented the publicity device of speaking to extremely hostile imaginary interviewers who always came away with good copy - an early anticipation of the "masochism strategy" with which Tony Blair was to seek re-election after the Iraq war. But if Shaw wanted to become his own fiercest critic, he failed: nothing made John Osborne angrier than Shaw. Shaw's genius cannot be doubted. Nor his astonishing range, from his major contribution to music criticism to his being the only Nobel laureate to also bag an Oscar. But he is all paradox - the deeply committed wag, the egotistical collectivist, who pioneered great causes and pursued absurd flights of fancy with equal vigour: against Shakespeare, against Darwin, for an entirely new alphabet. Michael Holroyd, author of the magisterial biography to which all discussion of Shaw is indebted, refers to "that mixture of rare sense and inspired nonsense that the world had come to refer to as Shavian".

The difficulty in working out when to take Shavian hyperbole seriously has meant that few have tried. Bernard Crick's 1991 essay "Shaw as political thinker, or the dogs that did not bark" pointed out the complete absence of any academic study of Shaw's political thought. (A monograph was about to appear.) But for Shaw, not being taken too seriously may be a blessing. The case against him seems compelling. Very few early Fabian arguments on economics, which they saw as foundational, survive. Much worse, Shaw ended his long career as an apologist for Stalin's Soviet Union and ventured dangerously into eugenics. Can any reputable Shaw with anything to say to us today really be rescued from all that?

The case for Shaw has been put by Robin Cook in an eloquent, short Fabian essay published less than a year before Cook's untimely death. Revealing that he first grew his beard in emulation of his political hero, Cook argues that Shaw can speak to us still, that Shaw's belief in the politics of rational persuasion, his feminism and advocacy of social justice and his hatred of war provide important lessons for our times.

Crucially, Shaw's unreasonableness in following thought through to a logical conclusion becomes a key virtue for early Fabian socialists seeking to change the world as well as to understand it, endorsing Shaw's view that: "The reasonable man adapts himself to the world; the unreasonable one persists in trying to adapt the world to himself. Therefore all progress depends on the unreasonable man." Equality and democracy are the key issues. An argument for Shaw's contemporary relevance must establish two premises: first, that his ideas about equality are worth discussing; and second, that his allegiance to Moscow and hostility to democracy marked a rupture with Shaw's Fabianism rather than a natural extension of it. There are arguments on both sides of each question.

On equality, Shaw seems wholly unpromising. He advocates literal equality of income and outcome (albeit gradually, and mainly by levelling up). Harold Laski complained: "For a man to tell you that the desirable thing is equality of income without telling you how to get it is simply irritating." Crick says Shaw is the only known socialist thinker since French revolutionary Gracchus Babeuf to take this impossibilist position but, perhaps generously, sees Shaw's position as a device to flush out and challenge stock objections to equality.

This would make Shaw a source of the argument, later developed by Crosland and Rawls, that it is departures from equality that require justification. As Crosland argued, "no justified inequalities" would give the left a project to pursue for some generations before the question of a theoretical endpoint arose. However, this arid, texbook debate, "equal opportunity" versus "equal outcome", misses the point: how today's unequal outcomes shape tomorrow's unequal opportunities. Nobody seriously advocates equality of outcome. Trust Shaw, perhaps only half seriously, to provide the counter-example.

Yet, having added to that muddle, Shaw brilliantly illuminates the case for equality. What would the test of an equal society be? Shaw chooses marriage - or rather "intermarriageability". If there were no social objections to any match, we would live in a classless society. So the object of social policy should be "to keep the entire community intermarriageable". Crick rightly salutes Shaw's masterly "sociological imagination", which anticipates Crick's own argument, in In Defence of Politics, that mortality rates capture a core truth about life chances (a classless society would, he says, have "an almost perfect correlation between mortality statistics and social class"). Equal life chances is the compelling public case for greater equality that today's left needs, and wide differences in infant mortality rates and life expectancy provide the starkest evidence for the absence of social justice. (Last weekend's newspapers report new research findings that marriage explains social mobility, and its absence.)

This egalitarian spirit made Shaw a persistent pioneer of both feminism and racial equality. "Marriages of White and Black: Startling Plan by Mr Shaw" screamed a Telegraph headline reporting Shaw's South African tour of 1931, where his argument that intermarriage would end racial tension proved unpopular.

On feminism, Shaw was not just always ahead of his own time but sometimes of ours, too. Much trouble over Cameroonian 'A lists' and all-women shortlists could have been saved had Shaw's idea been adopted of the "coupled vote": that each constituency should elect one man and one woman in order to get proper representation of women in parliament. On Ireland, Shaw talked more sense than any side was prepared to listen too. And his campaigns for public theatre as part of the necessary fabric of democracy, and against censorship, finally won the day.

But why did Shaw, champion of female suffrage, give up on democracy? One argument is that the elitism of Shaw and the Webbs did not require too great a shift on the road to Russia. Future Fabians revised and democratised top-down Fabianism, Tony Crosland famously asserting, in The Future of Socialism: "Total abstinence and a good filing system are not now the right signposts to the socialist utopia. Or at least, if they are, some of us will fall by the wayside." Shaw had always been torn about gradualism.

He could see that only Webb on the left had a political strategy, but William Morris's rejection of such pragmatism appealed to him too. The first world war proved a great turning point. Shaw's brave stance against it can be seen as his finest hour. But he felt let down by humanity and gave up on democracy. The failure of the first minority Labour governments to pursue socialism or cope with the great crash confirmed the point. He became an advocate of the "great man" in politics, tempted by Mosley and even Mussolini, and decided, as an act of faith, to support the Soviet experiment.

Shaw's hatred of war badly affected his later judgment. But in that, he represented a generation. He was neutral on Spain in an era when authors were supposed to take sides. He saw Nazi anti-semitism as "insanity", though he had judged that Hitler "shrinks from the massacre which the logic of his phobia demands". He was far from the only one - on left or right - to still be contemplating a negotiated peace with Hitler after war had broken out. (When Keynes tried to get Shaw's New Statesman essay censored, the foreign secretary, Lord Halifax, was extremely keen to see it published, in order to gauge reaction.) And by the war's end, he was against the Nuremberg trials, believing victors' justice could never do any good.

By his works, the earlier Shaw had shown himself to be a democrat. The great row that saw HG Wells join, shake up and storm out of the Fabians was really about Wells's inability to work collectively. Shaw painstakingly drafted pamphlets, circulated in draft to the entire membership for amendment, to hold the divided Fabians together over the Boer war and tariff reform. Wells, meanwhile, had the best lines in his attack on the Old Gang's gradualism: "In the end, the mouse did succeed in permeating the cat, but the cat is still living and the mouse can't be found." But the strength of the gradualist strategy was its ability to survive the desertion of its founders. "There is now nothing but communism and it is quite futile to go about calling yourselves Fabians," he wrote.

But he was ignored, and the institutional legacy of the Fabian Old Gang did its own work: through the LSE, the New Statesman, the influence of the 1909 Webb minority report on Beveridge and the Labour parliamentary party of the 1945 landslide, which "looked just like an enormous Fabian summer school".

Shaw may have given up, but they intended, if gradually,

to legislate what had once been his impossibilist dreams. (Shaw's institutional legacy continues: the Fabian Society lives still in the Dartmouth Street headquarters Shaw rather astutely purchased for £3,000 in 1928, while Rada and the National Gallery of Ireland also benefited immensely from his generosity).

The two great essayists of the British left both died in 1950 - Orwell at 46 and Shaw at 94. Since then, Orwell's stock has risen as Shaw's has plummeted. Orwell could have been thinking of Shaw in his caricatured complaint that "the mere words 'Socialism' and 'Communism' draw towards them with magnetic force every fruit juice-drinker, nudist, sandal-wearer, sex maniac, Quaker, 'nature cure' quack, pacifist and feminist in England."

Socialism for superior brains proved no match for plain-spoken common sense, at least when it came to the fundamental judgment call of the century. Orwell seems to be our contemporary, in a way that Shaw cannot be. As Robert Skidelsky has written: "The most striking revolution in the west has not been the socialist revolution, which the Fabians wanted, but the sexual revolution, which they feared." The overwhelming sense of duty of the early Fabians distances them from us.

Shaw's plays will one day return. If the prefaces became more eccentric, his plays retained their human complexity. There can be no great totalitarian literature. Shaw's Fabian contemporary Granville Barker has recently been revived to critical acclaim, and Michael Holroyd revisits the old Shaw v Shakespeare question in the current TLS to argue that it is Shaw has more to say about faith and fanaticism in the world after 9/11.

Yet how distant the age of Shaw seems to us now. Can you imagine Blair, Cameron and Ming getting together for a night at the theatre? But Balfour went to see John Bull's Other Island five times, taking the Liberal leaders Campbell Bannerman and Asquith with him. I have no doubt, however, that Shaw would have embraced our world of the blog. He found nothing more frustrating than his time as an undiscovered genius. He had five novels rejected by every house in London, and complained: "All my readers like the book, but they tell me that though they relish it they don't think the general public would." Nor would anybody publish Fabian essays. I can see him battling it out in the Comment is free fray, adopting multiple identities and cussing at the idea of waiting half an hour to make his next sally. In fact, he practically invented the art, as another of Holroyd's brilliant anecdotes shows:

However much he wrote, he still searched for opportunities elsewhere. Letters editors were harried with correspondence from George Bunnerd, Shendar Bwra, A. Donis, Redbarn Wash, GBS Larking, Amelia Mackintosh, Horatia Ribbonson and the Reverend CW Stiggins JR, as well as from "the milkman", "an English mistress", "inveterate gambler" and "a novelist". Under one name or another, or no name at all, he was everywhere, pleading for the retention of the split infinitive and the abolition of Christmas. Perhaps Shaw was, after all, truly a hero for our times.

## Chapter 11

# First Plays

When Shaw began writing for the English stage, its most prominent dramatists were Sir A.W. Pinero and H.A. Jones. Both men were trying to develop a modern realistic drama, but neither had the power to break away from the type of artificial plots and conventional character types expected by theatregoers. The poverty of this sort of drama had become apparent with the introduction of several of Henrik Ibsen's plays onto the London stage around 1890, when *A Doll's House* was played in London; his *Ghosts* followed in 1891, and the possibility of a new freedom and seriousness on the English stage was introduced.

Shaw, who was about to publish *The Quintessence of Ibsenism* (1891), rapidly refurbished an abortive comedy, *Widowers' Houses,* as a play recognizably "Ibsenite" in tone, making it turn on the notorious scandal of slum landlordism in London. The result (performed 1892) flouted the threadbare romantic conventions that were still being exploited even by the most daring new playwrights.

In the play a well-intentioned young Englishman falls in love and then discovers that his prospective father-in-law's fortune and his own private income derive from exploitation of the poor. Potentially this is a tragic situation, but Shaw seems to have been always determined to avoid tragedy. The unamiable lovers do not attract sympathy; it is the social evil and not the romantic predicament on which attention is concentrated, and the action is kept well within the key of ironic comedy.

The same dramatic predispositions control *Mrs. Warren's*

*Profession,* written in 1893 but not performed until 1902 because the lord chamberlain, the censor of plays, refused it a license. Its subject is organized prostitution, and its action turns on the discovery by a well-educated young woman that her mother has graduated through the "profession" to become a part-proprietor of brothels throughout Europe. Again, the economic determinants of the situation are emphasized, and the subject is treated remorselessly and without the titillation of fashionable comedies about "fallen women." As with many of Shaw's works, the play is, within limits, a drama of ideas, but the vehicle by which these are presented is essentially one of high comedy.

Shaw called these first plays "unpleasant," because "their dramatic power is used to force the spectator to face unpleasant facts." He followed them with four "pleasant" plays in an effort to find the producers and audiences that his mordant comedies had offended. Both groups of plays were revised and published in *Plays Pleasant and Unpleasant* (1898). The first of the second group, *Arms and the Man* (performed 1894), has a Balkan setting and makes lighthearted, though sometimes mordant, fun of romantic falsifications of both love and warfare.

The second, *Candida* (performed 1897), was important for English theatrical history, for its successful production at the Royal Court Theatre in 1904 encouraged Harley Granville-Barker and J.E. Vedrenne to form a partnership that resulted in a series of brilliant productions there. The play represents its heroine as forced to choose between her clerical husband—a worthy but obtuse Christian socialist—and a young poet who has fallen wildly in love with her. She chooses her confident-seeming husband because she discerns that he is actually the weaker.

The poet is immature and hysterical but, as an artist, has a capacity to renounce personal happiness in the interest of some large creative purpose. This is a significant theme for Shaw; it leads on to that of the conflict between man as spiritual creator and woman as guardian of the biological continuity of the human race that is basic to *Man and Superman.*

In *Candida* such speculative issues are only lightly touched on, and this is true also of *You Never Can Tell* (performed 1899), in which the hero and heroine, who believe themselves to be respectively an accomplished amorist and an utterly rational and emancipated woman, find themselves in the grip of a vital force that takes little account of these notions.

The strain of writing these plays, while his critical and political work went on unabated, so sapped Shaw's strength that a minor illness became a major one. In 1898, during the process of recuperation, he married his unofficial nurse, Charlotte Payne-Townshend, an Irish heiress and friend of Beatrice and Sidney Webb.

The apparently celibate marriage lasted all their lives, Shaw satisfying his emotional needs in paper-passion correspondences with Ellen Terry, Mrs. Patrick Campbell, and others. Shaw's next collection of plays, *Three Plays for Puritans* (1901), continued what became the traditional Shavian preface—an introductory essay in an electric prose style dealing as much with the themes suggested by the plays as the plays themselves.

*The Devil's Disciple* (performed 1897) is a play set in New Hampshire during the American Revolution and is an inversion of traditional melodrama. *Caesar and Cleopatra* (performed 1901) is Shaw's first great play. In the play Cleopatra is a spoiled and vicious 16-year-old child rather than the 38-year-old temptress of Shakespeare's *Antony and Cleopatra.* The play depicts Caesar as a lonely and austere man who is as much a philosopher as he is a soldier. The play's outstanding success rests upon its treatment of Caesar as a credible study in magnanimity and "original morality" rather than as a superhuman hero on a stage pedestal. The third play, *Captain Brassbound's Conversion* (performed 1900), is a sermon against various kinds of folly masquerading as duty and justice.

In *Man and Superman* (performed 1905) Shaw expounded his philosophy that humanity is the latest stage in a purposeful and eternal evolutionary movement of the "life force" toward ever-higher life forms. The play's hero, Jack Tanner, is bent on pursuing his own spiritual development in accordance with this philosophy as he flees the determined marital pursuit of the heroine, Ann Whitefield. In the end Jack ruefully allows himself to be captured in marriage by Ann upon recognizing that she herself is a powerful instrument of the "life force," since the continuation and thus the destiny of the human race lies ultimately in her and other women's reproductive capacity.

The play's nonrealistic third act, the "Don Juan in Hell" dream scene, is spoken theatre at its most operatic and is often performed independently as a separate piece. Shaw had already become established as a major playwright on the Continent by the performance of his plays there, but, curiously, his reputation lagged in England. It was only with the production of *John Bull's Other Island* (performed 1904) in London, with a special performance for Edward VII, that Shaw's stage reputation was belatedly made in England.

Shaw continued, through high comedy, to explore religious consciousness and to point out society's complicity in its own evils. In *Major Barbara* (performed 1905), Shaw has his heroine, a major in the Salvation Army, discover that her estranged father, a munitions manufacturer, may be a dealer in death but that his principles and practice, however unorthodox, are religious in the highest sense, while those of the Salvation Army require the hypocrisies of often-false public confession and the donations of the distillers and the armourers against which it inveighs.

In *The Doctor's Dilemma* (performed 1906), Shaw produced a satire upon the medical profession (representing the self-protection of professions in general) and upon both the artistic temperament and the public's inability to separate it from the artist's achievement. In *Androcles and the Lion* (performed 1912), Shaw dealt with true and false religious exaltation in a philosophical play about early Christianity. Its central theme, examined through a group of early Christians condemned to the arena, is that one must have something worth dying for—an end outside oneself—in order to make life worth living.

Possibly Shaw's comedic masterpiece, and certainly his funniest and most popular play, is *Pygmalion* (performed 1913).

It was claimed by Shaw to be a didactic drama about phonetics, and its antiheroic hero, Henry Higgins, is a phonetician, but the play is a humane comedy about love and the English class system.

The play is about the training Higgins gives to a Cockney flower girl to enable her to pass as a lady and is also about the repercussions of the experiment's success. The scene in which Eliza Doolittle appears in high society when she has acquired a correct accent but no notion of polite conversation is one of the funniest in English drama. *Pygmalion* has been both filmed (1938), winning an Academy Award for Shaw for his screenplay, and adapted into an immensely popular musical, *My Fair Lady*.

## WORKS AFTER WORLD WAR I

World War I was a watershed for Shaw. At first he ceased writing plays, publishing instead a controversial pamphlet, "Common Sense About the War," which called Great Britain and its Allies equally culpable with the Germans and argued for negotiation and peace. His antiwar speeches made him notorious and the target of much criticism. In *Heartbreak House* (performed 1920), Shaw exposed, in a country-house setting on the eve of war, the spiritual bankruptcy of the generation responsible for the war's bloodshed.

Attempting to keep from falling into "the bottomless pit of an utterly discouraging pessimism," Shaw wrote five linked plays under the collective title *Back to Methuselah* (1922). They expound his philosophy of creative evolution in an extended dramatic parable that progresses through time from the Garden of Eden to 31,920.

The canonization of Joan of Arc in 1920 reawakened within Shaw ideas for a chronicle play about her. In the resulting masterpiece, *Saint Joan* (performed 1923), the Maid is treated not only as a Catholic saint and martyr but as a combination of practical mystic, heretical saint, and inspired genius.

Joan, as the superior being "crushed between those mighty forces, the Church and the Law," is the personification of the tragic heroine; her death embodies the paradox that humankind fears—and often kills—its saints and heroes and will go on doing so until the very higher moral qualities it fears become the general condition of man through a process of evolutionary change. Acclaim for *Saint Joan* led to the awarding of the 1925 Nobel Prize for Literature to Shaw (he refused the award).

In his later plays Shaw intensified his explorations into tragicomic and nonrealistic symbolism. For the next five years, he wrote nothing for the theatre but worked on his collected edition of 1930–38 and the encyclopaedic political tract "The Intelligent Woman's Guide to Socialism and Capitalism" (1928).

Then he produced *The Apple Cart* (performed 1929), a futuristic high comedy that emphasized Shaw's inner conflicts between his lifetime of radical politics and his essentially conservative mistrust of the common man's ability to govern himself.

Shaw's later, minor plays included *Too True to Be Good* (performed 1932), *On The Rocks* (performed 1933), *The Simpleton of the Unexpected Isles* (performed 1935), *Geneva* (performed 1938), and *In Good King Charles's Golden Days* (1939). After a wartime hiatus, Shaw, then in his 90s, produced several more plays, including *Farfetched Fables* (performed 1950), *Shakes Versus Shav* (performed 1949), and *Why She Would Not* (1956), which is a fantasy with only flashes of the earlier Shaw. Impudent, irreverent, and always a showman, Shaw used his buoyant wit to keep himself in the public eye to the end of his 94 years; his wiry figure, bristling beard, and dandyish cane were as well-known throughout the world as his plays.

When his wife, Charlotte, died of a lingering illness in 1943, in the midst of World War II, Shaw, frail and feeling the effects of wartime privations, made permanent his retreat from his London apartment to his country home at Ayot St. Lawrence, a Hertfordshire village in which he had lived since 1906. He died there in 1950.

George Bernard Shaw was not merely the best comic dramatist of his time but also one of the most significant playwrights in the English language since the 17th century. Some of his greatest works for the stage—*Caesar and Cleopatra,* the "Don Juan in Hell" episode of *Man and Superman, Major Barbara, Heartbreak House,* and *Saint Joan*—have a high seriousness and prose beauty that were unmatched by his stage contemporaries.

His development of a drama of moral passion and of intellectual conflict and debate, his revivifying the comedy of manners, his ventures into symbolic farce and into a theatre of disbelief helped shape the theatre of his time and after. A visionary and mystic whose philosophy of moral passion permeates his plays, Shaw was also the most trenchant pamphleteer since Swift; the most readable music critic in English; the best theatre critic of his generation; a prodigious lecturer and essayist on politics, economics, and sociological subjects; and one of the most prolific letter writers in literature. By bringing a bold critical intelligence to his many other areas of interest, he helped mold the political, economic, and sociological thought of three generations.

## LITERARY CAREER AS A CRITIC

At 20, he joined his mother in London. He began his literary career as a respected drama, literary and music critic in his mid-20s. It was during this time that he encountered the work of the playwright Henrik Ibsen.

### IBSEN'S INFLUENCE

Before writing plays, he started writing novels, however, Ibsen's realistic dramas were of great influence on his thinking. His treatise *The Quintessence of Ibsenism* establishes his belief in the drama of socialism and realism, much an Ibsen factor. Aged 36, Shaw wrote his first play, *Widower's Houses,* which criticizes slum landlords.

This was the first of three plays that together Shaw labelled unpleasant plays because they dealt with subjects that many people would rather ignore. A lifelong socialist, Shaw helped found the Fabian Society, which believed in reforming society in a way that was just and fair to all people.

## SUCCESS AS PLAYWRIGHT

His plays, from 1903, for example, *Man and Superman, Major Barbara* and *Pygmalion,* and even *Back to Methuselah,* proved successful as plays instead of novels due to Shaw's mastery of witty dialogues. *Pygmalion* is probably Shaw's best-known play.

The story, which criticizes the British class system, was the basis for the popular musical *My Fair Lady*. However, *Saint Joan,* which tells the story of Joan of Arc, is widely regarded as his masterpiece. Shaw was a vegetarian, a supporter of women's rights and a strong critic of Victorian society. He defends his views in his essays, which are noted for their clarity of expression and his 'wit' trademark. As a playwright George Bernard Shaw is considered as an institution by the British people.

# Chapter 12

# How to Write a Popular Play

The formula for the well made play is so easy that I give it for the benefit of any reader who feels tempted to try his hand at making the fortune that awaits all manufacturers in this line. First, you "have an idea" for a dramatic situation.

If it strikes you as a splendidly original idea, whilst it is in fact as old as the hills, so much the better. For instance, the situation of an innocent person convicted by circumstances of a crime may always be depended on. If the person is a woman, she must be convicted of adultery. If a young officer, he must be convicted of selling information to the enemy, though it is really a fascinating female spy who has ensnared him and stolen the incriminating document. If the innocent wife, banished from her home, suffers agonies through her separation from her children, and, when one of them is dying (of any disease the dramatist chooses to inflict), disguises herself as a nurse and attends it through its dying convulsion until the doctor, who should be a serio-comic character, and if possible a faithful old admirer of the lady's, simultaneously announces the recovery of the child and the discovery of the wife's innocence, the success of the play may be regarded as assured if the writer has any sort of knack for his work.

Comedy is more difficult, because it requires a sense of humour and a good deal of vivacity; but the process is essentially the same: it is the manufacture of a misunderstanding. Having manufactured it, you place its culmination at the end of the last act but one, which is the point at which the manufacture of the play begins. Then you make your first act out of the necessary introduction of the characters to the audience, after elaborate explanations, mostly conducted by servants, solicitors, and other low life personages (the principals must all be dukes and colonels and millionaires), of how the misunderstanding is going to come about. Your last act consists, of course, of clearing up the misunderstanding, and generally getting the audience out of the theatre as best you can.

Now please do not misunderstand me as pretending that this process is so mechanical that it offers no opportunity for the exercise of talent. On the contrary, it is so mechanical that without very conspicuous talent nobody can make much reputation by doing it, though some can and do make a living at it. And this often leads the cultivated classes to suppose that all plays are written by authors of talent. As a matter of fact the majority of those who in France and England make a living by writing plays are unknown and, as to education, all but illiterate.

Their names are not worth putting on the playbill, because their audiences neither know nor care who the author is, and often believe that the actors improvise the whole piece, just as they in fact do sometimes improvise the dialogue. To rise out of this obscurity you must be a Scribe or a Sardou, doing essentially the same thing, it is true, but doing it wittily and ingeniously, at moments almost poetically, and giving the persons of the drama some touches of real observed character.

## WHY THE CRITICS ARE ALWAYS WRONG

Now it is these strokes of talent that set the critics wrong. For the talent, being all expended on the formula, at least consecrates the formula in the eyes of the critics. Nay, they become so accustomed to the formula that at last they cannot relish or understand a play that has grown naturally, just as they cannot admire the Venus of Milo because she has neither a corset nor high heeled shoes.

They are like the peasants who are so accustomed to food reeking with garlic that when food is served to them without it they declare that it has no taste and is not food at all.

This is the explanation of the refusal of the critics of all nations to accept great original dramatists like Ibsen and Brieux as real dramatists, or their plays as real plays. No writer of the first order needs the formula any more than a sound man needs a crutch.

In his simplist mood, when he is only seeking to amuse, he does not manufacture a plot: he tells a story. He finds no difficulty in setting people on the stage to talk and act in an amusing, exciting or touching way. His characters have adventures and ideas which are interesting in themselves, and need not be fitted into the Chinese puzzle of a plot.

**THE INTERPRETER OF LIFE**

But the great dramatist has something better to do than to amuse either himself or his audience. He has to interpret life. This sounds a mere pious phrase of literary criticism; but a moment's consideration will discover its meaning and its exactitude. Life as it appears to us in our daily experience is an unintelligible chaos of happenings. You pass Othello in the bazaar in Aleppo, Iago on the jetty in Cyprus, and Desdemona in the nave of St. Mark's in Venice without the slightest clue to their relations to one another.

The man you see stepping into a chemist's shop to buy the means of committing murder or suicide, may, for all you know, want nothing but a liver pill or a toothbrush. The statesman who has no other object than to make you vote for his party at the next election, may be starting you on an incline at the foot of which lies war, or revolution, or a smallpox epidemic or five years off your lifetime. The horrible murder of a whole family by the father who finishes by killing himself, or the driving of a young girl on to the streets, my be the result of your discharging an employee in a fit of temper a month before.

To attempt to understand life from merely looking on at it as it happens in the streets is as hopeless as trying to understand public questions by studying snapshots of public demonstrations.

If we possessed a series of cinematographs of all the

executions during the Reign of Terror, they might be exhibited a thousand times without enlightening the audiences in the least as to the meaning of the Revolution: Robespierre would perish as "un monsieur" and Marie Antoinette as "une femme." Life as it occurs is senseless: a policeman may watch it and work in it for thirty years in the streets and courts of Paris without learning as much of it or from it as a child or a nun may learn from a single play by Brieux.

For it is the business of Brieux to pick out the significant incidents from the chaos of daily happenings and arrange them so that their relation to one another becomes significant, thus changing us from bewildered spectators of a monstrous confusion to men intelligently conscious of the world and its destinies. This is the highest function that man can perform—the greatest work he can set his hand to; and this is why the great dramatists of the world, from Euripides and Aristophanes to Shakespeare and Molière, and from them to Ibsen and Brieux, take that majestic and pontifical rank which seems so strangely above all the reasonable pretensions of mere strolling actors and theatrical authors.

## HOW THE GREAT DRAMATISTS TORTURE THE PUBLIC

Now if the critics are wrong in supposing that the formula of the well made play is not only an indispensable factor in playwriting, but is actually the essence of the play itself—if their delusion is rebuked and confuted by the practice of every great dramatist, even when he is only amusing himself by story telling, what must happen to their poor formula when it impertinently offers its services to a playwright who has taken on his supreme function as the Interpreter of Life?

Not only has he no use for it, but he must attack and destroy it; for one of the very first lessons he has to teach to a play-ridden public is that the romantic conventions on which the formula proceeds are all false, and are doing incalculable harm in these days when everybody reads romances and goes to the theatre.

Just as the historian can teach no real history until he

has cured his readers of the romantic delusion that the greatness of a queen consists in her being a pretty woman and having her head cut off, so the playwright of the first order can do nothing with his audiences until he has cured them of looking at the stage through a keyhole, and sniffing round the theatre as prurient people sniff round the divorce court.

The cure is not a popular one. The public suffers from it exactly as a drunkard or a snuff taker suffers from an attempt to conquer the habit. The critics especially, who are forced by their profession to indulge immoderately in plays adulterated with falsehood and vice, suffer so acutely when deprived of them for a whole evening that they hurl disparagements and even abuse and insult at the merciless dramatist who is torturing them. To a bad play of the kind they are accustomed to they can be cruel through superciliousness, irony, impatience, contempt, or even a Rouchefoucauldian pleasure in a friend's misfortune.

But the hatred provoked by deliberately inflicted pain, the frantic denials as of a prisoner at the bar accused of a disgraceful crime, the clamor for vengeance thinly disguised as artistic justice, the suspicion that the dramatist is using private information and making a personal attack: all these are to be found only when the playwright is no mere *marchand de plaisir*, but, like Brieux, a ruthless revealer of hidden truth and a mighty destroyer of idols.

## Chapter 13

# Personal Quotes

He who can, does. He who cannot teaches.

The golden rule is that there are no golden rules.

I'm only a beer teetotaller, not a champagne teetotaller.

Nothing is ever done in this world until men are prepared to kill one another if it is not done.

There are two tragedies in life. One is not to get your heart's desire. The other is to get it.

There is no love sincerer than the love of food.

A lifetime of happiness! No man alive could bear it: it would be hell on earth.

I am a gentleman: I live by robbing the poor.

An Englishman thinks he is moral when he is only uncomfortable.

Do not unto others as you would they should do unto you. Their tastes may not be the same.

Marriage is popular because it combines the maximum of temptation with the maximum of opportunity.

Hell is full of musical amateurs: music is the brandy of the damned.

It's a woman's business to get married as soon as possible, and a man's to keep unmarried as long as he can

Democracy substitutes election by the incompetent many for appointment by the corrupt few.

Liberty means responsibility. That's why most men dread it.

Assassination is the extreme form of censorship.

The theory of legal procedure is that if you set two liars to expose one another, the truth will emerge.

Censorship ends in logical completeness when nobody is allowed to read any books except the books that nobody can read.

The things most people want to know about are usually none of their business.

Silence is the most perfect expression of scorn.

As long as I have a want, I have a reason for living. Satisfaction is death.

Beauty is all very well at first sight, but who ever looks at it when it has been in the house three days?

Dancing is a perpendicular expression of a horizontal desire.

Don't waste time collecting other people's autographs; rather devote it to making your own autograph worth collecting.

The more things a man is ashamed of, the more respectable he is.

If you eliminate smoking and gambling, you will be amazed to find that almost all an Englishman's pleasures can be, and mostly are, shared by his dog.

The worst sin towards our fellow creatures is not to hate them, but to be indifferent to them: that's the essence of inhumanity.

He treats a flower girl as if she was a duchess, and a duchess as if she was a flower girl.

We don't stop playing because we grow old; we grow old because we stop playing.

When a stupid man is doing something he is ashamed of, he always declares that it is his duty.

If you can't get rid of the skeleton in your closet, you'd best teach it to dance.

The power of accurate observation is frequently called cynicism by those who don't have it.

A perpetual holiday is a good working definition of Hell.

There are scores of human insects who are ready at a moment's notice to reveal the will of God on every possible subject.

You have a choice between the natural stability of gold

and the honesty and intelligence of the members of government. And with all due respect for those gentlemen, I advise you, as long as the capitalist system lasts, vote for gold.

Sister, you're trying to keep me alive as an old curiosity, but I'm done, I'm finished, I'm going to die.

"and there is, on the whole, nothing on earth intended for innocent people so horrible as a school. To begin with, it is a prison. But it is in some respects more cruel than a prison. In a prison, for instance, you are not forced to read books written by the warders (who of course would not be warders and governors if they could write readable books), and beaten or otherwise tormented if you cannot remember their utterly unmemorable contents. In the prison you are not forced to sit listening to the turnkeys discoursing without charm or interest on subjects that they don't understand and don't care about, and are therefore incapable of making you understand or care about.

In a prison they may torture your body; but they do not torture your brains; and they protect you against violence and outrage from your fellow-prisoners. In a school you have none of these advantages. With the world's bookshelves loaded with fascinating and inspired books, the very manna sent down from Heaven to feed your souls, you are forced to read a hideous imposture called a school book, written by a man who cannot write: A book from which no human can learn anything: a book which, though you may decipher it, you cannot in any fruitful sense read, though the enforced attempt will make you loathe the sight of a book all the rest of your life." "A Treatise on Parents and Children," preface to Misalliance (1909).

There is only one true happiness in life, to love and be loved.

When a thing is funny, search it carefully for a hidden truth.

Life isn't about finding yourself; it's about creating yourself.

The average age (longevity) of a meat eater is 63. I am on the verge of 85 and still work as hard as ever. I have lived quite long enough and am trying to die; but I simply cannot do it. A single beef-steak would finish me; but I cannot bring myself to swallow it. I am oppressed with a dread of living forever. That is the only disadvantage of vegetarianism.

Sister, you're trying to keep me alive as an old curiosity, but I'm done, I'm finished, I'm going to die. (his last words)

In 1866 the family moved to a better neighborhood. Shaw went to the Wesleyan Connexional School, and then moved to a private school near Dalkey, and from there to Dublin's Central Model School. Shaw finished his formal education at the Dublin English Scientific and Commercial Day School. At the age of fifteen, he started to work as a junior clerk. In 1876 he went to London, joining his sister and mother. Shaw did not return to Ireland for nearly thirty years.

During the next two years Shaw educated himself at the British Museum. He began his literary career by writing music, drama criticism, and novels, including the semi-autobiographical *Immaturity*, without much success. A vegetarian who eschewed alcohol and tobacco, Shaw joined the Fabian Society in 1884 and served on its executive committee from 1885 until 1911. The middle-class socialist group also attracted H.G. Wells - both writers sent each other copies of their new books as they appeared. "You are, now that Wilde is dead, the one living playwright in my esteem," wrote Wells after receiving Shaw's *Three Plays for Puritans* (1901).

A man of many causes, Shaw supported abolition of private property, radical changes in the voting system, and campaigned for the simplification of spelling, and for the reform of the English alphabet. As a public speaker, Shaw gained the status of one of the most sought-after orators in England. In 1895 Shaw became a drama critic for the *Saturday Review*. Articles written for the paper were later collected in *Our Theatres in the Nineties* (1932).

Music, art, and drama criticism Shaw wrote for *Dramatic Review* (1885-86), *Our Corner* (1885-86), *The Pall Mall Gazette* (1885-88), *The World* (1886-94), and *The Star* (1888-90) as 'Corno bi Basetto'. His music criticisms were collected in *Shaw's Music*

(1981). After lacing a shoe too tightly, an operation was performed on his foot for necrosis; Shaw was unable to put his foot on the ground for eighteen months. During this period he wrote *Caesar and Cleopatra* (1901) and *The Perfect Wagnerite* (1898). "...I have no reason to believe that they would have been a bit better if they had been written on two legs instead of one," he said in a letter to the playwright St. John Ervine. His friend had his leg amputated during WWI after being hit by a shell splinters.

In 1898 Shaw married the wealthy Charlotte Payne-Townshend. They settled in 1906 in the Hertfordshire village of Ayot St. Lawrence. Shaw remained with Charlotte until her death, although he was occasionally linked with other women. He carried on a passionate correspondence over the years with Mrs. Patrick Campbell, a widow and actress, who got the starring role in *Pygmalion*. All the other actresses refused to say the taboo word 'bloody' that the playwright had put in the mouth of Eliza. When she wanted to publish his love letters to her, Shaw answered: "I will not, dear Stella, at my time of life, play the horse to your Lady Godiva."

The Norwegian playwright Henrik Ibsen had a great influence on Shaw's thinking. For a summer meeting of the Fabian Society in 1890, he wrote *The Quintessence of Ibsenism* (1891), in which he said that he considered Ibsen a pioneer, "who declares that it is right to do something hitherto regarded as infamous." Shaw's early plays, *Widower's Houses* (1892), which criticized slum landlords, as well as several subsequent ones, were not well received. His 'unpleasant plays', ideological attacks on the evils of capitalism and explorations of moral and social problems, were followed with more entertaining, but just as principled productions.

"To a professional critic (I have been one myself) theatre-going is the curse of Adam. The play is the evil he is paid to endure in the sweat of his brow; and the sooner it is over, the better." (from 'Preface' to *Saint Joan*). *Candida* was a comedy about the wife of a clergyman, and what happens when a weak, young poet wants to rescue her from her dull family life. But it was not until *John Bull's Other Island* (1904) that

Shaw gained in England a wider popularity with his own plays. In the Unites States and Germany Shaw's name was already well-known. Between 1904 and 1907 The Royal Court Theatre staged several of his plays, including *Candida.*

Morell: Man can climb to the highest summits; but he cannot dwell there.

Marchbacks (springing up): It's false: there can he dwell for ever, and there only. It's in the other moment that he can find no rest, no sense of the silent glory of life. Where would you have spend my moments, if not on the summits?

Morell: In the scullery, slicing onions and filling lamps. (from *Candida*)

*Major Barbara* depicted an officer of the Salvation Army, who learns from her father, a manufacturer of armaments, that money and power can be better weapons against evil than love. Ironically the producer of the film version of the play, Gabriel Pascal, was eager to do business with Sir Basil Zaharoff, an arms dealer.

Pickering: Have you no morals, man?

Doolittle: Can't afford them, Governor. (from *Pygmalion*)

*Pygmalion* was originally written for the actress Mrs. Patrick Campbell. Later the play became the basis for two films and a musical. (Shaw's correspondence with the actresses Ellen Terry and Stella Campbell are available in book form.) Shaw's popularity declined after his essay *Common Sense About the War* (1914), which was considered unpatriotic. With *Saint Joan* (1924), his masterpiece, Shaw was again accepted by the post-war public.

Now he was regarded as 'a second Shakespeare', who had revolutionized the British theatre. Shaw did not portray Joan of Arc, his protagonist, as a heroine or martyr, but as a stubborn young woman. And as in classic tragedies, her flaw is fatal and brings about her downfall. Uncommonly Shaw showed some sympathy to her judges. The play was written four years after Joan was declared a saint.

In 1893 Shaw collaborated with Keir Hardie in writing the party programme for the new Independent Labour party. Many of his plays also were philosophical addresses on the subject of individual responsibility or freedom of spirit against the conformist demands of society. Shaw was cofounder with the Webbs of the London School of Economics, and launched the petition against the imprisonment of Oscar Wilde. In 1897 he entered local government.

In his plays Shaw combined contemporary moral problems with ironic tone and paradoxes "Shavian" wit (which has produced such phrases as "He who can, does. He who cannot, teaches.") Discussion and intellectual acrobatics are the basis of his dramas, and before the emergence of the sound film, his plays were nearly impossible to adapt into screen. During his long career, Shaw wrote over fifty plays. He continued to write them even in his 90's.

George Bernard Shaw died at Ayot St. Lawrence, Hertfordshire, on November 2, 1950. He was cremated, and it was his wish that his ashes be mixed with those of his wife, Charlotte. She had died seven years before, "an old woman bowed and crippled, furrowed and wrinkled," as Shaw depicted her in a letter to H.G. Wells.

Since the days of the silent films, Shaw had been a fan of motion-picture. He also played in the film *Rosy Rapture - The Pride of the Beauty*(1914). Shaw did not like much of the German film version of *Pygmalion* (1935). The penniless producer and director Gabriel Pascal persuaded the author to give him the rights to make films from his plays. "Mr. Pascal, you're the first honest film producer I have ever met," Shaw told him at their first meeting and gave him a pound note.

*Pygmalion*, produced by Pascal and directed by Anthony Asquith and David Lean (uncredited), was a great success. In one article, Pascal was picked with the Pope and Hitler as one of the ten most famous men of 1938, but his career ended in the financial fiasco of the spectacle *Caesar and Cleopatra* (1945). Among several other films inspired by Shaw's plays are *Saint Joan* (1927), *How He Lied to Her Husband* (1931), *Arms and the Man* (1932), *Major Barbara* (1941), and *My Fair Lady* (1964). Pascal's co-director in *Major Barbara* was David Lean, but for one thousand pounds, Lean agreed to give the full credit to Pascal.

## Chapter 14

# Misconceptions of the Mass

From its first performance in Vienna in 1867, Johannes Brahms' *German Requiem* has been the subject of critical debate, often polemical, controversial, and even contradictory. Even the conditions surrounding the composer's choice of the Requiem form have sparked numerous debates ranging from historical and personal motivating factors to Brahms' own religious beliefs and intentions.

On a musical level, the text has been praised, attacked, accepted, and reevaluated in a circular, cyclical progression: from the early debates between Brahms' and Wagner's respective supporters to the newfound acclaim from Schoenberg and other modern theorists, the only element of the *Requiem's* reception that has remained in any way constant is its continued popularity in concert performances.

Certain key issues, most notably Brahms' use of traditional compositional elements and the enigmatic religious debates surrounding his choice of texts, can be seen to be the motivating factors throughout the reception of the work and to the present day. By examining these and other factors in greater detail, we can arrive at an appraisal of the *Requiem's* sometimes puzzling historical and musicological position.

As with any such musical masterpiece, much study has been devoted to reconstructing the process by which Brahms came to produce the *German Requiem*. It appears, by all accounts, that the idea for the piece was already well-conceived by April of 1865, when Brahms mentioned his plans in several letters to Clara Schumann. He avoided particular details, but seemed to have the basic structure of the work clearly in mind, and he had apparently already decided on the individual texts (taken from the Luther Bible) as well. The writing of the *Requiem* began intensively in February of 1866, and the bulk of the piece — movements 1, 2, 3, 4, and 6 — was complete by August of the same year.

The next few months, through December of 1866, brought revisions and minor changes, which were also discussed with several of his correspondents, among them Clara Schumann and Joseph Joachim. The first two performances of the work, in Vienna and Bremen in 1867-8, led to further revisions of the existing movements and the final addition of the fifth movement, written from April to June of 1868 and performed in a private concert in September.

The motivations for Brahms' composition are a complicating factor in the work's production history. Early critics, among them Max Kalbeck, Brahms' first biographer, insisted that the idea for a Requiem mass was inspired by the death of the composer's mother, in 1865. This date does coincide with the letters written to Clara Schumann, and Brahms does in fact mention that his work was spurred on by the memory of his mother; in addition, the textual excerpts from the Luther Bible refer to a motherly comfort which consoles those whom the dead have left behind: "ich will euch trösten, wie einen seine Mutter tröstet." Later critics, however, have also noted that Brahms was greatly affected by the death of his friend and benefactor Robert Schumann, and had considered, within months after Schumann's death in 1856, composing some sort of musical memorial to him.

Undoubtedly, as Musgrave has concluded, "it seems unlikely that there was only one personal influence on the *Requiem*," and that both his mother's and Schumann's death were for Brahms "a stimulus to the completion of existing ideas, rather than the source of them." Indeed, on numerous later occasions Brahms was heard to insist that his *Requiem* was intended for all humanity, despite (or indeed because of) its title; its innate themes of melancholy and consolation are applicable to any number of occasions. Not surprisingly, some critics have searched for other possible motivating factors for the *Requiem*, often with quite surprising results: Erb, as cited in Evans, even claims that the Franco-Prussian War, ending in 1866, also played a role in Brahms' choice. Clearly, we cannot determine with certainty whether any one event became the impetus for the work's creation, although many separate issues can be found to connect with the Requiem's textual and musical message.

The *German Requiem* saw its first performance in a semi-private concert in Vienna on December 1, 1867. The programme was an evening concert given by the *Gesellschaft der Musikfreunde*, and dedicated to the memory of Franz Schubert. Johann von Herbeck, the conductor, had known of Brahms' composition and urged him to allow its early performance; somewhat reluctantly — for he had his sights set on the Protestant Bremen for the true premiere — Brahms agreed to the concert.

At this point in time, Brahms was known to the Viennese concert-goers chiefly as a producer of Baroque choral works with the *Wiener Singverein*; as such, Herbeck believed that the programme would draw only a limited and somewhat dedicated audience, and convinced Brahms to perform only the first three movements of the piece. Despite these obstacles, the concert was very well-attended and immediately, according to all critics, made Brahms a widely recognized force in Vienna musical life. Although not a scandal, the performance was nonetheless the subject of hefty critical debate, and played a decisive role in the division of critics into the "Brahms vs. Wagner" camps that were becoming so fatefully significant.

Perhaps the most vociferous complaints against the piece arose not from its inherent musical structure or composition, but from an unfortunate series of problems with the evening's performance. The first two movements, Kalbeck and others report, were accepted with little hesitation; the third (and for Vienna, final) movement, however, became immediately notorious because of a percussionist's misunderstanding of the score: in the pedal fugue section of the third movement, his repeated D's were played not as the written *pf*, but instead as *f* or even *ff*: the effect was to completely drown out the rest of the orchestra and the vocal soloists. Upon the conclusion of the movement, audience members (particularly from the conservative, old-school camp, Hanslick and others report) hissed and booed and behaved quite boorishly. Reviewers, both friend and foe alike, were quick to note this catastrophe: some, such as the Wagner supporter Hirsch, snubbed the entire work and dismissed the "heathenish noise of the percussion," while Brahms' supporters such as Hanslick, although forced to admit to the performance's imperfections, attempted to defend the work's positive qualities.

Hanslick in particular praised the *Requiem's* innovative quality and impressive construction, although he conceded that it was difficult for the listener to grasp, and was probably not destined for widespread popularity. Still, he insisted on placing the *Requiem* in a broad and distinguished historical perspective:

The *German Requiem* is a work of unusual significance and great mastery. It seems to us one of the ripest fruits to have emerged from the style of the late Beethoven in the field of sacred music. Since the masses for the dead and mourning cantatas of our classical composers the shadow of death and the seriousness of loss have scarcely been presented in music with such power. The harmonic and contrapuntal art which Brahms learnt in the school of Bach is inspired by him with the living breath of the present ...

Beginning a trend which later critics were to follow to extremes, Hanslick also expressed his reservations about the *Requiem's* suitability for the concert-room, implying instead that its religious nature required a less secular venue. Several other critics also focused on the religious aspects of the work — a topic which, as we shall see, was to become increasingly important in the work's reception.

Theodor Billroth, for example, frankly accepted the work's avoidance of excess emotionalism, and explained that, while many critics faulted the lack of sensuality, "I think it is as much as intentional avoidance of everything sensuous as it is a fault. His *Requiem* is nobly spiritual and so Protestant-Bachish that it was difficult to make it go down here."

Perhaps due to the religious scene in Bremen — in the overwhelmingly Protestant northern Germany — and also due to the composer's own connections to this region, Brahms had been in correspondence with Carl Reinthaler there, attempting to set up the *Requiem's* premiere as a complete work. After several delays, Reinthaler was eventually able to provide a venue, and rehearsed the orchestra himself before Brahms' arrival.

The concert, given on April 10, 1868, Good Friday of that year, was in the town cathedral, and conducted by Brahms himself, with Joseph Joachim, Amalie Weiss and Clara Schumann all in attendance. The concert was extremely well-publicized and a matter of great anticipation, as Brahms' position in the Bremen musical world had consistently been highly respected; as a result, the turnout was an astounding 2500 listeners, and by all accounts a fabulous success. The programme included all six of the then-composed movements (as stated, the fifth movement was added in the months following); in addition, Joachim performed excerpts of works by Bach and Schumann, and Amalie sang parts of Bach's *St. Matthew Passion* and Handel's *Messiah*, making not only for a rather lengthy concert, but also — not at all coincidentally — reinforcing the religious nature of the *Requiem* itself.

The Bremen performance was not marred by any such mistakes as had clouded the Vienna premiere, and the critical response was one of resounding approval and appreciation. Nearly all critics recognized the extraordinarily complex nature of the composition, stressing in particular the incorporation of traditional elements such as counterpoint together with a modern-sounding modulation and rhythmic structure.

Even the few negative comments, usually minor, were expressed with a respect for the composer's achievements, which had been completely lacking in the Viennese diatribes. One critic remarked on a "somewhat notable unease in modulation," while another lamented Brahms' "ascetic Greco-German composition" and hoped "that he will withdraw himself from this subjectivity in the course of time." Just as the regional preferences of Vienna played a role in the *Requiem's* reception there, so too in Bremen were the responses at least in part due to the city's Protestant heritage; telling is also the criticism of the second movement, which, with its slow tempo set in 3/4 time, was seen as a rather ridiculous-sounding Ländler waltz, so beloved in Austria; one critic even considered this movement an "undeniable lapse."

In general, however, critical and public acclaim was so positive that a second performance had to be immediately scheduled in Bremen, only two weeks later on April 28. Brahms had found his success; although Vienna would still present its own resistance, performances throughout Germany began immediately, and reception was, with a few notable exceptions, overwhelmingly respectful.

After the fifth movement had been added and performed in a special private performance in September of 1868, the *Requiem* began to be performed in nearly all the major cities of Germany. Cologne and Leipzig were the first to experience the entire seven-movement work in its final form: Cologne on February 16, 1869 under the conducting of Ferdinand Hiller, and Leipzig two days later, on the 18th of February, under Karl Reinecke. Cologne, like Bremen, was overwhelmingly supportive and immediately accepted the work into its regular repertoire — another performance occurred there in 1870, yet another the next year, and several in the following decade.

Leipzig, however, proved harder to conquer. As in Vienna and later Munich, the greatest stumbling block appeared to be not the musical qualities of the *Requiem,* but its Protestant religious text. Although the region was primarily Protestant, many critics objected to the *Requiem's* "mystical" and "contemplative" tone, which they found at odds with the straightforward Protestantism of Bach, Schütz, and other composers of religious music. This seeming contradiction in reception — as we recall, critics in both Vienna and Bremen had found the work to be lacking in emotion and sensuality, not overflowing with fervent appeal — may perhaps, however, be explained by the earlier resistance of Leipzig to Brahms' works: his first performances there, a few years earlier, had been met with marked hostility, and the Leipzig premiere of his first major orchestral work, the D minor piano concerto, had been disastrous.

The critical reception of the *Requiem*, however, seemed, at least in comparison to earlier voices, to consist of much less serious complaints: the work was seen to be weak because of its "lengths" and "empty passages," rather than because of any inherent compositional offense. Even the editor of the local music paper found these complaints to be superficial, and by the time of the *Requiem's* second performance in Leipzig in 1878, Brahms' standing had improved immeasurably; he had been accepted, if grudgingly, into the musical canon, and even his "mystical" *Requiem* had reached the status of a classic in the repertoire.

Indeed, the reactions of Leipzig and Bremen seem to mark the two possible paths which the *Requiem* was to follow throughout Germany. In many cities, nearly all of them Protestant and/or northern towns, reception was immediately positive, and the work encountered little, if any resistance. In Catholic and southern towns, however, the initial performances of the *Requiem* were more often than not met with critical scorn: opposition was expressed both in terms of textual and emotional issues — the foreign Protestant fervour being quite untenable — or in rather vague resistance to the heavy-handed, academic nature of Brahms' composition.

Generally critics recognized the craftsmanship involved in writing such a monumental and interconnected work; what they objected to was the constructed nature of the counterpoint and fugal passages, which stood at odds with their conception of 'modern' music. Both friend and foe alike devoted extensive attention to the use of older traditions in the *Requiem*; in addition, nearly everyone was able to recognize its importance as a new or reinvented model for religious orchestral music.

The 'modern' qualities of the work — the harmonic ambivalences and certain nearly untonal passages — became the foci of either praise or attack, depending on the particular critic's affinities. One reviewer, Adolf Schubring in the *Allgemeine musikalische Zeitung*, unfailingly praised the *Requiem's* "organic melody" and structural subtleties, while at the same time despairing over the "ascetic modern colouring" of the instrumentation.

Despite or even because of the critical attention paid to the *Requiem,* it continued to enjoy great success in the concert hall. In the year 1869 alone there were at least eleven performances besides Leipzig and Cologne: Basel, Hamburg, Karlsruhe, Münster, Zürich, Dessau, and Weimar all produced the work for public concerts. 1870 saw several additions to this list, as well as many repeat performances, particularly in Hamburg, Bremen, and Cologne, the strongest Brahms supporters. 1871, besides encores in the northern towns, brought the return of the *Requiem* to Vienna; reviews were certainly better than for the premiere four years earlier, but still fairly cool and reserved.

Similarly, when the *Requiem* finally came to Munich in Catholic Bavaria — not until 1872 — reviews were decidedly negative: Brahms was described as "scarcely more than a name" by one critic, and his *Requiem* was seen on a par with Franz Lachner's — hardly the same critical acclaim as he had won in Hamburg or Bremen. As with Leipzig and Vienna, however, the critics softened with time, and by the 1880's the protests and polemicism to be heard against the *Requiem* came almost entirely from the Wagnerian school; among the greater concert-going public, the *Requiem* had been embraced, and was to remain, as a `standard' and `classic' masterpiece.

Wagner's reception of and attitude toward Brahms is well-documented, and can only be touched on here. Clearly, he had nothing positive to say about the *Requiem*: not only did he abhor the Protestant-bourgeois musical ethics which the piece embodied, but he was also outraged by Brahms' claim to have written a piece for all of Germany, a truly German work — a claim reflected only, as far as I can determine, in the title *Ein deutsches Requiem.* (The historical moment of the *Requiem's* conception, shortly before German unity in 1871, surely played a role in this view as well.)

Wagner's contempt for the piece extended to sarcastic comments in letters and essays; in one, he scornfully remarks that when the present generation (his own) dies, "we will want no *German Requiem* to be played to our ashes." The importance of Wagner's stance toward Brahms cannot be overemphasized: many critics echoed Wagner's sentiments, and while some devoted serious attention to an analysis of what they considered to be the work's particular flaws, others continued with vague polemicisms and *ad hominem* attacks against the composer, his beliefs and religion, and above all his `academic' attitude toward music.

Not all analysts, however, found Brahms to be the conservative schoolmaster he was made out to be: Kleinert, for example, in a direct reference to Wagner's own claims, calmly declared that "the music of the future, for others a vogue, is for Brahms already a music of the past."

As Kross and others have documented, critical opposition to the *Requiem*, mostly on dogmatic grounds, continued through the end of the 19th century; by 1900 however, it had mostly disappeared, and the work had been accepted not only into the concert-hall repertoire, but was receiving increased favorable critical and analytical attention, both within Germany and abroad. Following the paradigm of reception that we have set up for Germany — the fact that Catholic towns were far more resistant to the *Requiem* than their Protestant counterparts — it comes as no surprise to learn that the *Requiem* was considerably better received in England and the United States than in Catholic countries such as France and Italy.

Indeed, we have little documentation of any reception whatsoever in these countries; in England, on the other hand, reviews, commentary, and performances were abundant from 1871 onwards. There is some statistical disagreement about the number of performances of the *Requiem* in Europe during Brahms' lifetime: while Musgrave cites the figure of 79 performances outside Germany between 1869 and 1876, Kalbeck reports 85 performances between 1867 and 1876; in any event, the work was most certainly performed in most major European cities, and subject to repeats on demand on several occasions. In Britain, which had by far the strongest and most positive reception (as was typical for choral and religious music, Musgrave notes), the *Requiem* premiered in a private performance in London in July 1871, conducted by Julius Stockhausen himself, on one of his frequent visits to Sir Henry Thompson. The public premiere, also in London, was in April of 1873, and was the subject of great critical attention — most of it quite positive.

The work was immediately recognized as difficult, but esteemed at the same time as a work of a great composer, already seen as the successor in the German tradition of Bach and Beethoven. The only major criticism came from those who felt, like Hanslick's original commentary, that the concert hall was the wrong place for such a religious funeral service; others also echoed their Continental counterparts and claimed, alternately, that the work was either too "contemplative" or that it was "unemotional." The second public performance in Britain, in 1876, was similarly received: critics remarked in glowing terms of the great masterpiece, and the only major flaw, they felt, was that English singers were not well-trained to sing the contrapuntal German passages.

Not surprisingly, when the London Bach Choir began performing the *Requiem* on a semi-regular basis, the reviewers raved: vocalists trained for Bach, they agreed, were by far the best-equipped to handle Brahms' difficult demands. In the United States, critical reception generally seemed to follow the leads of the European critics, although a tendency to dismiss the work as "difficult" and overly "academic" can also be discerned. American concert-hall performance records for the 1870-1900 period are sketchy at best, but the *Requiem* seems to have enjoyed modest popularity until shortly after 1930, when its performances (and those of Brahms' other works as well) skyrocketed, as we shall see.

The earliest documented performances were the partial performance of several movements by the New York *Liederkranz Society* in January 1875, and the full premiere of the entire work, together with a Bach Cantata and excerpts from Gluck's *Orpheus*, by the New York *Oratorio Society* in March 1877. Critics were tame in their enthusiasm, but appreciated the grandeur and earnestness of the work. One rather amusing review came from the *New York Times,* claiming that "it is exceedingly scholarly, but its length and monotonousness are such that it is scarcely likely to impress any but students."

Milwaukee, owing perhaps to its German heritage, saw an early premiere of movements 5 and 6 only in October of 1875, and Cincinnati produced a partial performance in 1878, but had to wait until 1884 for the entire work. 1888 marked the full performance of the *Requiem* in both Boston and Chicago, thus guaranteeing a greater audience as well as more critical attention. Again, contradiction was the rule: while the *Boston Transcript,* echoing Hanslick's historical contextualization, emotes that in order to find the *Requiem's* equal, we must "go back to the soulful conventionality of Handel and Haydn ... the inspired technique of Mozart's Masses and Requiem ... and the works of the preacher of the musical gospel, Sebastian Bach," another reviewer of the same concert writes in the *Boston Herald* that "while it shows the hand of a skilled musician, its vagueness and fragmentary themes do not offer much satisfaction."

As we have seen, critical attitudes in Germany slowly consolidated themselves during the latter years of the 19th century: where at first there had been sharp divisions in judgment, a consensus was reached by 1900 which acclaimed the *Requiem* for its technical as well as aesthetic appeal in combining older traditions such as counterpoint with new or "modern" tonal and harmonic structures. A delayed but similar consensus was also reached in England and America, not surprisingly: while concert-hall acceptance was never in question, music journalists and critics did express some distaste towards the academic nature of Brahms' use, but these voices were gradually replaced by a more appreciative younger generation, who recognized the innovative and even "progressive" qualities in Brahms' compositional style.

In Britain, for example, Bernard Shaw, a staunch Wagnerian, had disparaged the *Requiem* in no uncertain terms, comparing it unfavorably to Mozart's *Requiem* and lamenting the "Bachian" fugues and tedium in glib statements such as:

"I do not deny that the *Requiem* is a solid piece of musical manufacture. You feel at once as though it could only have come from the establishment of a first-class undertaker. But I object to requiems altogether."

Later critics such as Britten and Tippet were slightly more lenient, objecting not to the traditional elements but to what they considered its aesthetic failings: Tippet wrote that Brahms had tried to fill the "Beethovenian mould without realising its inherently dramatic nature." Gradually, however, in England as well as in the United States, negative criticisms disappeared, to be replaced by serious academic studies of the *Requiem's* origins and construction.

Spurred perhaps by the continued public interest in hearing the piece performed, more and more critics began to analyse the so-called "Bachian" elements of the counterpoint, the textual and musical connections to earlier German masses, and, eventually, the compositional form and structure as well. In the eyes of the critics and the public alike, Musgrave concludes, Brahms' standing "changed imperceptibly from the context of `modern' to that of `classic.'"

Perhaps the greatest reevaluation of the *Requiem* and indeed all of Brahms' oeuvre came with the 1950 publication of Schoenberg's essay "Brahms the Progressive." Here, refuting the Wagnerian image of Brahms as an unfruitful conservative, as "the classicist, the academician," Schoenberg acclaimed Brahms' more progressive musical moments and praised his innovative qualities.

This essay, not originally published in German, coincided with a dramatic increase in the number of Brahms' performances in the post-war period, among which the *Requiem* was well represented. In essence, then, the image of Brahms had come full-circle: from the 1860's view of his work as "modern" and "difficult" through a sort of controversy and critical disparagement in the 1880's, to a newfound appreciation and reevaluation of his progressive, modern compositions.

Generally, symphony orchestra performances of Brahms have peaked at a fairly high level during the twentieth century, but it is interesting to examine the changing place of the *Requiem* in the concert repertoire. Unfortunately, it is difficult to document the performance history of the *Requiem* in Europe in the 20th century, not least because of the intervening war years and the lack of adequate recordkeeping materials. Nonetheless, Döbertin mentions the lasting popularity of the work in Germany today: nearly every city in Germany, he writes, performs the *Requiem* at least once a year; traditional faviurite places such as Hamburg and Bremen often do so several times each year.

Its position in the German concert repertoire seems assured; as Kross points out, the number of performances has changed little since 1900. The situation in the United States is similar, but again, like the views of critics, indicates a delayed reaction. Between 1897 and 1969, there were at least 52 performances of the *Requiem* in the United States; nearly every major symphony orchestra performed it more than once, especially in the post-war period.

Particularly strong were the years 1946-1960, in which there were over 24 performances. In her extensive collection of data on symphony orchestra performances, Mueller notes that performances of Brahms' works, rather surprisingly, exceeded those of Beethoven's in the 1940-45 years; particularly favorably disposed towards the *Requiem* were Chicago, Los Angeles, and St. Louis. The following chart, based on data from Mueller, helps to demonstrate the surge in popularity of the *Requiem* during the post-war years.

Modern criticism and analysis of the *Requiem* is extensive, as even a short glance at bibliographical materials will indicate. Particularly popular seem to be examinations of the traditional elements of the composition — folk songs, older choral music, relation to other German masses — and, quite significantly, religious analyses of the texts and themes of the work.

Noticeably lacking, however, as Krummacher and a few others lament, are serious attempts to discuss the compositional structure — sonata form, motet, harmonic modulations, and so forth — of the *Requiem*. Such analyses are undoubtedly forthcoming, and recent years have seen a number of new approaches to the work, as well.

The religious aspects, however, seem to provide extremely fruitful ground in looking both at Brahms' own viewpoints toward his work, and at the traditional elements he incorporated. We have seen that religion played an important role in the early reception of the *Requiem*; thus it should not come as a surprise to discover than even modern analysts are subject to this fascination with the spiritual issues of Brahms and his work.

Still today, reviewers of modern concert performances remark on the heavy-handed religious issues surrounding the *Requiem*: Hadow has claimed, echoing and at the same time reversing the commentary of numerous predecessors, that the work is "less suited to the church than to the concert room," while others have again attempted to explain the *Requiem's* identity: it is "not a requiem mass; it is rather a cantata," claims Dickenson, while another reviewer considers it to be "the great funeral chant of modern music."

Above all, analysts are taken with the textual choices Brahms made in producing the *Requiem*, and with its identity and categorization. Brahms himself was aware of these issues: even early on, considerations of the work prompted inquiries as to the composer's own religious beliefs and examinations of the spiritual message of the text. Brahms, however, seemed to care little for such questions: as we have stated, he considered the work to be a "human" requiem. His choice of texts can be ascribed less to religious inspiration and more to personal choice and cultural identity: he referred to the Bible as "ein echt menschliches Buch," or, in Krummacher's words, "ein Dokument tiefer menschlicher Sehnsüchte und hoher ethnischer Gesinnung," i.e. not a dogmatic interpretation of religious commandments, but a cultural and emotional repository of views and values.

In choosing certain texts from Luther's translation of the Bible — taking excerpts from both the Old Testament, the New Testament, as well as the Apocrypha — Brahms avoided any specific mention of Christ or even a final redemption at the hands of God: instead, he focuses on the very human sentiments which surround the death of a loved one. The *Requiem*, like many other vocal works of Brahms, deals with the transience of life, the need for comfort, the hope of a final resolution, and a reward for effort.

This annoyed Reinthaler, an orthodox Lutheran, who cautioned Brahms against such omissions and requested more "specifically Christian content," but Brahms remained adamant in the preservation of his artistic freedom. Several recent critics have produced thorough analyses not of later reception of Brahms, but of Brahms' own reception of earlier religious and vocal music. Parallels are numerous and interesting: rather than following the Latin mass on the order of Mozart, Beethoven or even Schubert (who had written a German Requiem, the *Deutsche Trauermesse*, for his brother's personal use in 1818), Brahms instead picks up on the Protestant German masses of Bach and Schütz.

Schütz, in particular, has been the subject of several recent studies, which note the significant relations between a work such as the *Teutsche Begräbnismissa* of 1636 and Brahms' Requiem. In part, Brahms' avoidance of the Latin Mass can be understood from a purely confessional view: as one critic writes, "the Catholic Mass, with its tenets of purgatory, salvation, and resurrection was utterly aesthenic and alien for him, and impossible to set" because of his Lutheran upbringing and later agnosticism. More importantly, however, may be the very message of Brahms' text: it is clearly not intended to be performed as a mass *for* the dead, but rather as a comfort and consolation *about* the dead, *for* the living.

Why, then, did Brahms entitle his work a Requiem? Surely a more descriptive and less categorically strict title might have prevented much of the critical debate that has surrounded this issue. Some critics, forced into the role of apologist for Brahms' choice of title, have attempted to justify it: after all, they claim, the scope and magnitude of Brahms' work are equal to, if not greater than, most traditional Requiems; even the structure of the movements has certain parallels in the Latin liturgy, using a framed structure with a common beginning and end ("selig sind ...") and progressing toward a centre focused on blessedness (the fourth movement) and a type of *Dies Irae* (the sixth). In addition, critics claim, surely the term "requiem" has lost its strict identity and come into common parlance, thus `allowing' Brahms to use it as his title.

Such strained justifications strike me as unnecessary, although interesting enough in their own right. One critic, however, takes the religious controversy to an even further extreme, and seems very concerned with defending Brahms' own religious beliefs and "honesty" in writing the *Requiem*. Only if, he claims, Brahms honestly believed in the hope of eternal life and the reality of an existential comfort for the living, only then can we "accept" his honest intentions in choosing such unusual textual matter for his Mass.

Although such a claim was not uncommon in the late 19th century, I find it telling that modern critics have taken up these themes yet again in their attempts to analyse the *Requiem*: yet another instance, perhaps, of the circular nature of Brahms' reception, an indication of a recurring turn in Brahms scholarship. There is no doubt that Brahms' *Requiem* enjoys great popularity in the concert hall today, as well as critical acclaim and academic interest from nearly all sides.

Interestingly, this position has not changed dramatically since the early years of this century; the 1940's saw a boost in popularity due in part, surely, to the reevaluated view of Brahms' progressive nature sparked by Schoenberg, but even before this, critical and public attention had centered on Brahms' *Requiem* as a masterful fusion of new and old techniques.

Perhaps the most significant and puzzling debates have arisen over the religious issues which surround and cloud the work: the textual choices and themes have prompted some to search for the composer's own religious views, or forced others to become apologists for his appropriation of the term Requiem.

All in all, the critical appraisal of Brahms has undergone a cyclical turn: from his early controversial stance as both 'modern' and 'academic,' Brahms was seen to fulfill Schumann's prophesy of opening new doors in composition. Similarly, the *Requiem* itself, after a period of hefty debate and some disparagement, rose again to critical acclaim as an innovative and progressive work. Today its stature seems assured, given the overwhelming popularity of the work in concert.

However, as any historian will admit, a careful examination of historical trends and processes may help indicate future directions. For Brahms and the *Requiem*, a return to certain critical modes of thought may be a mere anomaly, but it may also indicate yet another reevaluation of the work is in the process of forming.

Chapter 15

# Socialism and Liberty

The dread of Socialism by nervous people who do not understand it, on the ground that there would be too much law under it, and that every act of our lives would be regulated by the police, is more plausible than the terrors of the ignorant people Who think it would mean the end of all law, because under Capitalism we have been forced to impose restrictions that in a socialized nation would have no sense, in order to save the proletariat from extermination, or at least from extremities that would have provoked it to rebellion.

Here is a little example. A friend of mine Who employed some girls in an artistic business in which there was not competition enough to compel him to do his worst in the way of sweating them, took a nice old riverside house, and decorated it very prettily with Morris wall-papers, furnishing it in such a way that the girls could have their tea comfortably in their workrooms, which he made as homelike as possible. All went well until one day a gentleman walked in and announced himself to my friend as the factory inspector. He looked round him, evidently much puzzled, and asked where the women worked.

'Here,' replied my friend, with justifiable pride, confident that the inspector had never seen anything so creditable in the way of a factory before. But what the inspector said was 'Where is the copy of the factory regulations which you are obliged by law to post up on your walls in full view of your employees?' Surely you dent expect me to stick up a beastly ugly thing like that in a room furnished like a drawingroom,' said my friend.

'Why, that paper on the wall is a Morris paper: I cant disfigure it by pasting up a big placard on it.' 'You are liable to severe penalties' replied the inspector 'for having not only omitted to post the regulations, but for putting paper on your walls instead of having them limewashed at the intervals prescribed by law.' 'But hang it all!' my friend remonstrated, 'I want to make the place homely and beautiful. You forget that the girls are not always working. They take their tea here.' 'For allowing your employees to take their meals in the room where they work you have incurred an additional penalty' said the inspector. 'It is a gross breach of the Factory Acts.' And he walked out, leaving my friend an abashed criminal caught redhanded.

As it happened, the inspector was a man of sense. He did not return; the penalties were not exacted; the Morris wall-papers remained; and the illicit teas continued; but the incident illustrates the extent to which individual liberty has been cut down under Capitalism for good as well as for evil. Where women are concerned it is assumed that they must be protected to a degree that is unnecessary for men (as if men were any more free in a factory than women); consequently the regulations are so much stricter that women are often kept out of employments to which men are welcomed.

Beside's the factory inspector there are the Commissioners of Inland Revenue inquiring into your income and making you disgorge a lot of it, the school attendance visitors taking possession of your children, the local government inspectors making you build and drain your house not as you please but as they order, the Poor Law officers, the unemployment insurance officers, the vaccination officers, and others whom I cannot think of just at present. And the tendency is to have more and more of them as we become less tolerant of the abuses of our capitalist system.

But if you study these interferences with our liberties closely you will find that in practice they are virtually suspended in the case of people well enough off to be able to take care of themselves: for instance, the school attendance officer never calls at houses valued above a certain figure, though the education of the children in them is often disgracefully neglected or mishandled. Poor Law officers would not exist if there were no poor, nor unemployment insurance officers if we all got incomes whether we were employed or not. If nobody could make profits by sweating, nor compel us to work in uncomfortable, unsafe, insanitary factories and workshops, a great deal of our factory regulations would become not only superfluous but unbearably obstructive.

Then consider the police: the friends of the honest woman and the enemies and hunters of thieves, tramps, swindlers, rioters, confidence tricksters, drunkards, and prostitutes. The police officer, like the soldier who stands behind him, is mainly occupied today in enforcing the legalized robbery of the poor which takes place whenever the wealth produced by the labour of a productive worker is transferred as rent or interest to the pockets of an idler or an idler's parasite.

They are even given powers to arrest us for 'sleeping out', which means sleeping in the open air without paying a landlord for permission to do so. Get rid of this part of their duties, and at the same time of the poverty which it enforces, with the mass of corruption, thieving, rioting, swindling, and prostitution which poverty produces as surely as insanitary squalor produces smallpox and typhus, and you get rid of the least agreeable part of our present police activity, with all that it involves in prisons, criminal courts, and jury duties.

By getting rid of poverty we shall get rid of the unhappiness and worry which it causes. To defend themselves against this, women, like men, resort to artificial happiness, just as they resort to artificial insensibility when they have to undergo a painful operation. Alcohol produces artificial happiness, artificial courage, artificial gaiety, artificial self-satisfaction, thus making life bearable for millions who would otherwise be unable to endure their condition. To them alcohol is a blessing. Unfortunately, as it acts by destroying conscience, self-control, and the normal functioning of the body, it produces crime, disease, and degradation on such a scale that its manufacture and sale are at present prohibited by law throughout the United States of America, and there is a strong movement to introduce the same prohibition here.

The ferocity of the resistance to this attempt to abolish artificial happiness shows how indispensable it has become under Capitalism.

A famous American Prohibitionist was mobbed by medical students in broad daylight in the streets of London, and barely escaped with the loss of one eye, and his back all but broken. If he had been equally famous for anything else, the United States Government would have insisted on the more ample reparation, apology, and condign punishment of his assailants; and if this had been withheld, or even grudged, American hotheads would have clamored for war.

But for the enemy of the anaesthetic that makes the misery of the poor and the idleness of the rich tolerable, turning it into a fuddled dream of enjoyment, neither his own country nor the public conscience of ours could be moved even to the extent of a mild censure on the police. It was evident that had he been torn limb from limb the popular verdict would have been that it served him jolly well right.

Alcohol, however, is a very mild drug compared with the most effective modern happiness producers, These give you no mere sodden self-satisfaction and self-conceit: they give you ecstasy. It is followed by hideous wretchedness; but then you can cure that by taking more and more of the drug until you become a living horror to all about you, after which you become a dead one, to their great relief.

As to these drugs, not even a mob of medical students, expressly educated to make their living by trading in artificial health and happiness, dares protest against strenuous prohibition, provided they may still prescribe the drug; nevertheless the demand is so great in the classes who have too much money and too little work that smuggling, which is easy and very profitable, goes on in spite of the heaviest penalties.

Our efforts to suppress this trade in artificial happiness has already landed us in such interferences with personal liberty that we are not allowed to purchase many useful drugs for entirely innocent purposes unless we first pay (not to say bribe) a doctor to prescribe it.

Still, prohibition of the fiercer drugs has the support of public opinion. It is the prohibition of alcohol that rouses such opposition that the strongest governments shrink from it in spite of overwhelming evidence of the increase in material well-being produced by it wherever it has been risked. You prove to people that as teetotallers they will dwell in their own houses instead of in a frowsy tenement, besides keeping their own motor car, having a bank account, and living ten years longer.

They angrily deny it; but when you crush their denials by unquestionable American statistics they tell you flatly that they had rather be happy for thirty years in a tenement without a car or a penny to put in the bank than be unhappy for forty years with all these things. You find a wife distracted because her husband drinks and is ruining her and her children; yet when you induce him to take the pledge, you find presently that she has tempted him to drink again because he is so morose when he is sobre that she cannot endure living with him. And to make his drunkenness bearable she takes to drink herself, and lives happily in shameless degradation with him until they both drink themselves dead.

Besides, the vast majority of modern drinkers do not feel any the worse for it, because they do not miss the extra efficiency they would enjoy on the water waggon. Very few people ~re obliged by their occupations to work up to the extreme limit of their powers. Who cares whether a lady gardener or a bookkeeper or a typist or a shop assistant is a teetotaller or not, provided she always stops well short of being noticeably drunk?

It is to the motorist or the aeroplane pilot that a single glass of any intoxicant may make the difference between life and death. What would be sobriety for a billiard marker would be ruinous drunkenness for a professional billiard player. The glass of stimulant that enlivens a routine job is often dropped because when the routineer plays golf 'to keep herself fit' she finds that it spoils her putting. Thus you find that you can sometimes make a worker give up alcohol partly or wholly by giving her more leisure. She finds that a woman who is sobre enough to do her work as well as it need be done is not sobre enough to play as well as she would like to do it.

The moment people are in a position to develop their fitness, as they call it, to the utmost, whether at work or at play, they begin to grudge the sacrifice of the last inch of efficiency which alcohol knocks off, and which in all really fine work makes the difference between first rate and second rate. If this book owed any of its quality to alcohol or to any other drug, it might amuse you more; but it would be enormously less conscientious intellectually, and therefore much more dangerous to your mind.

If you put all this together you will see that any social change which abolishes poverty and increases the leisure of routine workers will destroy the need for artificial happiness, and increase the opportunities for the sort of activity that makes people very jealous of reducing their fitness by stimulants.

Even now we admit that the champion athlete must not drink whilst training; and the nearer we get to a world in which everyone is in training all the time the nearer we shall get to general teetotalism, and to the possibility of discarding all those restrictions on personal liberty which the prevalent dearth of happiness and consequent resort to pernicious artificial substitutes now force us to impose.

As to such serious personal outrages as compulsory vaccination and the monstrous series of dangerous inoculations which are forced on soldiers, and at some frontiers on immigrants, they are only desperate attempts to stave off the consequences of bad sanitation and overcrowding by infecting people with disease when they are well and strong in the hope of developing their natural resistance to it by exercise sufficiently to prevent them from catching it when they are ailing and weak.

The poverty of our doctors forces them to support such practices in the teeth of all experience and disinterested science; but if we get rid of poor doctors and overcrowded and insanitary dwellings we get rid of the diseases which terrify us into these grotesque witch rituals; and no woman will be forced to expose her infant to the risk of a horrible, lingering, hideously disfiguring death from generalized vaccinia lest it should catch confluent smallpox, which, by the way, is, in a choice between the two evils, much to be preferred. Dread of epidemics: that is, of disease and premature death, has created a pseudo-scientific tyranny just as the dread of hell created a priestly tyranny in the ages of faith.

Florence Nightingale, a sensible woman whom doctors could neither humbug nor bully, told them that what was wrong with our soldiers was dirt, bad food, and foul water: in short, the conditions produced by war in the field and poverty in the slum. When we get rid of poverty the doctors will no longer be able to frighten us into imposing on ourselves by law pathogenic inoculations which, under healthy conditions, kill more people than the diseases against which they pretend to protect them.

And when we get rid of Commercialism, and vaccines no longer make dividends for capitalists, the fairy tales by which they are advertized will drop out of the papers, and be replaced, let us hope, by disinterested attempts to ascertain and publish the scientific truth about them, which, by the way, promises to be much more hopeful and interesting.

As to the mass of oppressive and unjust laws that protect property at the expense of humanity, and enable proprietors to drive whole populations off the land because sheep or deer are more profitable, we have said enough about them already. Naturally we shall get rid of them when we get rid of private property.

Now, however, I must come to one respect in which official interference with personal liberty would be carried under Socialism to lengths undreamed of at present. We may be as idle as we please if only we have money in our pockets; and the more we look as if we had never done a day's work in our lives and never intend to, the more we are respected by every official·we come in contact with, and the more we are envied, courted, and deferred to by everybody.

If we enter a village school the children all rise and stand respectfully to receive us, whereas the entrance of a plumber or carpenter leaves them unmoved. The mother who secures a rich idler as a husband for her daughter is proud of it: the father who makes a million uses it to make rich idlers of his children.

That work is a curse is part of our religion: that it is a disgrace is the first article in our social code. To carry a parcel through the streets is not only a trouble, but a derogation from one's rank. Where there are blacks to carry them, as in South Africa, it is virtually impossible for a white to be seen doing such a thing. In London we condemn these colonial extremes of snobbery; but how many ladies could we persuade to carry a jug of milk down Bond Street on a May afternoon, even for a bet?

Now it is not likely, human laziness being what it is, that under Socialism anyone will carry a parcel or a jug if she can induce somebody else (her husband, say) to carry it for her. But nobody will think it disgraceful to carry a parcel because carrying a parcel is work. The idler will be treated not only as a rogue and a vagabond, but as an embezzler of the national funds, the meanest sort of thief.

The police will not have much trouble in detecting such offenders. They will be denounced by everybody, because there will be a very marked jealousy of slackers who take their share without 'doing their bit'. The real lady will be the woman who does more than her bit, and thereby leaves her country richer than she found it. Today nobody knows what a real lady is; but the dignity is assumed most confidently by the women who ostentatiously take as much and give as nearly nothing as they can.

The snobbery that exists at present among workers will also disappear. Our ridiculous social distinctions between manual labour and brain work, between wholesale business and retail business, are really class distinctions. If a doctor considers it beneath his dignity to carry a scuttle of coals from one room to another, but is proud of his skill in performing some unpleasantly messy operation, it is clearly not because the one is any more or less manual than the other, but solely because surgical operations are associated with descent through younger sons from the propertied class, and carrying coals with proletarian descent.

If the petty ironmonger's daughter is not considered eligible for marriage with the ironmaster's son, it is not because selling steel by the ounce and selling it by the ton are attributes of two different species, but because petty ironmongers have usually been poor and ironmasters rich.

When there are no rich and no poor, and descent from the proprietary class will be described as 'criminal antecedents', people will turn their hands to anything, and indeed rebel against any division of labour that deprives them of physical exercise. My own excessively sedentary occupation makes me long to be a half-time navvy. I find myself begging my gardener, who is a glutton for work, to leave me a few rough jobs to do when I have written myself to a standstill; for I cannot go out and take a hand with the nawies, because I should be taking the bread out of a poor man's mouth; nor should we be very comfortable company for one another with our different habits and speech and bringing-up, all produced by differences in our parents' incomes and class.

But with all these obstacles swept away by Socialism I could lend a hand at any job within my strength and skill, and help my mates instead of hurting them, besides being as good company for them as I am now for professional persons or rich folk.

Even as it is a good deal of haymaking is done for fun; and I am persuaded (having some imagination, thank Heaven!) that under Socialism open air workers would have plenty of voluntary help, female as well as male, without the trouble of whistling for it. Laws might have to be made to deal with officiousness. Everything would make for activity and against idleness: indeed it would probably be much harder to be an idler than it is now to be a pickpocket. Anyhow, as idleness would be not only a criminal offence, but unladylike and ungentlemanly in the lowest degree, nobody would resent the laws against it as infringements of natural liberty.

Lest anyone should at this point try to muddle you with the inveterate delusion that because capital can increase wealth people can live on capital without working, let me go back just for a moment to the way in which capital becomes productive. Let us take those cases in which capital is used, not for destructive purposes, as in war, but for increasing production: that is, saving time and trouble in future work.

When all the merchandise in a country has to be brought from the makers to the users on packhorses or carts over bad roads the cost in time and trouble and labour of man and beast is so great that most things have to be made and consumed on the spot. There may be a famine in one village and a glut in another a hundred miles off because of the difficulty of sending food from one to the other.

Now if there is enough spare subsistence (capital) to support gangs of navvies and engineers and other workers whilst they cover the country with railways, canals, and metalled roads, and build engines and trains, barges and motor cars to travel on them, to say nothing of aeroplanes, then all sorts of goods can be sent long distances quickly and cheaply; so that the village which formerly could not get a cartload of bread and a few cans of milk from a hundred miles off to save its life is able to buy quite cheaply grain grown in Russia or America and domestic articles made in Germany or Japan.

The spare subsistence will be entirely consumed in the operation: there will be no more left of it than of the capital lent for the war; but it will leave behind it the roadways and waterways and machinery by which labour can do a great deal more in a given time than it could without them. The destruction of these aids to labour would be a very different matter from our annual confiscations of the National Debt by taxation. It would leave us much poorer and less civilized: in fact most of us would starve, because big modern populations cannot support themselves without elaborate machinery and railways and so forth.

Still, roadways and machines can produce nothing by themselves. They can only assist labour. And they have to be continually repaired and renewed by labour. A country crammed with factories and machines, traversed in all directions by roadways, tramways and railways, dotted with aerodromes and hangars and garages, each crowded with aeroplanes and airships and motor cars, would produce absolutely nothing at all except ruin and rust and decay if the inhabitants ceased to work. We should starve in the midst of all the triumphs of civilization because we could not breakfast on the clay of the railway embankments, lunch on boiled aeroplanes, and dine on toasted steam-hammers.

Nature inexorably denies to us the possibility of living without labour or of hoarding its most vital products. We may be helped by past labour; but we must live by present labour. By telling off one set of workers to produce more than they consume, and telling off another set to live on the surplus whilst they are making roads and machines, we may make our labour much more productive, and take out the gain either in shorter hours of work or bigger returns from the same number of hours of work as before, but we cannot stop working and sit down and look on while the roads and machines make and fetch and carry for us without anyone lifting a finger.

We may reduce our working hours to two a day, or increase our income tenfold, or even conceivably do both at once; but by no magic on earth can any of us honestly become an idler. When you see a person who does no productive or serviceable work, you may conclude with absolute certainty that she or he is sponging on the labour of other people. It may or may not be expedient to allow certain persons this privilege for a time: sometimes it is; and sometimes it is not. I have already described how we offer at present, to anyone who can invent a labour-saving machine, what is called a patent: that is, a right to take a share of what the workers produces with the help of that machine for fourteen years.

When a man writes a book or a play, we give him, by what is called copyright, the power to make everybody who reads the book or sees the play performed pay him and his heirs something during his lifetime and fifty years afterwards. This is our way of encouraging people to invent machines and to write books and plays instead of being content with the old handiwork, and with the Bible and Shakespear; and as we do this with our eyes open and with a definite purpose, and the privilege lasts no longer than enough to accomplish its purpose, there is a good deal to be said for it.

But to allow the descendants of a man who invested a few hundred pounds in the New River Water Company in the reign of James I to go on for ever and ever living in idleness on the incessant daily labour of the London ratepayers is senseless and mischievous.

If they actually did the daily work of supplying London with water, they might reasonably claim either to work for less time or receive more for their work than a water-carrier in Elizabeth's time; but for doing no work at all they have not a shadow of excuse. To consider Socialism a tyranny because it will compel everyone to share the daily work of the world is to confess to the brain of an idiot and the instinct of a tramp.

Speaking generally, it is a mistake to suppose that the absence of law means the absence of tyranny. Take, for example, the tyranny of fashion. The only law concerned in this is the law that we must all wear something in the presence of other people.

It does not prescribe what a woman shall wear: it only says that in public she shall be a draped figure and not a nude one. But does this mean that a woman can wear what she likes? Legally she can; but socially her slavery is more complete than any sumptuary law could make it. If she is a waitress or a parlormaid there is no question about it: she must wear a uniform or lose her employment and starve. If she is a duchess she must dress in the fashion or be ridiculous.

In the case of the duchess nothing worse than ridicule is the penalty of unfashionable dressing. But any woman who has to earn her living outside her own house finds that if she is to keep her employment she must also keep up appearances, which means that she must dress in the fashion, even when it is not at all becoming to her, and her wardrobe contains serviceable dresses a couple of years out of date.

And the better her class of employment the tighter her bonds. The ragpicker has the melancholy privilege of being less particular about her working clothes than the manageress of a hotel; but she would be very glad to exchange that freedom for the obligation of the manageress to be always well dressed. In fact the most enviable women in this respect are nuns and policewomen, who, like gentlemen at evening parties and military officers on parade, never have to think of what they will wear, as it is all settled for them by regulation and custom.

This dress question is only one familiar example of the extent to which the private employment of today imposes regulations on us which are quite outside the law, but which are none the less enforced by private employers on pain of destitution.

The husband in public employment, the socialized husband, is much freer than the unsocialized one in private employment. He may travel third class, wearing a lounge suit and soft bat, living in the suburbs, and spending his Sundays as he pleases, whilst the others must travel first class, wear a frock coat and tall hat, live at a fashionable address, and go to church regularly.

Their wives have to do as they do; and the single women who have escaped from the limitations of the home into independent activity find just the same difference between public work and private: in public employment their livelihood is never at the mercy of a private irresponsible person as it is in private. The lengths to which women are sometimes forced to go to please their private employers are much more revolting than, for instance, the petty dishonesties in which clerks are forced to become accomplices.

Then there are estate rules: that is to say, edicts drawn up by private estate owners and imposed on their tenants without any legal sanction. These often prohibit the-building on the estate of any place of worship except an Anglican church, or of any public house.

They refuse houses to practitioners of the many kinds that are now not registered by the General Medical Council. In fact they exercise a tyranny which would lead to a revolution if it were attempted by the King, and which did actually provoke us to cutoff a king's head in the seventeenth century.

We have to submit to these tyrannies because the people who can refuse us employment or the use of land have powers of life and death over us, and can therefore make us do what they like, law or no law. Socialism would transfer this power of life and death from private hands to the hands of the constitutional authorities, and regulate it by public law. The result would be a great increase of independence, self-respect, freedom from interference with our tastes and ways of living, and, generally, all the liberty we really care about.

Childish people, we saw, want to have all their lives regulated for them, with occasional holiday outbursts of naughtiness to relieve the monotony; and we admitted that the ablebodied ones make good soldiers and steady conventional employees.

When they are left to themselves they make laws of fashions, customs, points of etiquette, and 'what other people will say', hardly daring to call their souls their own, though they may be rich enough to do as they please. Money as a means of freedom is thrown away on these people.

It is funny to hear them declaring, as they often do, that Socialism would be unendurable because it would dictate to them what they should eat and drink and wear, leaving them no choice in the matter, when they are cowering under a social tyranny which regulates their meals, their clothes, their hours, their religion and politics, so ruthlessly that they dare no more walk down a fashionable street in an unfashionable hat, which there is no law to prevent them doing, than to walk down it naked, which would be stopped by the police. They regard with dread and abhorrence the emancipated spirits who, within the limits of legality and cleanliness and convenience, do not care what they wear, and boldly spend their free time as their fancy dictates.

But do not undervalue the sheepish wisdom of the conventional. Nobody can live in society without conventions. The reason why sensible people are as conventional as they can bear to be is that conventionality saves so much time and thought and trouble and social friction of one sort or another that it leaves them much more leisure for freedom than unconventionality does.

Believe me, unless you intend to devote your life to preaching unconventionality, and thus make it your profession, the more conventional you are, short of being silly or slavish or miserable, the easier life will be for you. Even as a professional reformer you had better be content to preach one form of unconventionality at a time. For instance, if you rebel against high-heeled shoes, take care to do it in a very smart hat.

## Chapter 16

# The Lysenko Muddle

The Lysenko controversy has been honored in *The Times* by a special article. To anyone who knows the ropes the rumpus is laughable. Lysenko is a neo-Lamarckian who believes that acquired characteristics are inherited, in flat contradiction to the neo Darwinist Weismann, who denied that any acquired characteristic can be inherited, and was so fanatically Determinist that he maintained that every act of a living creature was imposed on it by external circumstances, and could not be prevented or initiated or forwarded by any legislature or any purpose or desire or volition of its living agents.

As Butler had put it to Darwin, Determinism 'banishes mind from the universe.' Call it Fatalism and it becomes plain at once that it is a doctrine that no State can tolerate, least of all a Socialist State, in which every citizen shall aim at altering circumstances for the better purposely and conscientiously, and no criminal nor militant reactionary can be excused on the ground that his actions are not his own but the operation of external natural forces predetermined from the beginning of the world and entirely beyond his control or prevention. There is not a civilized country on earth which does not hold its citizens responsible for their conduct, persecuting ruthlessly all who act too irresponsibly, and in extreme cases certifying them as madmen and locking them up.

Lysenko is no Determinist. Following up Michurin's agricultural experiments he found that it is possible to extend the area of soil cultivation by breeding strains of wheat that flourish in a sub-Arctic climate, and transmit this acquired characteristic to its seed. This hard fact nullified Weismann and his Determinism, as facts are continually nullifying paper theories and hypotheses.

Lysenko is not the first in the field. Samuel Butler realised 80 years age the enormity of the Fatalism inherent in Darwinism, though Darwin, a Unitarian, was not a Darwinist, but a naturalist whose specialty was the semblance of evolution produced by what he called Natural Selection. Butler, in two books entitled *Life and Habit* and *Luck or Cunning?* fought Darwin tooth and nail.

Butler was followed in 1906 by myself. After a careful observation of my own acquired habits I pointed out, in the course of a lecture on Darwin to the Fabian Society, that evolution means that all habits are inherited.

I cited the fact that as breathing is an inborn habit, and speaking, like skating and bicycling, one which every generation has to acquire, proves that habits are acquired by imperceptible increments at each generation, the inborn habits being those already fully acquired, and the rest only in process of acquirement.

I was followed by Bergson, who supplemented Butler's views and mine with a philosophy of our Creative Evolution.

After Bergson, Weismannism lost its stranglehold on the scientific world. Scott Haldane (father of J.B.S.), Needham, and in Russia Michurin and Lysenko, broke away from Fatalism, not polemically, but by simply ignoring it.

And now comes the joke. Fatalism is now dropped or certified as Materialism gone mad. Creative Evolution is basically Vitalist, and, as such, mystical, intuitive, irrational, poetic, passionate, religious, and catholic; for neither Lamarck nor Butler nor I nor Bergson nor Lysenko nor anyone else can account rationally for the Life Force, the Evolutionary Appetite, the *Elan Vital*, the Divine Providence (alias Will of God), or the martyrdoms that are the seed of Communism. It has just to be accepted as a so far inexplicable natural fact.

Weismannism, dismissing this force as an illusion produced by Darwinian Natural Selection, is soulless, totally rationalist, fatalist, anarchist, mechanist, and arch-materialist.

It immobilises its votaries morally, driving Lysenko to the extremity of demanding its persecution as a Voodoo.

Lysenko is on the right side as a Vitalist; but the situation is confused by the purely verbal snag that Marx called his philosophy Dialectical Materialism. Now in Russia Marx is a Pontif; and all scientists who do not call themselves Materialists must be persecuted. Accordingly, Lysenko has to pretend that he is a Materialist when he is in fact a Vitalist; and thus muddles us ludicrously. Marxism seems to have gone as mad as Weismannism; and it is no longer surprising that Marx had to insist that he was not a Marxist.

The fault is wholly that of the detestable Hegelian jargon which hampered and bothered the Socialist movement in the eighteen sixties, and is mere abracadabra in England.

We have a parallel mix-up at home. In the Church of England no candidate for ordination can be inducted to a living unless when catechized by the Bishop he tells the flat lie, which the Bishop knows to be a lie, that he believes without mental reservations everything in The Bible literally.

His justification is that as he will not be allowed to exercise his vocation without going through this imposture, he does it under duress and is therefore not morally responsible for it. Lysenko has to tell the flat lie that he is a Materialist, and can make the same excuse for what it is worth. Meanwhile it is our business not to let this bogus controversy be used as a red herring to split us into two factions squabbling about nothing. The trick is an old one: Divide and Govern.

Anyone can be a good Christian without believing that Joshua stopped the sun, or Jesus raised Lazarus from the dead. So also is it possible to be a Socialist without, like Engels, making Das Kapital 'the Bible of the working class,' or accepting Marx's version of the exploded capitalist theory of value or his attempt to account for Surplus Value by an analysis of the circulation of commodities that is now tiresome nonsense.

He knew nothing of the theory of rent and interest; and his English translators, like those of Wagner, made a mess of the German philosophic lingo, not having the literary genius of Carlyle, who assimilated it superbly. If only they had read the Jacobean Bible and learnt from it how to write English as Bunyan did, Marx would not have had to wait twenty-five years for his doctrine to be put into plain English by Hyndman, Morris and the Fabians. By that time he was dead.

G.B.S.

P.S. Sir Henry Dale's resignation of his membership of the Soviet Academy of Science on the Lysenko issue is entirely conscientious and honorable in intention. But the real issue is between the claim of the scientific professions to be exempted from all legal restraint in the pursuit of knowledge, and the duty of the State to control it in the general interest as it controls ail other pursuits. To my old question 'May you boil your mother to ascertain at what temperature a mature woman will die?' the police have a decisive counter in the gallows.

To Lysenko's question 'Can the State tolerate a doctrine that makes every citizen the irresponsible agent of inevitable Natural Selection?' the reply is a short No. The Yes implied by Sir Henry Dale's resignation is a hangover from the faith of Adam Smith, who believed that God interferes continually in human affairs, overruling them to a divine purpose no matter how selfishly they are conducted by their human agents. Experience has not borne this faith out. Laissez-faire is dead. Sir Henry should think this out.

My long political experience has taught me that what we are hardest up against is not general ignorance of Communism and all the rival paper Isms, but of the status quo, our notions of which are so fantastically Utopian that we daily reproach Russians and foreigners in general for practices and institutions and codes that are in full blast here, and in fact mostly originated in Merry England.

## TREATISE ON PARENTS AND CHILDREN

### TRAILING CLOUDS OF GLORY

Childhood is a stage in the process of that continual remanufacture of the Life Stuff by which the human race is perpetuated. The Life Force either will not or cannot achieve immortality except in very low organisms: indeed it is by no means ascertained that even the amoeba is immortal. Human beings visibly wear out, though they last longer than their friends the dogs.

Turtles, parrots, and elephants are believed to be capable of outliving the memory of the oldest human inhabitant. But the fact that new ones are born conclusively proves that they are not immortal. Do away with death and you do away with the need for birth: in fact if you went on breeding, you would finally have to kill old people to make room for young ones.

Now death is not necessarily a failure of energy on the part of the Life Force. People with no imagination try to make things which will last for ever, and even want to live for ever themselves. But the intelligently imaginative man knows very well that it is waste of labour to make a machine that will last ten years, because it will probably be superseded in half that time by an improved machine answering the same purpose. He also knows that if some devil were to convince us that our dream of personal immortality is no dream but a hard fact, such a shriek of despair would go up from the human race as no other conceivable horror could provoke.

With all our perverse nonsense as to John Smith living for a thousand million eons and for ever after, we die voluntarily, knowing that it is time for us to be scrapped, to be remanufactured, to come back, as Wordsworth divined, trailing ever brightening clouds of glory. We must all be born again, and yet again and again. We should like to live a little longer just as we should like 50 pounds: that is, we should take it if we could get it for nothing; but that sort of idle liking is not will.

It is amazing—considering the way we talk—how little a man will do to get 50 pounds: all the 50-pound notes I have ever known of have been more easily earned than a laborious sixpence; but the difficulty of inducing a man to make any serious effort to obtain 50 pounds is nothing to the difficulty of inducing him to make a serious effort to keep alive.

The moment he sees death approach, he gets into bed

and sends for a doctor. He knows very well at the back of his conscience that he is rather a poor job and had better be remanufactured.

He knows that his death will make room for a birth; and he hopes that it will be a birth of something that he aspired to be and fell short of. He knows that it is through death and rebirth that this corruptible shall become incorruptible, and this mortal put on immortality. Practise as you will on his ignorance, his fears, and his imagination, with bribes of paradises and threats of hells, there is only one belief that can rob death of its sting and the grave of its victory; and that is the belief that we can lay down the burden of our wretched little makeshift individualities for ever at each lift towards the goal of evolution, which can only be a being that cannot be improved upon.

After all, what man is capable of the insane self-conceit of believing that an eternity of himself would be tolerable even to himself? Those who try to believe it postulate that they shall be made perfect first. But if you make me perfect I shall no longer be myself, nor will it be possible for me to conceive my present imperfections (and what I cannot conceive I cannot remember); so that you may just as well give me a new name and face the fact that I am a new person and that the old Bernard Shaw is as dead as mutton. Thus, oddly enough, the conventional belief in the matter comes to this: that if you wish to live for ever you must be wicked enough to be irretrievably damned, since the saved are no longer what they were, and in hell alone do people retain their sinful nature: that is to say, their individuality. And this sort of hell, however convenient as a means of intimidating persons who have practically no honour and no conscience, is not a fact.

Death is for many of us the gate of hell; but we are inside on the way out, not outside on the way in. Therefore let us give up telling one another idle stories, and rejoice in death as we rejoice in birth; for without death we cannot be born again; and the man who does not wish to be born again and born better is fit only to represent the City of London in Parliament, or perhaps the university of Oxford.

## THE CHILD IS FATHER TO THE MAN

Is he? Then in the name of common sense why do we always treat children on the assumption that the man is father to the child? Oh, these fathers! And we are not content with fathers: we must have godfathers, forgetting that the child is godfather to the man.

Has it ever struck you as curious that in a country where the first article of belief is that every child is born with a godfather whom we all call "our father which art in heaven," two very limited individual mortals should be allowed to appear at its baptism and explain that they are its godparents, and that they will look after its salvation until it is no longer a child.

I had a godmother who made herself responsible in this way for me. She presented me with a Bible with a gilt clasp and edges, larger than the Bibles similarly presented to my sisters, because my sex entitled me to a heavier article. I must have seen that lady at least four times in the twenty years following. She never alluded to my salvation in any way. People occasionally ask me to act as godfather to their children with a levity which convinces me that they have not the faintest notion that it involves anything more than calling the helpless child George Bernard without regard to the possibility that it may grow up in the liveliest abhorrence of my notions.

A person with a turn for logic might argue that if God is the Father of all men, and if the child is father to the man, it follows that the true representative of God at the christening is the child itself. But such posers are unpopular, because they imply that our little customs, or, as we often call them, our religion, mean something, or must originally have meant something, and that we understand and believe that something.

However, my business is not to make confusion worse confounded, but to clear it up. Only, it is as well to begin by a sample of current thought and practice which shews that on the subject of children we are very deeply confused.

On the whole, whatever our theory or no theory may

be, our practice is to treat the child as the property of its immediate physical parents, and to allow them to do what they like with it as far as it will let them. It has no rights and no liberties: in short, its condition is that which adults recognize as the most miserable and dangerous politically possible for themselves: namely, the condition of slavery. For its alleviation we trust to the natural affection of the parties, and to public opinion. A father cannot for his own credit let his son go in rags.

Also, in a very large section of the population, parents finally become dependent on their children. Thus there are checks on child slavery which do not exist, or are less powerful, in the case of manual and industrial slavery. Sensationally bad cases fall into two classes, which are really the same class: namely, the children whose parents are excessively addicted to the sensual luxury of petting children, and the children whose parents are excessively addicted to the sensual luxury of physically torturing them. There is a Society for the Prevention of Cruelty to Children which has effectually made an end of our belief that mothers are any more to be trusted than stepmothers, or fathers than slave-drivers.

And there is a growing body of law designed to prevent parents from using their children ruthlessly to make money for the household. Such legislation has always been furiously resisted by the parents, even when the horrors of factory slavery were at their worst; and the extension of such legislation at present would be impossible if it were not that the parents affected by it cannot control a majority of votes in Parliament. In domestic life a great deal of service is done by children, the girls acting as nursemaids and general servants, and the lads as errand boys.

In the country both boys and girls do a substantial share of farm labour. This is why it is necessary to coerce poor parents to send their children to school, though in the relatively small class which keeps plenty of servants it is impossible to induce parents to keep their children at home instead of paying schoolmasters to take them off their hands.

It appears then that the bond of affection between parents

and children does not save children from the slavery that denial of rights involves in adult political relations. It sometimes intensifies it, sometimes mitigates it; but on the whole children and parents confront one another as two classes in which all the political power is on one side; and the results are not at all unlike what they would be if there were no immediate consanguinity between them, and one were white and the other black, or one enfranchised and the other disenfranchised, or one ranked as gentle and the other simple. Not that Nature counts for nothing in the case and political rights for everything.

But a denial of political rights, and the resultant delivery of one class into the mastery of another, affects their relations so extensively and profoundly that it is impossible to ascertain what the real natural relations of the two classes are until this political relation is abolished.

## ENGLISH PHYSICAL HARDIHOOD AND SPIRITUAL COWARDICE

It is easier to convert most people to the need for allowing their children to run physical risks than moral ones. I can remember a relative of mine who, when I was a small child, unused to horses and very much afraid of them, insisted on putting me on a rather rumbustious pony with little spurs on my heels (knowing that in my agitation I would use them unconsciously), and being enormously amused at my terrors. Yet when that same lady discovered that I had found a copy of The Arabian Nights and was devouring it with avidity, she was horrified, and hid it away from me lest it should break my soul as the pony might have broken my neck.

This way of producing hardy bodies and timid souls is so common in country houses that you may spend hours in them listening to stories of broken collar bones, broken backs, and broken necks without coming upon a single spiritual adventure or daring thought.

But whether the risks to which liberty exposes us are moral or physical our right to liberty involves the right to run them. A man who is not free to risk his neck as an aviator or his soul as a heretic is not free at all; and the right to liberty begins, not at the age of 21 years but of 21 seconds.

## THE RISKS OF IGNORANCE AND WEAKNESS

The difficulty with children is that they need protection from risks they are too young to understand, and attacks they can neither avoid nor resist. You may on academic grounds allow a child to snatch glowing coals from the fire once. You will not do it twice. The risks of liberty we must let everyone take; but the risks of ignorance and self-helplessness are another matter. Not only children but adults need protection from them. At present adults are often exposed to risks outside their knowledge or beyond their comprehension or powers of resistance or foresight: for example, we have to look on every day at marriages or financial speculations that may involve far worse consequences than burnt fingers.

And just as it is part of the business of adults to protect children, to feed them, clothe them, shelter them, and shift for them in all sorts of ways until they are able to shift for themselves, it is coming more and more to be seen that this is true not only of the relation between adults and children, but between adults and adults.

We shall not always look on indifferently at foolish marriages and financial speculations, nor allow dead men to control live communities by ridiculous wills and living heirs to squander and ruin great estates, nor tolerate a hundred other absurd liberties that we allow today because we are too lazy to find out the proper way to interfere. But the interference must be regulated by some theory of the individual's rights. Though the right to live is absolute, it is not unconditional. If a man is unbearably mischievous, he must be killed.

This is a mere matter of necessity, like the killing of a man-eating tiger in a nursery, a venomous snake in the garden, or a fox in the poultry yard. No society could be constructed on the assumption that such extermination is a violation of the creature's right to live, and therefore must not be allowed.

And then at once arises the danger into which morality has led us: the danger of persecution. One Christian spreading his doctrines may seem more mischievous than a dozen thieves: throw him therefore to the lions. A lying or disobedient child may corrupt a whole generation and make human Society impossible: therefore thrash the vice out of him. And so on until our whole system of abortion, intimidation, tyranny, cruelty and the rest is in full swing again.

## THE COMMON SENSE OF TOLERATION

The real safeguard against this is the dogma of Toleration. I need not here repeat the compact treatise on it which I prepared for the Joint Committee on the Censorship of Stage Plays, and prefixed to The Shewing Up of Blanco Posnet. It must suffice now to say that the present must not attempt to schoolmaster the future by pretending to know good from evil in tendency, or protect citizens against shocks to their opinions and convictions, moral, political or religious: in other words it must not persecute doctrines of any kind, or what is called bad taste, and must insist on all persons facing such shocks as they face frosty weather or any of the other disagreeable, dangerous, or bracing incidents of freedom.

The expediency of Toleration has been forced on us by the fact that progressive enlightenment depends on a fair hearing for doctrines which at first appear seditious, blasphemous, and immoral, and which deeply shock people who never think originally, thought being with them merely a habit and an echo. The deeper ground for Toleration is the nature of creation, which, as we now know, proceeds by evolution.

Evolution finds its way by experiment; and this finding of the way varies according to the stage of development reached, from the blindest groping along the line of least resistance to intellectual speculation, with its practical sequel of hypothesis and experimental verification; or to observation, induction, and deduction; or even into so rapid and intuitive an integration of all these processes in a single brain that we get the inspired guess of the man of genius and the desperate resolution of the teacher of new truths who is first slain as a blasphemous apostate and then worshipped as a prophet.

Here the law for the child is the same as for the adult. The high priest must not rend his garments and cry "Crucify him" when he is shocked: the atheist must not clamor for the suppression of Law's Serious Call because it has for two centuries destroyed the natural happiness of innumerable unfortunate children by persuading their parents that it is their religious duty to be miserable.

It, and the Sermon on the Mount, and Machiavelli's Prince, and La Rochefoucauld's maxims, and Hymns Ancient and Modern, and De Glanville's apologue, and Dr. Watts's rhymes, and Nietzsche's Gay Science, and Ingersoll's Mistakes of Moses, and the speeches and pamphlets of the people who want us to make war on Germany, and the Noodle's Orations and articles of our politicians and journalists, must all be tolerated not only because any of them may for all we know be on the right track but because it is in the conflict of opinion that we win knowledge and wisdom. However terrible the wounds suffered in that conflict, they are better than the barren peace of death that follows when all the combatants are slaughtered or bound hand and foot.

The difficulty at present is that though this necessity for Toleration is a law of political science as well established as the law of gravitation, our rulers are never taught political science: on the contrary, they are taught in school that the master tolerates nothing that is disagreeable to him; that ruling is simply being master; and that the master's method is the method of violent punishment. And our citizens, all school taught, are walking in the same darkness. As I write these lines the Home Secretary is explaining that a man who has been imprisoned for blasphemy must not be released because his remarks were painful to the feelings of his pious fellow townsmen.

Now it happens that this very Home Secretary has driven many thousands of his fellow citizens almost beside themselves by the crudity of his notions of government, and his simple inability to understand why he should not use and make laws to torment and subdue people who do not happen to agree with him. In a word, he is not a politician, but a grown-up schoolboy who has at last got a cane in his hand. And as all the rest of us are in the same condition (except as to command of the cane) the only objection made to his proceedings takes the shape of clamorous demands that he should be caned instead of being allowed to cane other people.

### The Sin of Athanasius

It seems hopeless. Anarchists are tempted to preach a violent and implacable resistance to all law as the only remedy; and the result of that speedily is that people welcome any tyranny that will rescue them from chaos. But there is really no need to choose between anarchy and tyranny. A quite reasonable state of things is practicable if we proceed on human assumptions and not on academic ones. If adults will frankly give up their claim to know better than children what the purposes of the Life Force are, and treat the child as an experiment like themselves, and possibly a more successful one, and at the same time relinquish their monstrous parental claims to personal private property in children, the rest must be left to common sense.

It is our attitude, our religion, that is wrong. A good beginning might be made by enacting that any person dictating a piece of conduct to a child or to anyone else as the will of God, or as absolutely right, should be dealt with as a blasphemer: as, indeed, guilty of the unpardonable sin against the Holy Ghost.

If the penalty were death, it would rid us at once of that scourge of humanity, the amateur Pope. As an Irish Protestant, I raise the cry of No Popery with hereditary zest. We are overrun with Popes. From curates and governesses, who may claim a sort of professional standing, to parents and uncles and nurserymaids and school teachers and wiseacres generally, there are scores of thousands of human insects groping through our darkness by the feeble phosphorescence of their own tails, yet ready at a moment's notice to reveal the will of God on every possible subject; to explain how and why the universe was made (in my youth they added the exact date) and the circumstances under which it will cease to exist; to lay down precise rules of right and wrong conduct; to discriminate infallibly between virtuous and vicious character; and all this with such certainty that they are prepared to visit all the rigors of the law, and all the ruinous penalties of social ostracism on people, however harmless their actions maybe who venture to laugh at their monstrous conceit or to pay their assumptions the extravagant compliment of criticizing them.

As to children, who shall say what canings and birchings and terrifyings and threats of hell fire and impositions and humiliations and petty imprisonings and sendings to bed and standing in corners and the like they have suffered because their parents and guardians and teachers knew everything so much better than Socrates or Solon?

It is this ignorant uppishness that does the mischief. A stranger on the planet might expect that its grotesque absurdity would provoke enough ridicule to cure it; but unfortunately quite the contrary happens. Just as our ill health delivers us into the hands of medical quacks and creates a passionate demand for impudent pretences that doctors can cure the diseases they themselves die of daily, so our ignorance and helplessness set us clamoring for spiritual and moral quacks who pretend that they can save our souls from their own damnation.

If a doctor were to say to his patients, "I am familiar with your symptoms, because I have seen other people in your condition; and I will bring the very little knowledge we have to your treatment; but except in that very shallow sense I dont know what is the matter with you; and I cant undertake to cure you," he would be a lost man professionally; and if a clergyman, on being called on to award a prize for good conduct in the village school, were to say, "I am afraid I cannot say who is the best-behaved child, because I really do not know what good conduct is; but I will gladly take the teacher's word as to which child has caused least inconvenience," he would probably be unfrocked, if not excommunicated. And yet no honest and intellectually capable doctor or parson can say more.

Clearly it would not be wise of the doctor to say it, because optimistic lies have such immense therapeutic value that a doctor who cannot tell them convincingly has mistaken his profession. And a clergyman who is not prepared to lay down the law dogmatically will not be of much use in a village school, though it behoves him all the more to be very careful what law he lays down.

But unless both the clergyman and the doctor are in the attitude expressed by these speeches they are not fit for their work. The man who believes that he has more than a provisional hypothesis to go upon is a born fool. He may have to act vigorously on it. The world has no use for the Agnostic who wont believe anything because anything might be false, and wont deny anything because anything might be true. But there is a wide difference between saying, "I believe this; and I am going to act on it," or, "I dont believe it; and I wont act on it," and saying, "It is true; and it is my duty and yours to act on it," or, "It is false; and it is my duty and yours to refuse to act on it." The difference is as great as that between the Apostles' Creed and the Athanasian Creed. When you repeat the Apostles' Creed you affirm that you believe certain things.

There you are clearly within your rights. When you repeat the Athanasian Creed, you affirm that certain things are so, and that anybody who doubts that they are so cannot be saved. And this is simply a piece of impudence on your part, as you know nothing about it except that as good men as you have never heard of your creed. The apostolic attitude is a desire to convert others to our beliefs for the sake of sympathy and light: the Athanasian attitude is a desire to murder people who dont agree with us.

I am sufficient of an Athanasian to advocate a law for the speedy execution of all Athanasians, because they violate the fundamental proposition of my creed, which is, I repeat, that all living creatures are experiments.

## THE EXPERIMENT EXPERIMENTING

And now all the modern schoolmaster abortionists will rise up beaming, and say, "We quite agree. We regard every child in our school as a subject for experiment. We are always experimenting with them. We challenge the experimental test for our system. We are continually guided by our experience in our great work of moulding the character of our future citizens, etc. etc. etc." I am sorry to seem irreconcilable; but it is the Life Force that has to make the experiment and not the schoolmaster; and the Life Force for the child's purpose is in the child and not in the schoolmaster. The schoolmaster is another experiment; and a laboratory in which all the experiments began experimenting on one another would not produce intelligible results.

I admit, however, that if my schoolmasters had treated me as an experiment of the Life Force: that is, if they had set me free to do as I liked subject only to my political rights and theirs, they could not have watched the experiment very long, because the first result would have been a rapid movement on my part in the direction of the door, and my disappearance there-through. It may be worth inquiring where I should have gone to.

I should say that practically every time I should have gone to a much more educational place. I should have gone into the country, or into the sea, or into the National Gallery, or to hear a band if there was one, or to any library where there were no schoolbooks. I should have read very dry and difficult books: for example, though nothing would have induced me to read the budget of stupid party lies that served as a text-book of history in school, I remember reading Robertson's Charles V. and his history of Scotland from end to end most laboriously.

Once, stung by the airs of a schoolfellow who alleged that he had read Locke On The Human Understanding, I attempted to read the Bible straight through, and actually got to the Pauline Epistles before I broke down in disgust at what seemed to me their inveterate crookedness of mind. If there had been a school where children were really free, I should have had to be driven out of it for the sake of my health by the teachers; for the children to whom a literary education can be of any use are insatiable: they will read and study far more than is good for them.

In fact the real difficulty is to prevent them from wasting their time by reading for the sake of reading and studying for the sake of studying, instead of taking some trouble to find out what they really like and are capable of doing some good at. Some silly person will probably interrupt me here with the remark that many children have no appetite for a literary education at all, and would never open a book if they were not forced to.

I have known many such persons who have been forced to the point of obtaining University degrees. And for all the effect their literary exercises has left on them they might just as well have been put on the treadmill. In fact they are actually less literate than the treadmill would have left them; for they might by chance have picked up and dipped into a volume of Shakespear or a translation of Homer if they had not been driven to loathe every famous name in literature. I should probably know as much Latin as French, if Latin had not been made the excuse for my school imprisonment and degradation.

## TECHNICAL INSTRUCTION

Technical instruction tempts to violence (as a short cut) more than liberal education. The sailor in Mr Rudyard Kipling's Captains Courageous, teaching the boy the names of the ship's tackle with a rope's end, does not disgust us as our schoolmasters do, especially as the boy was a spoiled boy. But an unspoiled boy would not have needed that drastic medicine. Technical training may be as tedious as learning to skate or to play the piano or violin; but it is the price one must pay to achieve certain desirable results or necessary ends. It is a monstrous thing to force a child to learn Latin or Greek or mathematics on the ground that they are an indispensable gymnastic for the mental powers.

It would be monstrous even if it were true; for there is no

labour that might not be imposed on a child or an adult on the same pretext; but as a glance at the average products of our public school and university education shews that it is not true, it need not trouble us. But it is a fact that ignorance of Latin and Greek and mathematics closes certain careers to men (I do not mean artificial, unnecessary, noxious careers like those of the commercial schoolmaster). Languages, even dead ones, have their uses; and, as it seems to many of us, mathematics have their uses.

They will always be learned by people who want to learn them; and people will always want to learn them as long as they are of any importance in life: indeed the want will survive their importance: superstition is nowhere stronger than in the field of obsolete acquirements. And they will never be learnt fruitfully by people who do not want to learn them either for their own sake or for use in necessary work. There is no harder schoolmaster than experience; and yet experience fails to teach where there is no desire to learn. Still, one must not begin to apply this generalization too early. And this brings me to an important factor in the case: the factor of evolution.

## DOCILITY AND DEPENDENCE

If anyone, impressed by my view that the rights of a child are precisely those of an adult, proceeds to treat a child as if it were an adult, he (or she) will find that though the plan will work much better at some points than the usual plan, at others it will not work at all; and this discovery may provoke him to turn back from the whole conception of children's rights with a jest at the expense of bachelors' and old maids' children. In dealing with children what is needed is not logic but sense. There is no logical reason why young persons should be allowed greater control of their property the day after they are twenty-one than the day before it.

There is no logical reason why I, who strongly object to an adult standing over a boy of ten with a Latin grammar, and saying, "you must learn this, whether you want to or not," should nevertheless be quite prepared to stand over a boy of five with the multiplication table or a copy book or a code of elementary good manners, and practice on his docility to make him learn them.

And there is no logical reason why I should do for a child a great many little offices, some of them troublesome and disagreeable, which I should not do for a boy twice its age, or support a boy or girl when I would unhesitatingly throw an adult on his own resources. But there are practical reasons, and sensible reasons, and affectionate reasons for all these illogicalities. Children do not want to be treated altogether as adults: such treatment terrifies them and overburdens them with responsibility.

In truth, very few adults care to be called on for independence and originality: they also are bewildered and terrified in the absence of precedents and precepts and commandments; but modern Democracy allows them a sanctioning and cancelling power if they are capable of using it, which children are not. To treat a child wholly as an adult would be to mock and destroy it. Infantile docility and juvenile dependence are, like death, a product of Natural Selection; and though there is no viler crime than to abuse them, yet there is no greater cruelty than to ignore them. I have complained sufficiently of what I suffered through the process of assault, imprisonment, and compulsory lessons that taught me nothing, which are called my schooling.

But I could say a good deal also about the things I was not taught and should have been taught, not to mention the things I was allowed to do which I should not have been allowed to do. I have no recollection of being taught to read or write; so I presume I was born with both faculties; but many people seem to have bitter recollections of being forced reluctantly to acquire them.

And though I have the uttermost contempt for a teacher so ill mannered and incompetent as to be unable to make a child learn to read and write without also making it cry, still I am prepared to admit that I had rather have been compelled to learn to read and write with tears by an incompetent and ill mannered person than left in ignorance. Reading, writing, and enough arithmetic to use money honestly and accurately, together with the rudiments of law and order, become necessary conditions of a child's liberty before it can appreciate the importance of its liberty, or foresee that these accomplishments are worth acquiring.

Nature has provided for this by evolving the instinct of docility. Children are very docile: they have a sound intuition that they must do what they are told or perish. And adults have an intuition, equally sound, that they must take advantage of this docility to teach children how to live properly or the children will not survive. The difficulty is to know where to stop. To illustrate this, let us consider the main danger of childish docility and parental officiousness.

## THE COMINGS OF AGE OF CHILDREN

All this inculcated adult docility, which wrecks every civilization as it is wrecking ours, is inhuman and unnatural. We must reconsider our institution of the Coming of Age, which is too late for some purposes, and too early for others. There should be a series of Coming of Ages for every individual. The mammals have their first coming of age when they are weaned; and it is noteworthy that this rather cruel and selfish operation on the part of the parent has to be performed resolutely, with claws and teeth; for your little mammal does not want to be weaned, and yields only to a pretty rough assertion of the right of the parent to be relieved of the child as soon as the child is old enough to bear the separation.

The same thing occurs with children: they hang on to the mother's apron-string and the father's coat tails as long as they can, often baffling those sensitive parents who know that children should think for themselves and fend for themselves, but are too kind to throw them on their own resources with the ferocity of the domestic cat. The child should have its first coming of age when it is weaned, another when it can talk, another when it can walk, another when it can dress itself without assistance; and when it can read, write, count money, and pass an examination in going a simple errand involving a purchase and a journey by rail or other public method of locomotion, it should have quite a majority.

At present the children of laborers are soon mobile and able to shift for themselves, whereas it is possible to find grown-up women in the rich classes who are actually afraid to take a walk in the streets unattended and unprotected. It is true that this is a superstition from the time when a retinue was part of the state of persons of quality, and the unattended person was supposed to be a common person of no quality, earning a living; but this has now become so absurd that children and young women are no longer told why they are forbidden to go about alone, and have to be persuaded that the streets are dangerous places, which of course they are; but people who are not educated to live dangerously have only half a life, and are more likely to die miserably after all than those who have taken all the common risks of freedom from their childhood onward as matters of course.

## THE CONFLICT OF WILLS

The world wags in spite of its schools and its families because both schools and families are mostly very largely anarchic: parents and schoolmasters are good-natured or weak or lazy; and children are docile and affectionate and very shortwinded in their fits of naughtiness; and so most families slummock along and muddle through until the children cease to be children. In the few cases when the parties are energetic and determined, the child is crushed or the parent is reduced to a cipher, as the case may be.

When the opposed forces are neither of them strong enough to annihilate the other, there is serious trouble: that is how we get those feuds between parent and child which recur to our memory so ironically when we hear people sentimentalizing about natural affection. We even get tragedies; for there is nothing so tragic to contemplate or so devastating to suffer as the oppression of will without conscience; and the whole tendency of our family and school system is to set the will of the parent and the school despot above conscience as something that must be deferred to abjectly and absolutely for its own sake.

The strongest, fiercest force in nature is human will. It is the highest organization we know of the will that has created the whole universe. Now all honest civilization, religion, law, and convention is an attempt to keep this force within beneficent bounds. What corrupts civilization, religion, law, and convention (and they are at present pretty nearly as corrupt as they dare) is the constant attempts made by the wills of individuals and classes to thwart the wills and enslave the powers of other individuals and classes.

The powers of the parent and the schoolmaster, and of their public analogues the lawgiver and the judge, become instruments of tyranny in the hands of those who are too narrow-minded to understand law and exercise judgment; and in their hands (with us they mostly fall into such hands) law becomes tyranny. And what is a tyrant? Quite simply a person who says to another person, young or old, "You shall do as I tell you; you shall make what I want; you shall profess my creed; you shall have no will of your own; and your powers shall be at the disposal of my will."

It has come to this at last: that the phrase "she has a will of her own," or "he has a will of his own" has come to denote a person of exceptional obstinacy and self-assertion. And even persons of good natural disposition, if brought up to expect such deference, are roused to unreasoning fury, and sometimes to the commission of atrocious crimes, by the slightest challenge to their authority. Thus a laborer may be dirty, drunken, untruthful, slothful, untrustworthy in every way without exhausting the indulgence of the country house. But let him dare to be "disrespectful" and he is a lost man, though he be the cleanest, soberest, most diligent, most veracious, most trustworthy man in the county.

Dickens's instinct for detecting social cankers never served him better than when he shewed us Mrs Heep teaching her son to "be umble," knowing that if he carried out that precept he might be pretty well anything else he liked. The maintenance of deference to our wills becomes a mania which will carry the best of us to any extremity. We will allow a village of Egyptian fellaheen or Indian tribesmen to live the lowest life they please among themselves without molestation; but let one of them slay an Englishman or even strike him on the strongest provocation, and straightway we go stark mad, burning and destroying, shooting and shelling, flogging and hanging, if only such survivors as we may leave are thoroughly cowed in the presence of a man with a white face.

In the committee room of a local council or city corporation, the humblest employees of the committee find defenders if they complain of harsh treatment. Gratuities are voted, indulgences and holidays are pleaded for, delinquencies are excused in the most sentimental manner provided only the employee, however patent a hypocrite or incorrigible a slacker, is hat in hand. But let the most obvious measure of justice be demanded by the secretary of a Trade Union in terms which omit all expressions of subservience, and it is with the greatest difficulty that the cooler-headed can defeat angry motions that the letter be thrown into the waste paper basket and the committee proceed to the next business.

## THE DEMAGOGUE'S OPPORTUNITY

And the employee has in him the same fierce impulse to impose his will without respect for the will of others. Democracy is in practice nothing but a device for cajoling from him the vote he refuses to arbitrary authority. He will not vote for Coriolanus; but when an experienced demagogue comes along and says, "Sir: _you_ are the dictator: the voice of the people is the voice of God; and I am only your very humble servant," he says at once, "All right: tell me what to dictate," and is presently enslaved more effectually with his own silly consent than Coriolanus would ever have enslaved him without asking his leave. And the trick by which the demagogue defeats Coriolanus is played on him in his turn by his inferiors.

Everywhere we see the cunning succeeding in the world by seeking a rich or powerful master and practising on his lust for subservience. The political adventurer who gets into parliament by offering himself to the poor voter, not as his representative but as his will-less soulless "delegate," is himself the dupe of a clever wife who repudiates Votes for Women, knowing well that whilst the man is master, the man's mistress will rule. Uriah Heep may be a crawling creature; but his crawling takes him upstairs. Thus does the selfishness of the will turn on itself, and obtain by flattery what it cannot seize by open force. Democracy becomes the latest trick of tyranny: "womanliness" becomes the latest wile of prostitution.

Between parent and child the same conflict wages and the same destruction of character ensues. Parents set themselves to bend the will of their children to their own—to break their stubborn spirit, as they call it—with the ruthlessness of Grand Inquisitors. Cunning, unscrupulous children learn all the arts of the sneak in circumventing tyranny: children of better character are cruelly distressed and more or less lamed for life by it.

## OUR QUARRELSOMENESS

As between adults, we find a general quarrelsomeness which makes political reform as impossible to most Englishmen as to hogs. Certain sections of the nation get cured of this disability. University men, sailors, and politicians are comparatively free from it, because the communal life of the University, the fact that in a ship a man must either learn to consider others or else go overboard or into irons, and the habit of working on committees and ceasing to expect more of one's own way than is included in the greatest common measure of the committee, educate the will socially.

But no one who has ever had to guide a committee of ordinary private Englishmen through their first attempts at collective action, in committee or otherwise, can retain any illusions as to the appalling effects on our national manners and character of the organization of the home and the school as petty tyrannies, and the absence of all teaching of self-respect and training in self-assertion. Bullied and ordered about, the Englishman obeys like a sheep, evades like a knave, or tries to murder his oppressor.

Merely criticized or opposed in committee, or invited to

consider anybody's views but his own, he feels personally insulted and wants to resign or leave the room unless he is apologized to. And his panic and bewilderment when he sees that the older hands at the work have no patience with him and do not intend to treat him as infallible, are pitiable as far as they are anything but ludicrous.

That is what comes of not being taught to consider other people's wills, and left to submit to them or to over-ride them as if they were the winds and the weather. Such a state of mind is incompatible not only with the democratic introduction of high civilization, but with the comprehension and maintenance of such civilized institutions as have been introduced by benevolent and intelligent despots and aristocrats.

## Chapter 17

# Chronology

| | |
|---|---|
| 1856 | He was born in dublin, ireland. |
| 1876 | He moved to london. |
| 1879 | Immaturity. |
| 1880 | The irrational knot. |
| 1881 | Love among artists. |
| 1882 | Our corner: Cashel byron's profession. |
| 1883 | An unsocial socialist. |
| 1884 | He joined the fabian society. |
| 1889 | Fabian essays on socialism. |
| 1891 | The quintessence of ibsenism. |
| 1892 | Widower's houses. |
| 1893 | He cowrote the party programme for the independent labour party. |
| 1894 | Arms and the man. |
| 1895 | Cashel byron's profession; he became a drama critic for the saturday review. |
| 1897 | Candida; the man of destiny; the devil's disciple; he entered local government. |
| 1898 | The perfect wagnerite; plays plesant and unpleasant; the philander; he married charlotte payne-townshend. |
| 1899 | You never can tell. |
| 1900 | Tabianism and the empire; captain brassbound's conversion. |
| 1901 | Caesar and cleopatra; three plays for puritans. |
| 1902 | Mrs. Warren's profession. |
| 1904 | John bull's other island; the common sense of municipal trading. |

| | |
|---|---|
| 1905 | Man and superman; on going to church; major barbara. |
| 1906 | Doctor's dilemma; dramatic opinions and essays; he moved with his wife to ayot st. Lawrence. |
| 1908 | Getting married. |
| 1910 | Misalliance; socialism and superior brains. |
| 1911 | Fanny's first play. |
| 1912 | Overruled; androcles and the lion. |
| 1913 | Great catherine; pygmalion. |
| 1919 | Peace conference hints. |
| 1920 | Heartbreak house. |
| 1922 | Back to metuselah. |
| 1923 | Saint joan. |
| 1925 | Imprisonment; he was awarded the nobel prize for literature. |
| 1926 | The socialism of shaw. |
| 1928 | The intelligent woman's guide to socialism and capitalism. |
| 1929 | The apple cart. |
| 1930 | Bernard shaw and karl marx. |
| 1931 | What i really wrote about the war. |
| 1932 | Doctor's delusions, crude criminology, and sham education; essays in fabian socialism; the works of bernard shaw; major critical esays; too true to be good; our theatres in the nineties; music in london, 1890-94. |
| 1933 | American boobs. |
| 1934 | Prefaces; village wooing. |
| 1935 | The simpleton of the unexpected isles. |
| 1936 | The millionairess. |
| 1937 | London music in 1888-1889. |
| 1939 | "In good king charles's golden days". |
| 1944 | Everybody's political what's what. |
| 1948 | Sixteen self-sketches; buoyant billions. |
| 1950 | Farfetched fables; he died in hertfordshire, england. (November 2). |
| 1952 | Plays and players. |

| | |
|---|---|
| 1953 | Selected prose. |
| 1955 | Shaw on music. |
| 1956 | The illusions of socialism. |
| 1958 | Shaw on the theatre; an unfinished novel. |
| 1959 | Shaw's dramatic criticism: 1895-1898. |
| 1960 | How to become a musical critic. |
| 1961 | Platform and pupit; shaw on shakespeare. |
| 1962 | The matter with ireland; g.b.s. On music. |
| 1963 | Religious speeches. |
| 1964 | Heartbreak house. |
| 1965 | The complete prefaces of bernard shaw. |
| 1967 | Shaw on religion. |
| 1969 | Shaw: An autobiography, vol 1. |
| 1970 | Shaw: An autobiography, vol 2. |
| 1971 | The road to equality. |
| 1973 | Collected music criticism. |
| 1976 | Bernard shaw's practical politics. |
| 1977 | The portable bernard shaw. |
| 1978 | The great composers. |
| 1980 | The collected screenplays of bernard shaw 1981 Early texts; shaw's music. |
| 1984 | Shaw on dickens. |
| 1985 | Agitations; the diaries, 1885-1897. |
| 1987 | Selected shorter plays. |
| 1988 | Collected letters, 1965-88. |
| 1991 | Bernard shaw's book reviews. |
| 1993 | The complete prefaces; the dramA OBSERVED. |
| 1996 | Unpublished shaw. |

# Bibliography


Grene, Nicholas. *Bernard Shaw: A Critical View*. Macmillan, London, 1984.

Holroyd, Michael. *Bernard Shaw, Vol. II 1898-1918: The Pursuit of Power*, Chatto & Windus, London, 1989.

Holt, Charles, Lloyd. "*Mozart, Shaw and Man and Superman*", *The Shaw Review* (9), 1966, 102-116.

Irvine, William. "*G.B. Shaw's Musical Criticism*", *The Music Quarterly*, Vol. 32 (3), July, 1946, 319-332.

Osborne, Linda Payne. "*Shaw and Mozart: Dramaturgy and the Life Force*", *The Journal of Irish Literature* (12), January, 1983, 96-110.

Parmenter, Ross. "*Shaw and Mozart*", *The Shaw Bulletin* (3), May, 1952, 3-5.

Pollak, Paulina, Salz. "*Master to the Masters: Mozart's Influence on Bernard Shaw's Don Juan in Hell*", *The Shaw Review* (8), 1988, 39-68.

Shaw, George, Bernard. *Shaw's Music*, Vols. I-III, Dan Lawrence (Ed.), Bodley Head, London, 1981.

Shaw, George, Bernard. "*Don Giovanni Explains*", *The Black Girl in Search of God and Some Lesser Tales*, London, 1934.

Shaw, George, Bernard. *Man and Superman: A Comedy and a Philosophy*, London, 1903 (Penguin Ed. 1946/1965).

Tompkins, Peter (Ed.). *To a Young Actress: The Letters of Molly Tompkins*, London, 1960.

Weintraub, Stanley. "*Genesis of a Play: Two Early Approaches to Man and Superman*", *Shaw: Seven Critical Essays*, Norman Rosenblood (Ed.), Toronto, 1971, 23-35.

West, E.J. "*Disciple and Master: Shaw and Mozart*", *The Shavian II* (3), February, 1961, 16-23.